The Pet Partners®
Team Training Course

A Delta Society® Program
for animal-assisted activities and therapy

PETS HELPING PEOPLE MANUAL
PPN-300/302

Project Director:	Maureen Fredrickson, MSW
Writer and Contributing Editor:	Ann R. Howie, ACSW
Editorial Consultant:	Mary Burch, Ph.D.
Project Consultant:	Ellen Shay
Illustrator:	Terry Albert

5th Edition, December 2000

For information contact:

Delta Society®
580 Naches Ave SW Suite #101
Renton, WA 98055-1329
(425) 226-7357
E-mail: info@deltasociety.org
Web site: www.deltasociety.org

ISBN 1-889785-08-3
Printed in the United States of America.

Acknowledgments

In 1990, Delta Society® established the Pet Partners® Program at the request of volunteers who wanted information on the best ways to visit people with their pets. We also received many requests from human service providers who were concerned that people and their animals be well trained in the special needs of the people they visit. In addition, the staff of many facilities sought tools for evaluating animals so that only animals with excellent health, skills and aptitude will visit. *The Handbook for Animal-Assisted Activities and Animal-Assisted Therapy*, drafted in 1992, established basic guidelines for training volunteers to participate in visiting animal programs. The Handbook identifies criteria for volunteer training, evaluation and commitment. The criteria are outlined in Section 2c of the Handbook.

The Pet Partners *Team Training Course* is the result of hundreds of hours of work by dedicated members of the Pet Partners National Committee. We are grateful to the leadership provided by Shari Sternberger, Chair of the National Committee, in organizing so many volunteers in the production of this manual. In particular we would like to thank Jennifer Wilk for her work on Unit 1; Joanne Silver and Linda Case for their work on Unit 2; Ann Howie, MSW and Susan Zapf, OT for their work on Unit 3; Shari Sternberger, and Cathy Sigler, L/OTC and Robert Sigler, DVM for their work on Unit 4; Kathy Pontikes, Ph.D., and Linda Nebbe, MA for their work on Unit 5. We especially thank Mary Burch, Ph.D., Ellen Shay, MA and Shari Sternberger for their role as the driving force to begin and complete this course. We also thank the Pet Partners volunteers nationwide who provided suggestions based on their experiences. In addition, we thank the many Pet Partners who are health care professionals and provided invaluable advice on infection control, various medical conditions and treatment team dynamics.

We would like to thank Ellen Shay, MA, Delta Society Training Consultant, for her direction and guidance in the development of this course. We would like to thank Mary Burch, Ph.D. for her contribution of many hours in editing the preliminary version. Delta Society is grateful to the volunteers who edited the course through several versions— Marian Owczarczak, Kathy Pontikes, Ph.D., Shirley Fontes, RN, Kris Butler, Debbie Coultis, MA, Texas Coastal Pet Partners, Ellen Shay, MA, Pamela B. Thompson, Beverly Ann Babik and Nancy Warden. The course is a reflection of their extensive experience and dedication to quality visiting animal programs.

Delta Society gratefully acknowledges Hill's® Pet Nutrition, Inc., makers of Science Diet,® HealthBlend,® and Prescription Diet,® for a generous grant to develop the *Team Training Course*. We also thank Jane Dale Owen, and The Marc Haas and Helen Hotze Haas Foundation for providing additional funding for this project.

Because of the cooperation and generosity of so many people and sponsors, this course will give thousands of volunteers the skills they need to change the lives of hundreds of thousands of individuals in their communities through their very special animals.

IMPORTANT!!!

The information in the following section supercedes some of the training material outlined in this manual. Please read this section before continuing.

September 14, 2001

Dear Student:

There are some important and recent changes to the Pet Partners® Program. This section (between the two green sheets of paper) includes the new information. The information in this section takes precedence over what is presented in the remainder of the Manual. For example, the manual permits unlimited slip collars (choke chains). But, the new policy, as stated in this section, prohibits these collars. You should follow the policy in this section

The new policies emphasize the need to evaluate the handler and the animal as a team. What that means is you and your animal will be scored individually for each exercise. The "team" score will be the lower of the two scores.

Who is affected?

> New Pet Partners

> Current Pet Partners as they renew their certification

When are the new policies effective?

The new policies and procedures will be phased-in over a 6 ½ month period. Delta is the process of retraining all the current evaluators in the new policies and procedures. It is important for you to understand this because some evaluators will use the "old" policies until they are retrained.

1. Beginning on **September 14, 2001** evaluators who have been trained in the new policies will be required to apply them.

   Evaluators who have not yet been retrained must continue to use the "old" procedures.

2. After **March 31, 2002** all evaluators **must** use the new policies and procedures.

   Evaluators who have not been retrained will not be allowed to perform evaluations until they complete the retraining.

In effect, Delta will run two evaluation systems until **March 31, 2002**.

What do I have to do?

If you want to be evaluated before **March 31, 2002** you will need to know whether your evaluator has been trained in the new policies. There are several ways to check:

> Check the Team Evaluator listing on the Delta Society web site (www.deltasociety.org). Evaluators who have completed the training will be identified.

- Check the Course and Event Schedule on the Delta Society web site for Team Evaluations. If the evaluator's status isn't listed, contact the evaluator and ask.

- Contact Delta Society and ask about the evaluators in your area.

What do I need to know?

- There are some major changes in the Pet Partners Program. Changes of this nature will be in **bold, *italics*** to call your attention to the change. This document will also provide you with some additional information to help you prepare for the evaluation.

Handler Requirements

General
- Both the animal and the handler should be groomed and/or dressed appropriately as if they were going on a volunteer visit.

- Handlers must be at least 10 years old to be evaluated. Handlers younger than 16 must be accompanied by a parent or guardian and must have written permission to participate from a parent or guardian.

- The team shall not be evaluated and shall be scored as "Not Appropriate for Visiting" if the handler is under the influence of drugs or alcohol or smells of alcohol.

Items to Be Provided by the Handler

You must bring the following items to the evaluation. (If you do not you will not be evaluated that day.)

- A completed Handler's Questionnaire for the Evaluator's review.

- The animal's current rabies vaccination certificate. Rabies tags alone are not sufficient.

- A towel or small blanket if the animal will be carried (e.g., cat, very small dog).

- Acceptable collar or harness.

- Acceptable leash.

- Signed indemnity form.

- The animal's brush or comb.

- Written permission to register with the animal as a Pet Partners team and to visit with the animal if the handler is not the animal's owner.

It is critical that you bring the proper equipment with you when you go on visits. The evaluation is like a simulated visit. You wouldn't visit if you forgot your animal's leash or collar. In the same way, it is important that you bring all the required items to your evaluation.

One of the exercises will have the evaluator offer your animal treat. If your animal has special food requirements you will want to also bring a treat.

Evaluating Handlers with Disabilities

➤ If you have a disability and require accommodations please discuss your needs with the evaluator before the evaluation takes place.

➤ The evaluator will respect your right to privacy when discussing the accommodations. There is no need, nor will you be expected to discuss your disability with the evaluator.

Animal Requirements

➤ Dogs and cats must have lived with the handler for at least 6 months.

➤ Dogs and cats must be at least 1 year old at the time of the evaluation.

➤ A dog of any breed or mix of breeds may participate, in accordance with the local animal control laws.

➤ If a person other than the animal's owner will be evaluated with the animal, he or she must have written permission from the animal's owner to register with the animal as a Pet Partners team and to visit with the animal.

➤ Only domesticated animals will be evaluated and registered as Pet Partners. Wild or exotic animals will not to be evaluated.

Animals **will not** be evaluated if they:

➤ have any infections, open sores, wounds, or stitches;

➤ are ill, injured, or otherwise in pain;

➤ are taking antibiotics or anti-fungal medication; or

➤ are not well groomed.

The evaluator may decide whether or not to evaluate an animal in season. Please discuss this with the evaluator before the day of the evaluation.

Certain dogs will no longer be permitted to be Pet Partners

➤ Dogs trained to aggressively protect and/or encouraged to actively bite, even as a component of a dog sport (e.g., bite work that is part of Schutzhund) shall not be evaluated.

> This is primarily a liability issue. Although many dogs that have been trained for bite-work are wonderful and under very good control, it is a risk that the Pet Partners Program can no longer take. We are concerned about the reaction of the dog should a handler be approached in a threatening manner during a visit. Even though the handler may be able to bring the dog under control immediately, the dog has already reacted.

Evaluating Animals with Disabilities

Animals with physical disabilities may require accommodations during the evaluation. Please discuss these with the evaluator before the evaluation.

> The team will complete all required exercises in the Pet Partners Skills and Aptitude Tests.

> The animal's veterinarian, in consultation with the handler, will determine if the animal is physically able to participate in the evaluation and AAA/T as part of the health examination to be a Pet Partner.

> The evaluator's responsibility is to assess the team as he or she would any other team.

Equipment

> All animals must wear a collar or harness and be attached to a leash while on the test grounds.

> Animals brought to the test site in a carrier or crate must have the leash attached once they are out of the carrier.

Acceptable equipment:

> Well-fitted buckle, quick-release connection, or snap closure collars or harnesses made of leather or fabric;

> Martingales (i.e., limited slip) and *halters (e.g., Gentle Leader, Promise, Snoot Loop, Halti);*

> Metal buckles, slip rings, and D-rings are acceptable.

> All leather or fabric leashes, no more than 6 feet in length.

Unacceptable equipment:

> *Metal collars and harnesses, including martingales with metal links;*

> *Slip collars of any type;*

> Special training collars such as "pinch," "spike," electric, or spray collars;

➤ Metal chain and retractable leashes (e.g., Flexi-leash)

The collars, harnesses, and leashes teams use when visiting must be safe and humane for the animal, handler, and people being visited by the animal. Metal collars and leashes are not acceptable due to concerns about the safety of the people being visited. Slip collars of any material are unacceptable due to concerns about the safety of the people being visited and the safety of the animal.

If a dog wears a halter during the evaluation, the dog must also wear the halter while visiting as a Pet Partner. The evaluator shall mark the "must wear halter while visiting" checkbox in the Recommended Special Qualifications section of the Pet Partners Team Evaluation Score Sheet

Animals Handled by More Than One Person

➤ The person who will handle the animal on visits must be the same person handling the animal during the evaluation

➤ A person other than the animal's owner may register as a Pet Partner with the animal, as long as the person successfully completes the tests with the animal.

➤ If two people wish to register with the same animal (e.g., family members or friend), both handlers must individually complete the entire tests with the animal.

Evaluating Service Dogs

➤ If you are being evaluated as a Pet Partners team with your service dog, you may choose to use the dog's normal equipment, as long as it not included in the "Unacceptable" list in the previous Collars, Harnesses, and Leashes section.

➤ The dog's harness may include metal components in the structure or handle, as long as the harness will be safe for the people being visited.

➤ If the equipment you want to use is specifically identified as unacceptable, you will not be allowed to use that equipment, even if you state that it is required to control the dog. The safety of the people being visited takes precedence.

In some instances, a service dog's response during an exercise might be considered appropriate for its role as a service dog, but not normally be considered a desirable response for AAA/T. For example, a dog that helps a handler who uses a wheelchair reposition his/her arm should it fall off the armrest, may pick up the handler's arm in its mouth to put the arm back on the armrest. This is an example where the requirement that the dog not mouth the handler would be waived because the dog is performing a necessary task for the handler. If that same dog were to mouth the evaluator's hand when the evaluator picks up the dog's foot, then the requirement would apply, and the animal would be scored as "Not Appropriate for Visiting" or "Not Ready," as appropriate. Make sure to identify such potential responses for the evaluator prior to the evaluation. Such responses will be documented on your evaluation form.

Familiarity with the Facility or Evaluator

➢ An important purpose of the evaluation is to determine how the team will respond when it goes into a new setting, visiting people it doesn't know. If the team is evaluated in a facility it is familiar with, by an evaluator it knows, it is difficult to measure this response. This only applies to teams that are not yet Pet Partners.

➢ The evaluator will try to have a facility or setting different from the place where the team has practiced or trained. If a different facility is not available, the team will only be eligible for a "Predictable Environment" qualification.

➢ The evaluator should not have had a relationship with the team that could influence the animal's performance positively or negatively

During the Evaluation

All dogs except "very small dogs" (see the next section) must perform the entire evaluation walking on the floor and may not be carried by the handler.

Animals That Are Carried

➢ Handlers will present their cats and very small dogs as they will on a visit. For example, the animal may be held in the handler's arms or in a basket.

➢ If the handler would normally carry the animal, the evaluation makes sure that the animal will respond appropriately when carried.

➢ It is the handler's option whether and how the animal is carried.

Evaluating "Very Small Dogs"

➢ *A dog is considered a "very small dog" if it is about 10 inches tall at the shoulder and 10 to 15 pounds in weight, no matter what its breed or mix of breeds.*

➢ *Typically, a dog is a very small dog if an average person can easily pick up and carry the dog with one hand. The evaluator will not weigh and measure the dog.*

➢ *Very small dogs may be carried during the evaluation, except as noted for some exercises (e.g., Exercise 5, Out for a Walk).*

➢ *If the dog is carried during the evaluation, the dog must be carried with visiting.*

➢ *It is not necessary that the dog be carried during the entire evaluation. There may be some exercises that the handler prefers that the dog walk or stand on the floor.*

Definitions and Explanations Related to the Evaluation

On the Test Premises, Grounds, or Site

- ➢ Your evaluation starts at the point you and your animal get out of your car in the facility's parking lot and extends up into the actual area in which the evaluations occur.

Proactive, Reactive, and Inactive Handlers

- ➢ When visiting (and when being evaluated), a handler should be proactive.

- ➢ Proactive handlers anticipate the animal's response, and set the animal up to succeed.

- ➢ If you feel that your animal is becoming stressed or over stimulated during a particular exercise, you may request that the exercise stop or the level of activity be reduced.

- ➢ Handlers who respond to the animal's behavior after the fact are considered "reactive."

- ➢ Inactive handlers do not anticipate the animal's behavior; nor do they do much of anything after the animal has responded. During exercises, the inactive handler just stands like a statue, not giving the animal any direction.

Handlers who are consistently reactive and/or inactive during the evaluation will be scored as "Not Ready," causing the team to be scored as "Not Ready" for the overall evaluation, no matter how well the animal scored. Such handlers are not ready to be visiting.

Simultaneous vs. Multiple Cues

- ➢ When a handler gives two or more cues at the same time, it is to be considered a single cue. For example, many handlers give simultaneous verbal and hand cues to Sit.

- ➢ When the handler gives a verbal cue and the animal doesn't respond as desired, the handler might repeat the same verbal cue or try a hand cue. This is an example of multiple cues, and the animal should be scored as requiring multiple cues.

Encouragement vs. Multiple Cues vs. Nervous Chatter

The evaluation is not an obedience competition; therefore, the handler is allowed to give the animal multiple cues.

- ➢ An example of an appropriate situation for multiple cues would be if the animal didn't respond to the first cue. The handler may wait a moment to see if the animal will respond and, if it doesn't, give a second cue that might include gentle, appropriate physical guidance (e.g., light touch on the dog's hip to cue it to sit or light hand on a cat to cue it to stay in the basket).

- ➢ The handler might encourage or reassure an animal by repeating the cue, interspersed with praise, such as when a cat is performing the Exercise 10, Stay in Place.

➢ An example of inappropriate multiple cues is if the team is performing Exercise 10, Stay in Place, and the handler continues to cue the dog to stay, even though the dog is staying, with no movement to not continue to stay. This may be a case of nervous chatter and/or the handler trying to calm his/herself.

Role Playing or Pretending to Be on a Visit

➢ The purpose of the evaluation is to assess how the team will do on a visit.

➢ To assess this the handler must do some role-playing. Both ends of the leash are critical to successful visits.

➢ The handler should interact comfortably with the evaluator. Likewise during exercises where there are "pretend" patients the handler should interact as if on a visit.

➢ Some patients may prefer to visit with the animals, but most also want to talk with another person.

➢ Handlers need to have good "people skills" to make the visit successful and satisfying.

➢ Handlers who do not demonstrate good "people skills" will be scored as "Not Ready".

During the PPST, you will be assessed on how you interact with the evaluator, the evaluator's assistants, the animal, and the environment around you.

During the PPAT, you will be assessed on how appropriately you interact with the evaluator and evaluator's assistants as though you are on a visit. They will be acting as though they are in a facility. Your interactions may be in the form of questions, responses to the evaluator and evaluator's' comments, eye contact, smiling, head nodding, directing the animal to interact, or other verbal and nonverbal methods of communicating.

What Makes a Team Appropriate?

The Handler

➢ Handlers should have an interest in and enjoy people and not be put off in a healthcare setting. The handler must also have good control of and communication with the animal.

➢ Handlers should be confident and natural in their interactions.

➢ Handlers should inspire confidence.

➢

The Animal

➢ Animals should have a basic level of training so that they are reliable, predictable, and under control, even in crowded situations and when there are loud noises.

➢ Pet Partners animals should be well behaved, have good manners, and enjoy people.

> The animal should inspire confidence.

General Desirable Responses

During the evaluation, the evaluator will look for the following responses from you and your animal.

Handler

> Is friendly making eye contact, smiling, etc.

> Is aware of possible animal responses, behavior, and position, and reassures, cues, or commands (as needed) to help animal be successful.

> Ensures the animal's well being.

> Does not yell or use a loud voice, or forcefully jerk on the leash.

> Demonstrates gentle interaction with the animal. Speaks to the animal in a friendly, conversational, normal tone of voice.

> Is confident, natural, and relaxed in the performance of each exercise and toward evaluator and animal.

> May talk to, praise, cue, encourage, and reassure the animal as needed throughout the exercises, but cannot offer food or use toys.

Animal

> Shows no shyness, aggression, or fear.

> Does not eliminate.

> May change position.

> Demonstrates non-threatening or neutral body posture.

> Friendly wagging or relaxed tail.

> Has soft body, relaxed face.

> If the animal vocalizes, it does so only once or twice, and the handler acts to stop the vocalization. Exuberant or excited vocalizations that are quickly controlled by the handler and contented noises (e.g., grunting, snuffling, sighs, purring) are allowed at appropriate points during exercises.

> Vocalizations such as continually barking, loud whining, howling, and aggressive vocalizations are indications of stress or aggression and not allowed.

Scoring for Individual Exercises

In each exercise, the evaluator is looking at four aspects of the team's performance:

> How the animal relates to the handler

> How the handler relates to the animal

> How the animal reacts to the evaluator and assistants

> How the handler interacts with the evaluators and assistants

Teams will be scored according to 4 categories

Handler Not Appropriate for Visiting

> The handler behaves in an inappropriate or inhumane way towards any animal or person while on the test grounds.

> There is a low possibility that the handler's behavior and skills can be corrected and/or improved.

Handler Not Ready

> The handler's animal handling skills interfere with or do not support the animal's performance of the exercise.

> The handler is reactive or inactive, rather than proactive, or the handler may provide unnecessary repetitive commands or cues.

> The handler has few or inappropriate interactions with the evaluator and assistants.

> The handler is stressed, awkward, or otherwise uncomfortable during the exercise.

> There is a high possibility that the handler's behavior and skills can be corrected and/or improved.

Score Handler a "1" If:

> The handler's animal handling skills often support the animal's performance of the exercise.

> The handler is sometimes reactive or inactive and sometimes proactive, and seldom provides unnecessary repetitive commands or cues.

> The handler usually interacts with the evaluator and assistants, and the interactions are appropriate.

> The handler is usually relaxed, smooth, and comfortable during the exercise, but occasionally shows stress or awkwardness.

Score Handler a "2" If:

> The handler is consistently proactive in handling the animal, always providing the appropriate level of commands and cues to support the animal's performance of the exercise.

> The handler consistently and appropriately interacts with the evaluator and assistants as though on a visit.

> The handler is consistently relaxed, smooth, and confident during the exercise.

Animal Not Appropriate for Visiting

> The animal behaves in an aggressive way towards any animal or person while on the test grounds.

> The animal is so fearful that continuing would be inhumane treatment of the animal.

Animal Not Ready

> The animal does not perform the skills required by the exercises.

> The animal displays clusters of displacement signals indicating stress, or is fearful, or aggressive.

> The animal avoids or only tolerates interactions with the evaluator and assistants.

Score Animal a "1" If:

> The animal is able to perform the skills required by the exercise, but sometimes needs additional direction or guidance from the handler.

> The animal may show some signals or signs of stress or fear, but recovers quickly and is often relaxed.

> The animal accepts and sometimes enjoys interactions with the evaluator and assistants.

Score Animal a "2" If:

> The animal performs the skills required by the exercise with little or no direction from the handler.

> The animal is relaxed and confident.

> The animal seeks out, welcomes, and enjoys interactions with the evaluator and assistants.

Determining the Team's Score

> The responses of the handler are equally as important as the animal's responses. Therefore the handler and the animal each receive a score.

> *The team score will be the lower of the two scores. Poor performance by either member of the team will affect the overall score for an exercise.*

General Procedures for the Evaluation

The Evaluator will explain the procedures to you before each exercise.

> Unlike obedience competitions, you are encouraged to talk to your animal during the entire evaluation. The main point is that the animal is under control.

> Treat your animal, the evaluator, and the assistants as though you are on a visit.

> If you're uncomfortable with or unsure of what's going on during the evaluation, please let the evaluator know. Please be your animal's advocate.

What to Do when Unsure about Responses or Pushing an Animal or Handler Too Far

> As your animal's advocate, it is your responsibility to ensure your animal's safety and comfort. You may ask the evaluator to reduce the level of activity or to stop the exercise if you feel your animal is becoming too stressed, fearful, or otherwise uncomfortable.

> You may also ask the evaluator to interact, at least initially, with your animal in the way that would make your animal most comfortable (e.g., kneeling down next to the dog instead of leaning over the dog), as long as it is in accordance with the policies and procedures and the evaluator is comfortable doing so.

Stopping the Evaluation Due to Clusters of Stress and Other Behaviors

> If a handler or animal displays undue stress behaviors or signals the evaluator will stop the evaluation and score the team as "Not Ready."

> If the handler does not recognize his/her own signs of stress or the stress, fear, or other signals of his/her animal, it is the evaluator's responsibility to protect the team and stop the evaluation, if necessary.

The Pet Partners Skills Test (PPST)

> The team may be given up to 3 attempts to successfully complete skills of the PPST only if the mistake is due to handler error.

> The exercises of the PPST are performed at stations. The exercises may be combined, but must be performed in the correct order.

The PPST Exercises

Exercise 1: Review the Handler's Questionnaire

> Purpose--his exercise allows the evaluator to ask questions about the team that may alert the evaluator to circumstances that may affect the evaluation. The team is also allowed to familiarize itself with the testing area.

Exercise 2: Accepting a Friendly Stranger

> Purpose--This exercise demonstrates that the team can greet strangers appropriately.

Exercise 3: Accepting Petting

> Purpose--This exercise demonstrates that the team has suitable social skills and control for visits.

Exercise 4: Appearance and Grooming

> Purpose--This exercise demonstrates that the team's appearance is suitable for visits, the animal welcomes being groomed and examined and permits a stranger to do so, and the handler's care, concern, and responsibility.

Exercise 5: Out for a Walk

> Purpose--This exercise demonstrates that the handler is in control of the animal and the animal is comfortable moving with the handler.

Exercise 6: Walking through a Crowd

> Purpose--This exercise simulates a crowded corridor and demonstrates that the team can move about politely in pedestrian traffic and under control in public places.

Exercise 7: Reaction to Distractions

> Purpose--This exercise demonstrates that the animal remains confident when faced with common distracting situations.

Exercise 8–10: Sit on Command, Down on Command, Stay in Place

> Purpose--These exercises demonstrate that the dog has training and will sit, lie down, and stay at the handler's command. These exercises demonstrate that animal other than dogs will accept being passed from one person to another and remain where placed.

Exercise 11: Come when Called

> Purpose--This exercise is for dogs only. This test demonstrates that the dog will leave pleasant distractions to come to the handler and allow the handler to attach a leash. *(Very small dogs that have been carried during other parts of the evaluation, must complete this exercise on the floor.)*

Exercise 12: Reaction to a Neutral Dog

> ➤ Purpose--This exercise demonstrates the animal can behave politely around an approaching dog, the handler is aware of the animal's potential response to a dog, can help the animal succeed, and the handler can be polite and friendly to a stranger.

The Pet Partners Aptitude Test (PPAT)

The PPAT is a combination of scenarios in which the individual exercises flow from one to another.

The current order of the exercises allows for escalation of stressors during testing.

> ➤ *During the PPAT, the handler and animal should interact (i.e., role play) with the evaluator and assistants as though they are people being visited at a facility.*

> ➤ The handler should be able to work with the animal while at the same time interacting socially with the "client" (evaluator and assistants) as if on a visit.

> ➤ The handler should pay close attention to the animal during exam, giving cues to help the animal accept and welcome handling.

> ➤ The animal should accept interaction in a pleasant, forgiving or welcoming manner as opposed to endures, tolerates, or avoids interactions with people.

PPAT Exercises

Exercise A: Overall Exam

> ➤ Purpose--This exercise demonstrates that the animal will accept and is comfortable being examined by a stranger and the handler knows how to present the animal on a visit and how to help the animal accept and welcome being touched all over.

Exercise B: Exuberant and Clumsy Petting

> ➤ Purpose--This exercise demonstrates that the animal will maintain self-control and will tolerate clumsy petting by people who have differing physical abilities or who do not know proper etiquette around the animal and the handler can work with the animal to help it tolerate such attention.

Exercise C: Restraining Hug

> ➤ Purpose--This exercise demonstrates that the animal will accept or welcome restraint and that the handler can assist the animal to accept or welcome such a situation.

Exercise D: Staggering, Gesturing Individual

> Purpose--This exercise demonstrates that the animal will exhibit confidence when a person acting in an unusual manner approaches and then interacts with it and the handler has the social skills to interact with such a person while attending to the animal.

Exercise E: Angry Yelling

> Purpose--This exercise demonstrates that the animal will not be upset when someone exhibits angry emotions and that the handler can help the animal tolerate such a situation.

Exercise F: Bumped from Behind

> Purpose--This exercise demonstrates that the animal is able to recover when a person bumps into it and that the handler can not only tolerate the animal being bumped, but can also assist the animal to recover.

Exercise G: Crowded and Petted by Several People

> Purpose--This exercise demonstrates that the animal will tolerate crowding and petting by several people at once and the handler has the social skills to visit with a group of people while still attending to the animal and maintaining its well-being.

Exercise H: Leave It

> Purpose--This exercise demonstrates the animal will ignore a toy left on the floor.

Exercise I: Offered a Treat

> Purpose--This exercise demonstrates the animal will take a treat politely and gently.

Exercise J: Overall Assessment

> Purpose--This item determines that the handler is proactive, not reactive or inactive, in the handling and management of his/her animal.

After the Evaluation

Overall Scoring for the Evaluation

With this version of the Team Evaluator Course, determining the score has been made much simpler than previous versions.

If all requirements are met, teams may be scored as:

> **Not Appropriate for Visiting**

> **Not Ready**

> **Predictable Environment**

> **Complex Environment**

>

Predictable Environment

To qualify for a Predictable Environment placement, the team must have:

> Received at least a score of "1" on all exercises of the PPST; Exercise A, Overall Exam; Exercise B, Exuberant and Clumsy Petting; or Exercise C, Restraining Hug of the PPAT.

> Received 2 or fewer "Not Ready" scores on the PPAT

Complex Environment

> To qualify for an Complex Environment placement, the team must have received at least a score of "1" on all PPST and PPAT exercises, and must have received a score of "2" on **all** the following exercises:

Exercise 2	Exercise A
Exercise 4	Exercise B
Exercise 5	Exercise C
Exercise 6	Exercise G
Exercise 10	Exercise J

Team Qualification Matrix

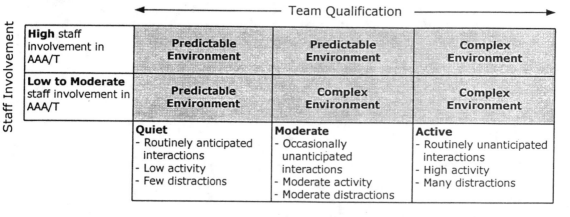

Figure 1: Team Qualification Matrix

Note:

The PPST/PPAT may only be performed for the purpose of evaluating teams for Pet Partners, and may not be performed in conjunction with evaluations for other therapy animal organizations, the American Kennel Club's Canine Good Citizenship test, to certify an animal as a service animal, or any other purpose.

Therapy Animals Are Not the Same As Service Animals

Many people are under the mistaken impression that therapy animals and their handlers have the same rights of access as people with disabilities and their service animals. In some cases, people have their animals evaluated and registered as therapy animals with the intention of insisting on access to public spaces with their animals, as if the animal were a service animal. They may be trying to have their animals accompany them in airplanes, into stores, or in restaurants that have "no pets/animals" policies. Essentially, this is fraudulent and, in many areas, illegal. Unless the handler meets the definition of a person with a disability and the animal meets the definition of a service animal, the team has no more rights of access than a person with a companion animal or pet. Delta Society will not tolerate Pet Partners who fraudulently pass off their therapy animals as service animals.

For information about service animals, visit the Delta web site (www.deltasociety.org) or contact Delta Society.

Contents

Introduction

Welcome

Welcome to Delta Society Pet Partners® *Team Training Course*. Our goal is to raise and maintain the standards of professionalism for the field of animal-assisted therapy and animal-assisted activities so that they will become widely recognized as valuable forms of treatment.

By completing the *Pets Helping People Manual* or attending an equivalent Delta Society workshop, you can meet the volunteer training requirements to become registered as a Pet Partner. In addition to the volunteer training requirements, you must also complete the skills and aptitude screening with your animal. Everything required to become a registered Pet Partner is described in this course. When you complete this process, you'll be able to share your animal teammate and your friendship with a variety of people in need, including lonely elderly people, school-aged children, individuals with disabilities, and others.

Thank you for joining us. We want to help you share your animal and your special skills with others as a Pet Partners volunteer.

Course Overview

This course provides you with information and activities that will prepare you and your animal to work effectively as a Pet Partners team.

As you proceed through the *Pets Helping People Manual*, read each lesson and complete the accompanying learning activities. It is important that you complete all of the assignments, which include watching videotapes and reading related articles.

When you have completed all five units, locate the Registration Packet in the back of this course and answer the Volunteer Review questions. This packet has all forms necessary to complete the Pet Partners registration for you and your animal(s). After you have completed the Registration Packet, mail it to Delta Society.

Learning Activities

There are several types of activities that will help you learn and practice the information in the course. Each type of activity is identified with a small graphic. The learning activities will be most effective if you complete them at the point in the course in which they appear.

 Video

Throughout the course, this small graphic lets you know when to watch the video. At the end of each video segment, you will be told to stop the tape and return to the text. The video segments will be on the tape in the same order they are used during the course. Watch as many times as needed in order to understand the information.

If you are completing this course at home and don't own a VCR for viewing the video, ask a family member or friend if you can watch the video at their house. Many community and school libraries also have VCRs you may use.

 Articles

The articles referred to in the text are provided in Appendix A. The full bibliographic reference is provided for each article.

Activity

Activities will provide you with the opportunity to observe, first hand, concepts presented in the course. They will also be used to show you good examples of how you and/or your animal should act when you're visiting. You'll also be able to practice some new skills.

 Research

You will be encouraged to research information that is unique to your local situation and to learn more information about the topic being discussed.

Sidebars

Short stories and examples will be set off from the main text in sidebars.

Layout

Units

Complete the five units in order. Each unit begins with an introduction, which provides an overview of the unit and includes the Unit Map.

The Unit Map

The five units are made up of lessons. There is a map at the beginning of each unit. Unit maps show the sequence in which you should complete the lessons. In most units, you will be able to choose the order in which the lessons are completed. This allows some flexibility as you proceed through the course.

xii

Unit 1
Volunteers

Unit Overview:

You, the volunteer, are the focus of this unit. You will be provided with some background information and terminology required for understanding the units that follow. This unit also helps you consider your needs and responsibilities as a Pet Partner.

Unit Map:

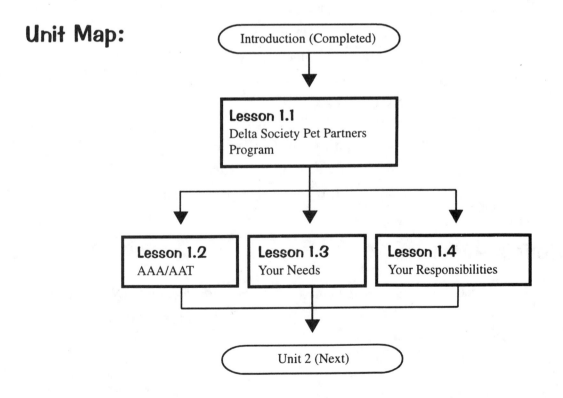

Introduction (Completed)

Lesson 1.1
Delta Society Pet Partners
Program

Lesson 1.2
AAA/AAT

Lesson 1.3
Your Needs

Lesson 1.4
Your Responsibilities

Unit 2 (Next)

Delta Society
Pet Partners Program

Lesson Overview:

This lesson introduces Delta Society, and Delta Society Pet Partners Program and familiarizes you with general procedures related to becoming registered as a Pet Partner.

Lesson Objectives:

1. State the purpose of Delta Society.
    a. Identify the mission of Delta Society.
    b. Identify the goals of Delta Society.
    c. Identify the services provided by Delta Society.

2. State the purpose of the Pet Partners Program.
    a. Describe the purpose of the Pet Partners Program.
    b. Describe the requirements of Pet Partners registration.
    c. Identify the benefits of becoming a Pet Partner.

Materials Required:

Video: *Welcome to the Course and Introduction to Delta Society and the Pet Partners Program.*

Delta Society — What Is It and What Does It Do?

Founded in 1977, the Delta Society is an international, not-for-profit organization of pet owners, volunteers, therapists, educators, health professionals, veterinarians, and other professionals.

Mission

Delta Society promotes *animals helping people* improve their health, independence and quality of life.

Goals

- *Expand* public awareness of the positive effects of animals on family health, and human development

- *Reduce* barriers to involvement of animals in everyday life

- *Bring* animal-assisted therapy to more people

- *Increase* the number of well-trained service dogs available to people with disabilities

The Pet Partners Program — A Special Program

The Pet Partners Program is one service program of the Delta Society. A person and his/her animal can register as Pet Partners when the animal has successfully completed a health, skills and aptitude screening, and the person has completed volunteer training requirements. Registered Pet Partners share the physical and emotional benefits of human-animal interactions with people in a variety of settings.

People without pets can register by fulfilling the volunteer requirements. A person without an animal of his/her own, can go on visits with a registered team (animal and handler). In order to act as a handler, s/he should complete the skills and aptitude screening with the registered animal s/he will take on visits. This allows assessment of the team and how they work together.

This program assures human service providers that the volunteers who enter their facilities are well-prepared and their animals have been carefully screened.

How to Become Registered as a Pet Partners Team

The forms needed for registration are in Appendix D.

Step 1:

❑ Complete Pet Partners *Team Training Course*
(at a workshop or by studying at home).

❑ Complete the Volunteer Review.

The Volunteer Review is used to ensure that you have completed the course and have the knowledge and skills required to be an effective Pet Partner.

- The Volunteer Review is an open-book test, so you may refer to this document while you complete the questions.

- Once you have completed the course, read the Volunteer Review questions and fill out the answer sheet.

Step 2:

❑ Have your animal's health screened by a veterinarian.
Take the Health Screening Forms for the veterinarian to fill out.

❑ Pass the Pet Partners Skills Test (PPST) with your animal.
See Lesson 2.1 for a detailed description of the PPST. The skills and aptitude tests can be completed in any order.

❑ Pass the Pet Partners Aptitude Test (PPAT) with your animal.
See Lesson 2.1 for a detailed description of the PPAT.

Step 3:

❑ Submit completed forms to:

Delta Society Pet Partners
289 Perimeter Rd. E.
Renton, WA 98055-1329

Benefits of Becoming a Pet Partner

Once you and your pet register as Pet Partners, you receive the following benefits:

- A special tag for your animal teammate, and an identification badge for you that includes a picture of you with your animal teammate.

- The Pet Partners Newsletter that provides "how-to" tips and information on programs throughout the country.

- Personal liability insurance (for volunteers).

- Networking opportunities with Pet Partners all across the United States (and in several other countries).

- Chances for recognition. You will have the opportunity to apply for the "Spirit of Jingles Award." This national award was named after Dr. Boris Levinson's dog. Dr. Levinson was one of the first professionals to document the benefits of animal-assisted therapy. The "Spirit of Jingles Award" winners are recognized each year at a special event. Winners usually receive national media exposure including television and magazine coverage.

 **Video**

Video: *Welcome to the Course and Introduction to Delta Society and the Pet Partners Program.*

Lesson 1.2 AAA and AAT

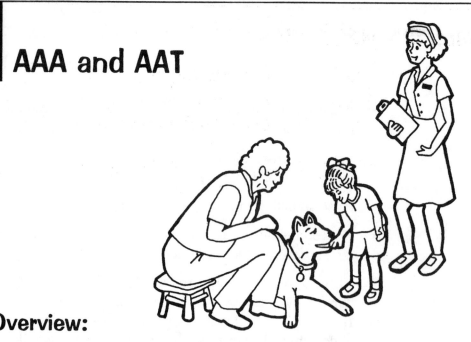

Lesson Overview:

The history of human-animal interactions is outlined in this lesson. As the field of animal-assisted activities (AAA) and animal-assisted therapy (AAT) has become more organized, documented and well-known, there has been a movement toward identifying common terminology. This lesson introduces the terms "AAA" and "AAT," identifies the differences and describes the benefits of each. The lesson also identifies situations in which AAA/AAT would be inappropriate.

Lesson Objectives:

1. Describe the history of human-animal interaction programs.

   a. Identify ways human-animal interaction has been used in the past.

   b. Identify settings where human-animal interaction can be used.

2. Identify the differences between AAA and AAT.

   a. Define AAA.   d. Identify the goals of AAT.

   b. Identify examples of AAA.   e. Identify examples of AAT.

   c. Define AAT.

3. Identify the benefits of AAA and AAT.

   a. Identify benefits human-animal interactions may provide to people in institutions.

   b. Identify instances when AAA and AAT would not be beneficial.

Materials Required:

Video:	*How Animals Help People Heal.*
Video:	*Differences Between AAA and AAT.*
Video:	*A Look at Beneficial and Non-Beneficial Visits.*
Article #1:	"Historical Perspectives on Human–Animal Interactions."
Article #2:	Pages from *Nature as a Guide*.

 **Article**

AAA/AAT is a field with an exciting and rich history. Before you proceed with this course, turn to the Articles in Appendix A and read,

Article #1:   "Historical Perspectives on Human-Animal Interactions."

▣ Video

Now watch the video: *How Animals Help People Heal.*

AAA Versus AAT — What's the Difference?

When you and your animal visit as Pet Partners, you participate in animal-assisted activities (AAA) or animal-assisted therapy (AAT). These are the terms that human service providers and volunteers use when referring to the involvement of animals in human treatment programs.

Although AAA and AAT are the preferred terms, you may also hear the terms "pet-facilitated therapy" and "animal-facilitated therapy." The term "pet therapy" should be avoided because it is inaccurate and misleading. This term was widely used several decades ago to refer to animal behavior training programs. The preferred terms (animal-assisted therapy and animal-assisted activities) suggest that the animal is the motivating force that enhances treatment provided by a well-trained person.

What is AAA?

Definition

The formal definition of animal-assisted activities is:

> *"AAA provides opportunities for motivational, educational, recreational, and/or therapeutic benefits to enhance quality of life. AAA are delivered in a variety of environments by specially trained professionals, para-professionals, and/or volunteers, in association with animals that meet specific criteria."*[1]

---

[1] Delta Society. 1992. *Handbook for Animal-Assisted Activities and Animal-Assisted Therapy.* Renton, WA: Delta Society.

What does this really mean? Animal-assisted *activities* are basically the casual "meet-and-greet" activities that involve pets visiting people. The same activity can be repeated with many people, unlike a therapy program that is tailored to a particular person or medical condition.

The Key Features of AAA Are:

- Specific treatment goals are not planned for each visit.

- Volunteers and treatment providers are not required to take detailed notes.

- Visit content is spontaneous and visits last as long or as short as needed.

Examples of AAA

- A group of volunteers takes their pets to a nursing home once a month to "visit." The visit occurs as a large-group activity with some direction and assistance provided by facility staff. The volunteer group facilitator keeps an informal log about who was visited.

- An individual brings her dog to a children's long-term care facility to "play" with residents. Although the staff is involved in the visits, the staff has not set treatment goals for the interactions. Aside from signing in and out, no records are kept.

- A dog obedience club gives an obedience demonstration at a residential facility for teenagers with delinquent behavior.

What is AAT?

Definition

The formal definition of animal-assisted therapy is:

> *"AAT is a goal-directed intervention in which an animal that meets specific criteria is an integral part of the treatment process. AAT is directed and/ or delivered by a health/human service professional with specialized expertise, and within the scope of practice of his/her profession.*

AAT is designed to promote improvement in human physical, social, emotional, and/or cognitive functioning [Cognitive functioning refers to thinking and intellectual skills]. AAT is provided in a variety of settings and may be group or individual in nature. This process is documented and evaluated."[1]

The Key Features of AAT Are:

- There are specified goals and objectives for each individual.

- Progress is measured.

In most therapeutic settings, there are requirements for measuring progress. In nursing homes, goals may be recorded in Nursing Care Plans. In facilities for people with developmental disabilities, goals are written on Habilitation Plans. In educational settings, school-aged children will have Individualized Educational Plans (IEPs). The names of these plans for recording individualized goals may vary slightly from state to state.

Examples of AAT

- An occupational therapist is assisted by a dog and its handler in work to increase a person's range of motion in her shoulder. The person has the specific goal of increasing her ability to reach towards one of her feet. The dog knows specialized commands that are used during the sessions. The progress made during each session is documented by the Occupational Therapist.

- A mental health professional incorporates a guinea pig in working with a small group of adults with developmental disabilities. People in the group are working on improving their communication and social skills. The professional documents the results of each session in each person's chart.

Goals of AAT Programs

Animals can be incorporated into a variety of programs. If you become involved in an AAT program, ask the treatment provider to explain the person's goals to you. The following are some examples of AAT goals.

Physical

- Improve fine motor skills
- Improve wheelchair skills
- Improve standing balance

Mental Health

- Increase verbal interactions between group members
- Increase attention skills (i.e., paying attention, staying on task)
- Develop leisure/recreation skills
- Increase self-esteem
- Reduce anxiety
- Reduce loneliness

Educational

- Increase vocabulary
- Aid in long- or short-term memory
- Improve knowledge of concepts such as size, color, etc.

Motivational

- Improve willingness to be involved in a group activity
- Improve interactions with others
- Improve interactions with staff
- Increase exercise

Differences between AAA and AAT

At first glance, it may be difficult to tell the difference between AAA and AAT. The following are some critical differences you can learn to identify. Although AAA may have one or more of these characteristics, AAT must have all three. AAT is a more formal process than AAA.

➤ **AAT is directed by health/human services professionals as a normal part of their practice.**

This person may be a physician, OT, PT, CTRS, teacher, nurse, social worker, speech therapist, mental health professional, etc. The animal may be handled by the professional or by a volunteer under the direction of a professional. To be considered AAT, a professional must use the animal as a part of his/her own specialty. For example, a social worker must use the animal in the context of social work. If this same social worker were to visit a group of children on an informal basis, the activity would be considered AAA.

➤ **AAT is goal-directed.**

There is a specific end in mind, such as improvement in social skills, range of motion, verbal skills, attention span, etc. Any visit with an animal may result in the achievement of one or more of these goals. Unless the goals have been identified and defined before the session, the session would not be considered AAT.

➤ **AAT is documented.**

Each session is documented in the person's record with the progress and activity noted.

 Video

Now watch the video: *Differences Between AAA and AAT.*

Some Terms You Should Know

You may come in contact with or work with a variety of therapists when you and your animal visit. The following descriptions will familiarize you with some of them.

Occupational Therapist (OT)

OTs generally work on physical, social, and cognitive skills with clients. They work on activities that may include daily living skills (e.g., eating, meal preparation, cleaning), and vocational skills. OTs also work on helping the client regain the functional use of the hands and upper body. OTs work on goals such as increasing range of motion. (Range of motion is how much the client can move a particular part of the body.) OTs can use equipment such as splints to keep a client's hands from becoming contracted. (Contracted means reduced in size and mobility; cramped or constricted.)

Physical Therapist (PT)

Generally, PTs work on improving gross motor abilities (using the larger muscle groups). For example, PTs work on goals such as strengthening one's legs and walking.

Note:

PTs and OTs often work closely together in their treatment approach. If a facility has both, very often OTs will work on movement of the upper body and functional living skills. PTs will work on movement of the lower body, ambulation (ambulation means moving around or walking), and the client's living environment.

Certified Therapeutic Recreation Specialist (CTRS)

A CTRS provides therapeutic recreation training for clients. This involves measuring progress and having specific recreation goals and objectives for clients. Goals are designed to provide leisure education and support other therapies. For example, if a person has motor problems, the CTRS may plan a program that involves teaching the person to play baseball. Throwing the ball and running to bases might result in improved motor abilities. A CTRS has specialized and advanced training (i.e. a college degree) and national certification in therapeutic recreation.

Recreational Therapist (RT) or Activity Director

An RT or Activity Director provides people with recreational activities. While s/he may plan various recreational activities like a CTRS does, the activities may not involve the same level of documentation and measurement of progress. An RT or Activity Director has formal education and is responsible for planning weekly or monthly activities for facility residents.

Other Staff Members

Your AAA/AAT setting will probably have a number of other staff members including psychologists, speech therapists, counselors, social workers, nurses, doctors, teachers, aides and technicians. You may be involved in working with any of these people in your AAA/AAT activities. If you have questions about the role of a staff member at a facility, your facility contact person should be able to answer them.

Benefits of AAA and AAT

Human-animal interactions may provide the following benefits to adults and children in a variety of human care facilities.

Empathy

(Identifying with and understanding the feelings and motives of another.)

Studies report that children who live in homes in which a pet is considered a member of the family are more empathetic than children in homes without pets.

Children see animals as peers. It is easier to teach children to be empathetic with an animal than with a human. With animals, what you see is what you get. Humans are not as direct. Children can be taught to read an animal's body language. Understanding what an animal is feeling is easier than determining what a person is feeling because the animal is straightforward and lives in the moment. As children get older, their ability to empathize with animals will carry over into their experiences with people.

Outward Focus

(Bringing individuals out of themselves.)

Individuals who have mental illness or low self-esteem focus on themselves; animals can help them focus on their environment. Rather than thinking and talking about themselves and their problems, they watch and talk to and about the animals.

Nurturing

(Promoting the growth and development of another living thing.)

Nurturing skills are learned. Many at-risk children have not learned nurturing skills through the traditional channel—their parents. By being taught to take care of an animal, the children can develop these skills. Psychologically, when a person nurtures, his/her need to be nurtured is being fulfilled.

Rapport

(A relationship of mutual trust or a feeling of connection or bonding.)

Animals can open a channel of emotionally safe, non-threatening communication between client and therapist.

In therapy settings, animals help present an air of emotional safety. If a therapist has an animal in his/her office, s/he "can't be all bad." The animal's presence may open a path through a person's initial resistance. Children are especially likely to project their feelings and experiences onto an animal.

Acceptance

(Favorable reception or approval.)

Animals have a way of accepting without qualification. They don't care how a person looks or what they say. An animal's acceptance is non-judgmental, forgiving, and uncomplicated by the psychological games people often play.

Entertainment

At a minimum, the presence of an animal can be entertaining. Even people who don't like animals often enjoy watching their antics and reactions. Especially in long-term care facilities, it seems everyone is entertained by animal visits in some way.

Socialization

(Seeking out or enjoying the company of others.)

Studies have shown that when dogs and cats come to visit a care facility, there is more laughter and interaction among residents than during any other "therapy" or entertainment time. In an in-patient setting, the presence of animals encourages socialization in three ways: between clients; between clients and staff; and between clients, staff and family or other visitors. Staff members have reported that it is easier to talk to residents during and after animal visits. Family members often come during the animal visits and some have reported that it is an especially comfortable and pleasant time to come.

Mental Stimulation

Mental stimulation occurs because of increased communication with other people, recalled memories, and the entertainment provided by the animals. In situations that are depressing or institutional, the presence of the animals serves to brighten the atmosphere, increasing amusement, laughter and play. These positive distractions may help to decrease people's feelings of isolation or alienation.

Physical Contact, Touch

Much has been written about the correlation between touch and health. Infants who are not touched do not develop healthy relationships with other people and often fail to thrive and grow physically. For some people, touch from another person is not acceptable, but the warm, furry touch of a dog or cat is. In hospitals where most touch is painful or invasive, the touch of an animal is safe, non-threatening, and pleasant.
There are a number of programs for people who have been physically or sexually abused in which staff and volunteers are not allowed to touch the clients. In cases like these, having an animal to hold, hug, and touch can make a world of difference to people who would otherwise have no positive, appropriate physical contact.

Physiological Benefits

(Positive effects on the basic functioning of the body.)

Many people are able to relax when animals are present. Tests have shown that the decrease in heart rate and blood pressure can be dramatic. Even watching fish swim in an aquarium can be very calming.

Something More

When they are with animals, some people feel spiritual fulfillment or a sense of oneness with life and nature. This is hard to define or explain. Some well-known authors have described their relationships with animals and nature as part of their sustaining life energy and/or part of their communion and relationship with God. Albert Schweitzer, George W. Carver, and J. Allen Boone (author of *Kinship with All Life*), among others, express this "something more" in their writing and work.

Article

Before proceeding, turn to Appendix A and read,

Article #2:   Pages from *Nature as a Guide*.

Instances When AAA/AAT Would Not Be Beneficial[2]

As beneficial as AAA and AAT can be, it is not always appropriate for every situation. Remember, "Good intention is not an adequate substitute for common sense." The following guidelines will help you identify those situations when AAA/AAT may not be beneficial.

For the People You Visit

AAA/AAT may not be beneficial for the people you visit in the following situations:

- When animals are a source of rivalry and competition in a group.

- When someone becomes possessive and attempts to "adopt" a visiting animal for him or herself.

- Injury may occur from inappropriate handling, animal selection, or lack of supervision.

- People with brain injury, developmental disabilities, or senility may provoke an animal without realizing it.

---

[2] Adapted from McCulloch, M. 1983. Pet Therapy – An Overview. *The Human-Pet Relationship: International Symposium on the 80th birthday of Nobel Prize Winner Prof. Konrad Lorenz.* Vienna: Institute for Interdisciplinary Research on Human-Pet Relationships. 25-31.

- People with unrealistic expectations may think an animal is rejecting them. This may deepen their feelings of low self-esteem.

- Allergies may create breathing problems, such as asthma, for the person.

- Zoonotic diseases (diseases that can be passed between people and other animals) may be transmitted, particularly if precautions are not taken. (This will be covered in Lesson 5.4, Reducing Risk).

- People with open wounds or low resistance to disease must be carefully monitored. Participation may need to be restricted.

- Someone may be fearful of some animals.

- People may view animals differently due to their cultural background.

For the Caregiver

Caregivers may consider AAA/AAT to be inappropriate when:

- Staff and other caregivers are not allowed to participate in the decision-making process about AAA/AAT, and are not properly oriented.

- Some see animals in a facility as totally inappropriate.

- Some do not like animals or fear them.

- Caregivers may be allergic to animals.

For the Institution

Institutions may consider AAA/AAT inappropriate when:

- Legal liability for an accident or injury involving a resident or staff member is a concern.

- Legal obstacles may have to be overcome.

- Noise, sanitation, disease, and other environmental concerns exist.

- Cost factors must be weighed.

For the Animal

AAA/AAT may be inappropriate for the animals when:

- Injuries from rough handling or from other animals may occur.

- Basic animal welfare cannot be assured. This includes veterinary care, and access to water and exercise areas.

- The animal does not enjoy visiting.

▶ Video

Now watch the video: *A Look at Beneficial and Non-Beneficial Visits.*

Lesson 1.3 Your Needs

Lesson Overview:

As you visit in AAA/AAT settings, you will notice some behaviors and feelings that occur in you, your animal, the people you visit, and the facility staff. This lesson will help you think about your animal's role as your teammate, the emotional and social benefits you will receive as a volunteer, and your level of comfort in various AAA/AAT situations. This lesson also provides information on identifying and reducing stress.

Lesson Objectives:

1. Identify benefits you receive from other volunteers, staff and your pet.

2. Identify your pet's role as a teammate.

3. Identify the settings you prefer.

4. Identify signs of stress in people.

Materials Required:

Video: *A Look at Different Settings.*

Article #3:   "Plain Talk About Handling Stress"

Benefits You Receive

People volunteer and/or get involved with animals and other people for a lot of reasons. Below are some of the benefits you might receive from other volunteers, staff, clients and your animal partner while you volunteer. You may want to mark those that apply to you.

- ❑ Meeting new people.
- ❑ Helping people who need help.
- ❑ Gaining a sense of inner peace.
- ❑ Sharing concern for others.
- ❑ Being recognized.
- ❑ Having pride in seeing your animal help others.
- ❑ A chance to talk about your pet.
- ❑ Meeting others who love animals.

Your Pet's Role As a Teammate

People will be very attracted to your animal and want to know its name, how old it is, etc. People will remember your pet if you visit the same place frequently and see the same people. You'll find that this happens in AAA and AAT settings also. However, don't be surprised when they don't know *your* name!

Your animal may become closely attached to someone you visit. There may be times when the person wants to talk to the animal and not to you. Be aware of your feelings. If you feel left out or jealous, explore this issue with an understanding friend or fellow Pet Partner. If left unresolved, these feelings could jeopardize your visits through your words or body language (e.g., you may hold the leash too tight).

 **Activity**

- Go to a park without your animal. Take a walk by yourself. Do people notice you? Do they smile at you? Do they talk to you? What are peoples' reactions? Keep a journal of your observations now and during future activities.

- Now visit the park with your pet. How are the reactions different? Do people notice you? Do they smile at you? Do they talk to you? How do they relate to your animal? How does your animal relate to the people?

Choosing a Setting

There are a variety of settings that you and your animal can visit. To answer the question, "Where should I visit?" you need to consider the characteristics of the people at the facility, your personality and preferences, and the skill level and aptitude of your animal. For example, you may have a wonderful, well-trained, well-behaved, quiet cat. Your cat may have the potential to be a great Pet Partner but may not do well around loud teenagers in a program for delinquent behavior. On the other hand, you may have an energetic dog who is not afraid of anything and is very active. This dog might not be best visiting in a nursing home with frail, elderly people who may be easily injured or fall.

Matrix of Environmental Dynamics

There are many types of facilities that one might visit as a Pet Partners team. Pet Partners teams differ broadly in such areas as experience, confidence, and capability.

The often-asked question, "Where should I visit?" has been considered in light of diversity in environmental dynamics. Animal-handler teams can develop additional skills, which gives them greater ability to visit safely in a wider variety of environments and with more diverse populations. Figure 1.3-1, the Matrix of Environmental Dynamics, shows in graphic form a structure of varying environmental characteristics and the skill level needed to visit safely in those environments.

Environments which are more difficult for visiting animal teams are those which have the challenge of more distractions and higher activity levels, combined with less help from staff. Thus, for the safety of patients *and* Pet Partners teams, teams which visit in highly challenging areas must have advanced skills and aptitude.

The Matrix (see Figure 1.3-1) shows you a combination of environmental and Pet Partners team characteristics and how these characteristics overlap and relate to each other. Stop for a minute and think about where you and your animal would like to visit:

• Think about the level of activity in the facility you would like to visit – is it quiet or a beehive of activity?

• Think about your animal – is s/he reliable and under control when at the end of the leash? Or does s/he need you right there to "remind" what should be done? Is s/he comfortable around groups of strangers? Around noise?

	Quiet Facility	Average Facility	Active Facility
High staff involvement in AAA/AAT visits	**Novice**		
Moderate staff involvement in AAA/AAT visits	**Novice**	**Intermediate**	
Low staff involvement in AAA/AAT visits	**Intermediate**	**Intermediate**	**Advanced**

Team Skills and Aptitude

Staff Involvement

Quiet Facility
• Routinely predictable interactions
• Low facility activity
• Few distractions

Average Facility
• Occasionally unpredictable interactions
• Moderate facility activity
• Moderate distractions

Active Facility
• Routinely unpredictable interactions
• High facility activity
• Many distractions

Environmental Dynamics

Figure 1.3-1, Matrix of Environmental Dynamics

- Think about what you would prefer – do you feel at ease visiting with your animal in a setting with many distractions? Or would you feel like your hands are full with just one person? Do you interact easily with strangers? Are you able to focus on several things at once – like ensuring your animal's well-being while having fun talking with people?

- Are you or your animal easily distracted by noises or unusual equipment or people who have strong odors?

- Do sudden or unpredictable events frighten you or your animal or make either of you nervous?

As you can see in the Matrix, most environments need teams with novice or intermediate skills and aptitude. Very few environments require advanced abilities. Many teams would not feel comfortable with the challenges of an environment which needs advanced skills and aptitude. Some teams may aspire to be more diverse or to visit in more challenging AAA/T settings. For these teams, it is important to develop a higher skill level and gain greater experience. The combination of advanced skills and confidence in visiting active and unpredictable environments is what makes a team advanced. Advanced testing is provided only by specially trained and licensed Pet Partners Evaluators.

Teams may visit in many environments. Advanced teams may visit side-by-side with novice teams. On special occasions, a team may have the opportunity to visit very challenging environments. Every team will be unique in its abilities, desires, and level of interest.

How does Delta determine whether a team is considered novice, intermediate, or advanced? Delta Society considers each of the following pieces of the Pet Partners registration packet equally in making this determination:

- Score on the Handler Review (for new Pet Partners)

- Experience (for renewing Pet Partners)

- Handler's answers to the Handler's Questionnaire

- Score and Evaluator's comments on the PPST and PPAT

Pet Partner identification badges will be color coded to indicate the areas they are qualified to visit. Novice teams will receive a green badge. Intermediate teams will receive a blue badge. Advanced teams will receive a red badge.

Below are some examples of typical settings and experiences. Not all items listed may be present in each facility but are listed as examples only, to help you get a picture in your mind of what these kinds of settings are like. Individual facilities will vary, and different wings in the same facility may have completely different dynamics.

Quiet

- Staff don't move around much

- Clients are too sick to be active – they may stay mostly in bed or sit quietly

- Clients may not talk much, or talk in a quiet voice

- Floors are carpeted and don't echo sounds

- There are few noisy machines or carts

Average

- Staff are somewhat active – moving from room to room, supervising the clients, etc.

- Clients are able to be up and moving around, may be sitting or walking, perhaps with equipment such as walkers, canes, wheelchairs

- Clients are talking, and there may be occasions of loud talking or laughing or arguing

- Clients may be gesturing occasionally as they talk or move about

- Music may be playing, or sounds of other activities may be heard through the walls

- Floors may be linoleum or tile, windows may not have curtains, and walls seem to echo sounds

- Machines in the environment may include a machine which dispenses canned soft drinks (clunk!), a pneumatic tube communication system (whoosh, thump!), IV or body systems monitor (beep beep), etc.

Active

- Staff are quite active virtually all the time – rushing from room to room, walking hurriedly and with purpose, wheeling carts (medicine, food, linens) in front of them, etc.

- Clients are active during the visit, or you may be visiting a *group* of active clients

- Client behaviors are unpredictable – clients may lack muscle coordination, causing sudden movements, or they may be living in a delusional world inhabited by people or things the rest of us cannot see, or they may be impulsive and full of excitement

- There is lots of consistent noise– from client talking or crying or shouting, from music, from neighboring rooms, from intercom systems, being near an emergency room or airport, etc.

- The general noise may be amplified because of hard flooring, lack of upholstery on furniture, lack of curtains, etc.

In any of these environments, the staff may be highly involved with your visit or may be barely involved. The more staff help you have, the safer you are and the less skill you need to have a successful visit. Some examples of staff involvement are:

- Give you a list of who is approved for a visit and then let you visit on your own (low staff involvement)

- Place everyone who is approved for a visit into a group room and then leave you alone for the visit (low staff involvement)

- Be with you in the milieu part of the time, with visual supervision from the nursing station the rest of the time (moderate staff involvement)

- Introduce you to a group of clients, then stay with you to help you with names and activities with the group (high staff involvement)

- Work with you with each individual client, telling you what goals you are working toward with each client, and helping you know what to do with each client (high staff involvement)

Important:

The first time you visit a new setting, you should go *without* your animal. If you encounter situations that cause you to have emotional reactions, your emotions might confuse your animal. It is best to deal with these issues before taking your animal to visit. When you visit with confidence, your animal will too.

Your Comfort Level

If you find yourself in an uncomfortable setting, what will you do? If you can't completely accept a person because of personal conflict, ask to visit someone else. Don't feel bad about having a difficult time dealing with a particular person or setting. Most likely, you will be able to make a contribution in a setting where another volunteer would not be able to visit.

Assess your preferences as you continue through this course. You may change your mind as you learn more about clients, your animal and the different facilities you have to choose from.

Are you more comfortable with:

☑ One-on-one interactions

☑ Small-group interactions

☐ Demonstrations

☐ Large groups

☐ Certain groups—youth, elderly, children, people with terminal illness

☑ Certain types of facilities—hospitals, jails, psychiatric units

What are your needs in terms of:

☑ Time commitment

☑ Travel

☐ People skills

☑ Level of comfort with strangers

What are your animal's needs in terms of:

☑ Socialization

☐ Quality time

☑ Level of comfort with strangers

☐ Application of skills

▣ Video

Video: *A Look at Different Settings.*

Stress in People

As you begin visiting in AAA/AAT settings, you will develop some sensitivity about the special needs of the people you visit. No matter how skilled and well-trained you become, there will be times when visits are stressful for you, your animal, or the people you visit.

In Lesson 2.2, you will learn about recognizing and dealing with stress in animals. You also need to learn about stress in people. The people you visit may be under stress, which could affect how they react to you and your animal. In addition, you may find yourself under stress. This section will help you identify symptoms of stress and what you can do to cope with that stress.

Recognizing Stress

There are many signs of stress in people. You have probably dealt with a person who is usually nice and easy to get along with. Then inexplicably, the person has seemed irritable and short-tempered when dealing with people. You may have discovered that the person was under tremendous stress at work or at home, and the stress was the cause of the change in behavior. Basically, stress is the body's response to demands.

Recognizing the signs of stress in people will help you handle situations more effectively. As you visit, you may see signs of stress in clients, staff, or yourself.

When a person first begins to experience stress, the symptoms may be mild. A mild sign of stress could be temporary grouchiness. For example, if the person is nervous about a deadline at work, s/he may act irritable with people who come into the office over a period of several days.

If stress is prolonged and intense, the person may develop some stress-related diseases such as ulcers, high blood pressure, or migraine headaches.

The first step to eliminating stress is being able to recognize the symptoms.

Signs of Stress

- Irritability, lack of patience with routine events (e.g., waiting for a traffic light)

- Moodiness, outbursts of anger

- Decrease in talking or increase in talking (excessive)

- Nervousness

- Yawning

- Withdrawal (verbal, physical and emotional)

- Disorganization

- Memory problems

- Does not complete tasks on time or at all

- Sleep disorders

- Mild headaches

- Stomach/digestive problems

- Fever blisters, rashes, or blotchy skin

- Menstrual irregularities

- Physical tension

Signs of Extreme Stress

- Heart disease, high blood pressure

- Stomach and digestive disorders (severe)

- Manic speech (rapid, rambling) and behavior

- Severe depression

 # Articles

Before proceeding, turn to Appendix A and read about how your body reacts to stressful situations.

Article #3:   "Plain Talk About Handling Stress."

Tips for Reducing Stress[3]

As you read this section, think about how the suggestions can apply to your AAA/AAT situation.

➤ Learn to plan

Disorganization can create stress. Having too many projects going simultaneously often leads to confusion, forgetfulness and the sense that uncompleted projects are hanging over your head. When possible, take on projects one at a time and work on them until completed.

As AAA/AAT volunteers, many of us get so excited about what we are doing that we want to share it with everyone. This might cause us to commit to too many people or projects. Be careful that you are not promising to go to too many facilities or see too many people. It is better to do a few things well than to disappoint people because you cannot fulfill all of your promises.

➤ Recognize and accept limits

Many of us set unreasonable and perfectionistic goals for ourselves. We can never be perfect, so we often have a sense of failure or inadequacy no matter how well we perform. Set achievable goals for yourself.

Setting reasonable goals as an AAA/AAT volunteer will help you enjoy visiting for a long time. When you expect too much of yourself, you will cause yourself to be disappointed much of the time. AAA and AAT should be both rewarding and fun.

---

[3] Adapted from Richardson, Dr. F.C., Associate Professor. Tips for Reducing Stress. Department of Educational Psychology.

➤ **Learn to play**

You need to escape from the pressures of life occasionally and have fun. Find pastimes that are absorbing and enjoyable to you, no matter what your level of ability is.

This applies to both you and your animal teammate. When you are feeling as though you may be experiencing stress, it may be time to take an afternoon and do something different with your pet. For example, take your animal on a nature trail at a park or spend time sitting in your favorite chair together. If your teammate is a dog, you may wish to participate together in activities such as flyball, agility, tracking, etc.

In some cases, you may need a short break from animal activities. Go to a movie, read a book, or spend time doing another kind of activity.

➤ **Be a positive person**

Avoid criticizing others. Learn to praise the things you like in others. Focus on the good qualities possessed by those around you.

Following this advice will help you be happier. Unfortunately, many people who participate in activities with their pets are intensely competitive. Remember that in this field, there is plenty of room for excellence. We need to support each other and the concept of AAA/AAT.

➤ **Learn to tolerate and forgive**

Intolerance of others leads to frustration and anger. An attempt to really understand the way other people feel can help you be more accepting.

You will be visiting with many different people and all of them will be unique individuals. When you feel yourself getting angry with people, try to look at the world from their perspective. Maybe they were trained to think the way they do, such as a nurse who strongly believes that animals cause infections. They may never have received correct and adequate information about a particular issue.

➤ **Avoid unnecessary competition**

There are many competitive situations in life that we can't avoid. Too much concern with winning in too many areas of life can create excessive tension and anxiety and make us unnecessarily aggressive.

In this field, there doesn't have to be a winner. You should never let yourself think, "my animal is better than that person's." All of us, people and animals included, will have something special that we can contribute. Individual Pet Partners teams will have strengths and characteristics which will appeal to different residents in the same facility, as well as in different facilities. Rise above it all—take the high road and be the best person you can be.

➤ **Get regular physical exercise**

Check with your physician before beginning any exercise program. You will be more likely to stay with an exercise program if you choose one that you really enjoy rather than one that feels like pure hard work and drudgery.

Regular exercise can make a big difference for both you and your animal. You don't have to join a gym. You can find a nice place to take a brisk walk on a regular basis. Exercise can actually lower blood pressure and relieve stress.

➤ **Learn a systematic, drug-free method of relaxing**

If you are volunteering in AAA/AAT, chances are you're a busy person. In addition to volunteering, you might be training your animal and spending time every day caring for it. You may also have a regular job.

Many relaxation techniques can be done in a few minutes every day in your own home. Meditation, yoga and progressive relaxation can be learned from various accredited teachers and professionals such as psychologists or psychotherapists. You can get some training to get started, or use some of the excellent instructional books and videotapes available.

➤ Talk out your troubles

Find a friend, member of the clergy, counselor, or psychotherapist you can be open with. Expressing your "bottled up" tension to a sympathetic ear can be incredibly helpful.

If you experience stress, you may also find it helpful to talk to another volunteer. Some AAA/AAT programs set up support groups for volunteers. You may contact the Delta office for the names of other Pet Partners teams in your area. Sometimes it helps to know you aren't in this alone.

➤ Change your thinking

How we feel emotionally often depends on our outlook or philosophy of life. Changing one's beliefs is a difficult and painstaking process. There is little practical wisdom in the modern world to guide us through our lives. No one has all the answers, but some answers are available.

As an AAA/AAT volunteer, you will be making a wonderful contribution to the lives of many people. If you are responsible, dependable, and work hard, you can be proud of yourself and your animal.

Your Responsibilities

Lesson Overview:

As you visit in AAA/AAT settings, it is important that you understand your responsibilities as a volunteer. Understanding your responsibilities will ensure that you have a safe, successful experience. This lesson will describe your responsibilities as a volunteer, Pet Partners policies and procedures, and human rights considerations.

Lesson Objectives:

1. Identify your responsibilities as a volunteer.

    a. State your responsibilities to the people you visit.

    b. State your responsibilities to your animal.

    c. State your responsibilities to the facility.

2. State the Pet Partners Policies and Procedures.

3. State the Code of Ethics.

Responsibilities and Skills of Volunteers

As a Pet Partners volunteer, you will be in a helping relationship with other people. In any therapeutic setting, establishing helping relationships with others can assist them in their growth toward personal goals and in strengthening their ability to cope with life.

The most important thing you can do for others is to help them:

- Help themselves

- Reach their potential

- Learn how to use their own resources

- Learn techniques for solving problems

You can encourage freedom, responsibility and individuality. To facilitate this process as a volunteer:

➤ Live up to your commitment

Volunteering is not something that can be done in a few odd hours when there is nothing more exciting to do. Rather, it is a job — with responsibilities that requires a definite allotment of time, energy, intelligence, and a real desire to prepare adequately.

➤ Be responsible at all times for your animal

Consider the animal's needs first and provide humane care. Always stay with the animal and be in control of the situation.

➤ Be present and on time for every commitment you make

If you find yourself unable to meet an obligation, notify the facility as far in advance as possible. *Remember*, if you don't come, someone will be disappointed.

➤ Be ethical and maintain confidentiality

If a helping relationship is formed, "secrets" may be told to you. These discussions are only to be shared with the treatment team/staff if necessary. Never promise "not to tell anyone" — you are making a promise you might not be able to keep. Inspire trust, confidence and dependability.

➤ **Show empathy to people — not sympathy**

Relate to the people you meet and try to understand each person's feelings without acting superior or getting too involved.

➤ **Be respectful**

Treat others as you would like to be treated. The world is made up of individuals, each with his/her own way of doing things. Don't degrade others because they don't fit a set "standard" or "role."

➤ **Ask questions**

Ask a staff member, team leader, or coordinator about anything you do not understand. Don't harbor any doubts or frustrations.

➤ **Be part of the team**

Be willing to accept supervision from the professional staff. Don't show partiality to one over another.

➤ **Be concrete**

Be specific and present oriented. Use open-ended questions.

➤ **Provide a supportive, encouraging emotional climate with your presence**

Respect a person's need for privacy and withdrawal. Don't push yourself on him/her. Be a good listener.

➤ **Continue to learn**

➤ **Enjoy the company of others**

Sharing with another person is a unique and exciting experience. There is something to be gained by all in each relationship.

➤ **Have a really good visit!**

Code of Ethics for AAA and AAT[1]

- Treat people, animals and nature with respect, dignity and sensitivity.

- Promote the quality of life in their work.

- Abide by the professional ethics of their professions and/or organizations.

- Perform duties commensurate with their training and position.

- Comply with all applicable Delta Society policies and local, state and federal laws relating to their work.

Important Human Rights Considerations

If you can be a responsible volunteer in all the ways that are mentioned above, you will make an important contribution to the lives of others. Being aware of what is *not* your responsibility is equally important.

Remember:

You are not there to diagnose or treat the people you visit.

AAA/AAT is Not Filler

In some facilities, volunteers are used to fill in the gaps and provide services to people who are not involved in other programs. While we don't like to think of this happening, sometimes volunteers are simply given a list of names by a facility staff person who did not determine if these people have any interest in animals.

Pet Partners should be open-minded, eager to help and willing to be team players at a facility. However, in cases where you do not feel that your visits would be beneficial, consult with your facility contact person and express your concerns. If you can't resolve this and continue to feel uncomfortable, call Delta Society for advice. It is not your responsibility to visit everyone. Your responsibility is to provide services to people who can benefit from the visits that you and your animal provide.

---

[1] Delta Society. 1992. *Handbook for Animal-Assisted Activities and Animal-Assisted Therapy*. Renton, WA: Delta Society.

Respect the Person's Choice

Some people think that it is acceptable to assign an AAA/AAT team to a person who clearly states that s/he does not like animals. They think you and your animal will change the person's opinion. We want you to treat the people you visit as you would like to be treated in the same situation. It is important to give people dignity and the right to make choices when they are capable of doing so.

When a person does not want to receive AAA/AAT visits, don't feel badly. There are plenty of people who need you and your animal and you will be able to fill many of their moments with joy.

Phobias

(Extreme fear.)

It is never appropriate to visit with a person who has an animal phobia, unless trained personnel are helping to deal with this problem. An animal phobia should be clearly documented in a person's chart. In contrast, when a person doesn't want to interact with your animal because of a lack of information or education regarding animals (e.g., "the dog's teeth are big—that means he will bite me."), it may be appropriate to provide AAA/AAT. In these cases, proceed cautiously and work with facility staff.

The Client's Choice

At one nursing home, a resident made it quite clear that she did not like dogs or cats and that she believed they should not be used in her facility. Instead of staying away from this woman, the social worker requested that the volunteer and her dog try to visit the resident every week.

During each visit, the scene was repeated. The volunteer and the dog would head down to the woman's room where she seemed to be waiting by her door. As she saw the volunteer approaching, she would begin to shout, "Get that animal out of here!" The volunteer would get close enough for the woman to hear her say, "I'm sorry to bother you. We will leave now." The volunteer and the dog would turn and head back down the hall.

The social worker believed this strong woman was in a situation (the nursing home) in which she had very little control. This weekly event gave her the chance to state her opinion strongly and get results. The social worker's theory was soon validated. The woman, who always enjoyed seeing her daughter, began declining her invitations to go out on days when pet visits were planned.

by Linda Nebbe, M.A.

Watch the Person's Behavior

Sometimes people will say they don't like animals. After several visits, you may discover that despite how loud and vocal they might be about their dislike of animals, they are the first ones to go to the visiting area on the days you visit. The story in the sidebar, on the previous page, shows us that we should watch a person's behavior in addition to listening to his/her words.

Pet Partners Policies and Procedures

1. Handlers shall visit with only one animal at a time.

2. Handlers shall visit only with animals registered with the Pet Partners Program.

3. Handlers shall ensure that policies and procedures are in place regarding Animal-Assisted Activities/Animal-Assisted Therapy by providing the facility(s) they visit with a copy of the Facility Policy Agreement. (The Facility Policy Agreement form is located on page 223. Call Delta Society for additional copies.)

4. Handlers shall abide by all policies, procedures and precautions of each facility visited.

5. Handlers shall check-in with the staff/supervisor upon arrival for each visit.

6. Handlers shall observe all rules of privacy and confidentiality.

7. Handlers shall be on time for every commitment made.

8. Handlers shall be responsible at all times for the animal, considering the animal's needs and humane care, first. Always stay with the animal and in control of the situation. For safety, all animals must wear a collar/harness and be on lead at all times. This is true during Pet Partners testing as well as during visits.

   Dogs shall wear a nylon, cloth or leather buckle collar, or metal or nylon slip collar. If you use a slip collar, be aware of the potential for someone to harm the animal. Consider snapping the lead to the non-slip ring while visiting. Dogs shall be on a cloth, nylon, or leather leash that is no more than 6' long. Dog head halters, prong or pinch collars and retractable leads are prohibited during visits.

Animals such as cats, rabbits, guinea pigs, etc. shall be carried in a basket and/or on a towel and must wear a collar/harness and be on lead at all times.

Caged birds that leave their cage for visits must be in a harness and on lead at all times. Caged birds that visit in their cage do not require a harness.

9. Prior to each visit, handlers shall:

   - Assess animal's overall health and attitude

   - Clean and brush the animal according to facility/program requirements

   - Cut and file nails, clean eyes and ears

   - Allow the animal time to exercise and eliminate

10. Handlers shall dress appropriately for the volunteer assignment. Be comfortable, neat, washable, and well groomed.

11. Handlers shall clean up after the animal inside and outside the facility.

12. Handlers shall *not* tie animals to people, equipment or furniture while visiting.

13. Use of drugs and/or alcohol is strictly prohibited on the day of the visit.

14. Handlers shall *not* routinely give or accept gifts from people they visit.

15. Handlers shall not charge fees for their services.

16. In case of an accident or unusual occurrence handlers shall:

   - Secure the animal.

   - Get help for the injured person.

   - Notify your facility contact person in writing so that it can be documented in the person's medical file.

   - Fill out all necessary documentation at the facility.

   - End the visit.

   - Notify the organization sponsoring the visit.

   - Notify Delta Society for insurance purposes. Call (425) 226-7357.

   - Evaluate the situation for future prevention.

Unit 2
Animals

Unit Overview:

Your animal is the focus of this unit. First, the unit covers how animals are selected for AAA/AAT and matched to the best environment for them. Next, information is presented to help you ensure your animal's safety, health and happiness.

Unit Map:

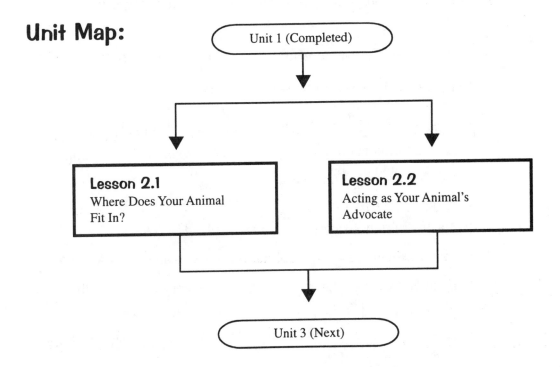

Where Does Your Animal Fit In?

Lesson Overview:

This lesson provides information on the health, aptitude, and skill requirements for Pet Partners animals. This lesson also provides additional information on determining which setting would best suit your animal.

Lesson Objectives:

1. Identify the steps for screening animals.
    a. Identify health requirements.

    b. Identify skills requirements.

    c. Identify aptitude requirements.

2. Analyze a specific animal. Identify whether it would be a good AAA or AAT animal, its limitations, and what environments or visiting activities would be appropriate for the animal.

    a. Identify the purposes of animal evaluations.

    b. Name different species that can be involved in AAA/AAT.

    c. List characteristics of animals that are appropriate for AAA/AAT.

    d. Identify characteristics of animals that are appropriate for different facilities/populations.

    e. Identify characteristics of animals that are inappropriate for different facilities/populations.

Materials Required:

Video: *Pet Partners Skills Test.*
Video: *Pet Partners Aptitude Test.*

Article #4: "Helping Your Pet Work in New Environments."

Screening Animals

All animals accepted as Pet Partners must have passed a three-part screening of health, skills and aptitude. The skills and aptitude screenings evaluate the animal/handler team and how well they communicate with each other.

The health screening is done by a veterinarian and ensures that animals are healthy and free from parasites, disease and infections.

Skills are tested with the Pet Partners Skills Test (PPST). This is a test that shows whether the animal can be controlled by the handler and follow basic commands.

The Pet Partners Aptitude Test (PPAT) is designed to simulate conditions that may be encountered on a visit. This screening helps determine the most appropriate environment for you and your animal. Many people compare this to a temperament test.

One of the goals of the Pet Partners Program is to have visiting animals that we can all be proud of because they are safe and reliable. The screening process gives a complete picture of each animal. Delta-certified evaluators actually see and work with the animals in the testing process. This process is the safest way to identify acceptable visiting animals. Be honest about your animal. If your animal exhibits unpredictable behavior, *don't* use it in AAA/AAT, even if it passes the screening.

Remember:

At no time will your animal be put in a situation that is dangerous to the animal's welfare. Our evaluators are trained and learn that the well-being of animals comes first, no matter what. At no point during the evaluation will animals be hurt or intentionally frightened. The PPAT is designed to resemble an AAA/AAT visit with situations that might occur when the animal goes on a visit.

Health Requirements

The health screening is completed by a veterinarian. We want to make sure that all animals who participate in the program are healthy and free from parasites, disease, infections and illnesses. Veterinarians will complete the forms related to the health screening of animals. (Forms are provided in the registration packet.) To participate in Pet Partners, the animal must meet the following health requirements:

1. **Current on all vaccinations, which include:**

   - Rabies
   - DHLPP (dogs)
   - FVRLP (cats)
   - Corona (dogs)
   - Bordatella (dogs)

   If possible, vaccination tags should be on the animal or carried by the handler. Vaccinations shall be documented by a licensed veterinarian. Whenever vaccinations are renewed, provide copies of the latest documentation to the supervisor at the facility so s/he can update the files. Other vaccinations may be required for other species.

   Note: Some facilities require veterinary examinations every six months.

2. **Animal shall be free of any signs of ill health.**

   Animals shall not visit when any of the following symptoms are present:

   - Skin rashes
   - Lameness
   - Extreme hair shedding
   - Runny nose
   - Change in eating and/or elimination habits (e.g., frequent urination)
   - Odd smelling ears or breath
   - Vomiting
   - Eye infections
   - Diarrhea and/or bloody stools
   - Sutures (stitches)
   - Medications for infections, or illness (excludes heartworm prevention)
   - Chronic illness

   Note: In addition, animals in season shall not visit.

3. **Dogs and cats *must* be house-trained. Other animals, such as birds and rabbits must be carried in baskets or carriers.**

   The handler must carry clean-up equipment.

4. **Animals must be free of internal and external parasites which include:**

   - Fleas
   - Lice
   - Ticks
   - Ear mites
   - Skin mites, diseases such as mange
   - Intestinal parasites

   Note: Fecal exams must be completed at least once per year to check for internal parasites.

5. The animal shall be cleaned and groomed within 24 hours prior to the visit.

The animal must then be kept clean until the visit. Attention should be given to the following areas:

- Bath, if necessary
- Nails (do not cut nails on the day of the visit unless you file the edges smooth)
- Eyes
- Ears
- Coat—animal shall be brushed well, especially if the animal sheds
- Teeth

Note: Do not use flea powder or sprays the day of your visit. These can cause allergic reactions in humans. Flea collars should be removed 24 hours prior to visits.

6. All animals except "pocket pets" must be at least one year old. Rabbits, guinea pigs, rats, etc. must be at least six months old. Birds must have lived in the handler's home at least one year.

Skill Requirements

In order to test basic "good behavior" skills, animals and handlers will complete the Pet Partners Skills Test (PPST) together. This test was modeled (with permission) after the American Kennel Club's (AKC) Canine Good Citizen Test. Health care equipment (such as wheelchairs, walkers) has been added to the test. Food treats cannot be used during the test.

We also use the test for cats and other animals. These animals do not complete all of the test items or perform them in the same way. For example, instead of walking on a leash, rabbits and cats must show that they can be carried in a basket or in the handler's arms. For specific test modifications, see Pet Partners Skills Test in the registration packet.

The items on the Pet Partners Skills Test are:

1. Accepting a Friendly Stranger

The Evaluator will shake your hand.

This exercise demonstrates that the team knows how to greet strangers appropriately. The Evaluator and handler shake hands and exchange pleasantries. The animal must show no sign of resentment or shyness and must not break position or try to go to the Evaluator. The handler is relaxed and friendly.

2. Accepting Petting

The Evaluator will ask to pet your animal.

This exercise demonstrates that the animal will allow a friendly stranger to touch it while it is out with its handler. The animal should allow the stranger to approach with or without medical equipment. The Evaluator pets the animal and then circles the animal and handler. The animal must not show shyness or resentment.

3. Appearance and Grooming

The Evaluator will lightly brush your animal and examine its mouth, feet and ears.

This exercise demonstrates that the team's appearance is suitable for visits. The handler will be dressed in clean and appropriate clothing. The animal will welcome being groomed and examined and will permit a stranger to do so. It also demonstrates the owner's care, concern, and responsibility. The Evaluator inspects the animal, then combs or brushes the animal and

lightly examines the ears and each front foot. Special attention is given to handling the ears, head, paws or wings, and tail. During examination there should be no sign of aggression, fear, or elimination. (These could also be signs of pain, injury, or extreme stress. See Lesson 2.2.)

4. Out For a Walk (Walking on a Loose Leash)

Handler and animal walk a short course.

Dogs walk on a leash; other animals are carried as they would be when visiting. All animals must be wearing a collar or harness and be on leash.

This exercise demonstrates that the handler is in control of the animal. The course will include a left turn, a right turn, and an about turn, with at least one stop in between and another at the end. Dogs need not be perfectly aligned with the handler and need not sit when the handler stops. Animals other than dogs are carried through the course. The animal may be on either the left or right side of the handler.

The animal should walk on a loose lead or be carried without:

- Pulling
- Jumping
- Struggling
- Barking or crying
- Sniffing
- Refusing to walk past medical equipment

The handler should be aware of the animal's behavior and should speak to the animal in a friendly tone.

5. Walking Through a Crowd

The handler and animal walk through a "crowd" of three or four people.

This exercise demonstrates that the team can move about politely in pedestrian traffic and public places. The animal and handler walk around and pass close to several people and equipment. The animal may show some interest in the strangers, without appearing over-exuberant, shy, frightened, or resentful.

Dogs walk and other animals are carried. The handler should be aware of the animal's behavior and help the animal in a friendly tone.

6. Reaction to Distractions

Distractions may include wheelchairs, a falling crutch, someone running, rolling metal carts or dropping metal items.

This test demonstrates that the animal and handler remain confident when faced with common distracting situations. The animal may express a natural interest and curiosity and may appear slightly startled, but should not:

- panic
- struggle or try to run away
- show aggressiveness
- eliminate
- vocalize

The handler should be aware of the animal's needs and give praise or encouragement as needed.

7. Sit on Command
8. Down on Command
9. Stay in Place

Dogs:
The handler will attach a 20-foot line to the dog, walk to the end of the line, and return.

These exercises demonstrate that the dog has training and will lie down, sit and stay at the handler's command. When told by the handler, the dog must stay/remain in place in a sit or down position (whichever the handler prefers).

The handler may not force the animal into position, use a loud voice, or jerk on the leash. The handler may take a reasonable amount of time and use more than one command in a friendly tone.

Other Animals:

Stay in Place—The animal will be placed in a stranger's lap for 30 seconds. The stranger will not pet or interact with the animal. The animal must stay in the stranger's lap.

Sit and Down—The animal will be passed to three strangers.

10. Come When Called

The handler may pat the floor, use verbal praise, and other encouragement (no food) to bring the dog close enough to grasp its collar.

This exercise is for dogs only. This test demonstrates that the dog will come to the handler and allow the handler to attach a leash.

11. Reaction to a Neutral Dog

Two handlers and their animals approach each other from a distance of about ten yards, stop, shake hands, and exchange pleasantries, and continue on for about five yards.

This exercise demonstrates that the team can behave politely around an approaching dog. The handler must be aware of the animal's potential response to a dog, help the animal succeed and at the same time be polite and friendly to a stranger. If the test is done with two dogs, they should show no more than a casual interest in each other. Cats and other animals can be held by the handler or placed in a carrier and walked past a dog.

The animal should not:

- Growl or Bite

- Stare

- Bark or Cry

- Chase

- Raise its Hackles

- Attack

- Attempt to Jump on a Person or an Animal

 **Video**

Video: *Pet Partners Skills Test.*

Aptitude Requirements

The Delta Society Pet Partners Aptitude Test (PPAT) determines if you and your animal have the ability, capacity, desire, and potential for participating in AAA/AAT programs. This part of the screening is similar to what many people would call a temperament test. We did not use the word temperament because so many people think that animals are born with a certain temperament and it can never be changed. We know that with training, many animals can learn to be reliable. For this reason, we use the word "aptitude" to suggest that the test applies to the animal's ability or potential for AAA/AAT. The PPAT is a role play of common visiting situations. It evaluates the aptitude of the animal/handler team.

The PPAT is based on research. To develop the test, over 600 qualified evaluators of visiting animals were surveyed. The people surveyed received a list of the 35 most frequently used items on temperament tests from all over the country. Many of those who responded to the survey stressed that the aptitude test should be functional and resemble a visit.

A: Overall Exam

This exercise demonstrates that the animal will accept and be comfortable being examined by a stranger. It also shows that the handler knows how to present the animal on a visit and how to help the animal tolerate being touched all over. The Evaluator will look in the animal's ears, hold its tail, put fingers in its mouth and handle its feet.

B: Exuberant and Clumsy Petting

This exercise demonstrates that the animal will maintain self-control and that the handler works with the animal to help it tolerate clumsy petting. Can your animal handle being petted if someone is excited, has a high voice, is clapping and has clumsy movements? The Evaluator will use elbows and feet to pet the animal. The Evaluator will also become very exuberant, speaking in a high pitched voice, squealing and jiggling the animal. The Evaluator may wave or bounce a toy around the animal and offer a treat.

C: Restraining Hug

This exercise demonstrates that the animal will tolerate restraint and that the handler can assist the animal. Will your animal allow someone to hug them without resisting? The Evaluator will, unexpectedly, give the animal a full body hug that restricts the animal's movement. If the animal is a bird or other small animal, the Evaluator will restrain the animal's movement with both hands.

D: Staggering/Gesturing Individual

This exercise demonstrates that the animal will exhibit confidence when a person, acting in an unusual manner, approaches it. It also shows that the handler has the social skills to interact with a stranger while attending to the animal. Can your animal be approached by a person who could be staggering, gesturing, and yelling? A person with an unsteady gait and wearing a shawl, or someone using an assistive device (such as a wheelchair) will approach the animal. The person will gesture wildly and/or wail.

E: Angry Yelling

This exercise demonstrates that the animal and handler will not be upset when someone is angry. Will your animal continue to feel comfortable around yelling and strong emotions displayed by an unfamiliar person? Two people will begin to shout angrily and wave their arms.

F: Bumped from Behind

This exercise demonstrates that the animal is able to recover when a person bumps into it and that the handler will help the animal recover. While the team is distracted by the angry yelling, a person will bump into the animal's body. With small dogs and other animals, a hard stomp or loud slap will be made behind the animal.

G: Crowded and Petted by Several People

This exercise demonstrates that the animal will tolerate crowding and petting by several people at once. The handler must have the social skills to interact with the group while attending to the animal and maintaining its well being. At least three people will gather closely around the animal and begin to touch it. All three people will be talking and trying to gain the animal's attention. At least one person will be using health care equipment. Food may be offered.

H: Animal Held by Stranger

This exercise demonstrates that the animal will not get upset when left with a stranger. The Evaluator will hold the animal's leash or basket while the handler goes out of sight for two minutes. There should be no vocalizing, crying, pacing, or extreme nervousness.

I: Sociability

This item determines that the team has the proper sociability for AAA/AAT. The Evaluator will score the team's overall interest in people.

J: Overall Reaction

This item determines if the animal/handler team is appropriate for AAA/AAT. The Evaluator will score the overall reaction of the team (you and your animal) to the test. The Evaluator will determine whether the team has developed the level of trust and understanding needed to work well together in unpredictable environments.

Testing and Scoring

The Pet Partners Skills Test (PPST) and Pet Partners Aptitude Test (PPAT) simulate visiting situations and ask that you and your animal (as a team) role play as if you are on a visit with the testers.

If there will be more than one handler for the animal (for example, husband and wife or mother and daughter), *each* handler (separately) must go through the PPST and PPAT with the animal. Remember: the scores are based on *teamwork*, how well the person and animal work together as a team. Different handlers may work differently with the same animal. Thus, each person-animal team must pass the PPST and PPAT.

You will receive a score on each exercise. Possible scores are: Not Suitable, Not Ready, or Pass 1, 2, or 3. The Evaluator may make comments on the test exercises to help you understand the scoring.

Not Suitable

A score of Not Suitable means that the team is showing responses which are not suitable in visiting situations. Receiving one Not Suitable score means that the team does not pass the PPST and PPAT. A team will receive a score of Not Suitable with the following responses:

- The animal shows aggression (growl, snap, lunge, snarl, etc.) toward a person or animal during testing or while on the testing grounds

- The animal shows extreme fear or anxiety

- The animal (other than birds or "pocket pets") eliminates during testing or on the testing grounds (in an area other than that marked for elimination)

- The handler treats animals or people inappropriately at any time while on the test grounds

If you receive a Not Suitable score, ask your Evaluator to explain if the problem is something which can be improved so that you can be retested. Some Not Suitable scores mean that the animal would *not* be happy in a visiting situation and should not be forced to visit (no matter how much the handler wants to visit). The animal *must* enjoy the work. Not every animal – or person – enjoys meeting strangers and interacting with them.

Not Ready

A score of Not Ready means that the team is showing responses which are not ready for the demands of visiting situations.

A team will *not* pass the PPST if they receive even *one* Not Ready score. In the PPST, training is often all that is needed to improve a Not Ready score. An animal can be trained to do a task (for example, to sit or lie down or walk quietly by your side). After training, the team can retake the tests.

An animal *may* be trained to accept a situation (for example, to tolerate loud, angry voices). However, we do *not* want to place animals in visiting situations which are uncomfortable to them. That does not respect the animal's needs, and it increases the risk that the animal may retaliate to protect itself. For this reason, Not Ready scores in the PPAT give information about the area(s) that are best for you and your animal and the kinds of situations to avoid. A team may receive up to three Not Ready scores in the PPAT and still pass.

Teams must pass both the PPST and PPAT to register as Pet Partners. A team will receive a score of Not Ready with the following responses:

- A dog barks at a person or animal during testing or while on the testing grounds

- The animal mouths the tester

- The animal does not enjoy interactions with people

- The handler is unaware of possible negative effects of the animal's behavior and may allow the behavior to continue

- The handler shows extreme nervousness, is unable to make eye contact with testers, or in other ways shows inability to enjoy interactions

- The handler does not have adequate control over the animal or teamwork between the handler and animal is not adequately developed

If you receive a score of Not Ready and you don't understand why, ask your Evaluator to explain.

Pass

A score of 1 indicates that on the day of the test the team showed entry-level skills or aptitude. A score of 2 indicates that the team showed intermediate skills or aptitude. A score of 3 indicates that the team was extraordinary, showing high-level, advanced skills or aptitude.

Pass 1

A team will receive a score of Pass 1 with the following responses:

Handler -

- Is nervous or stiff, unable to pretend to be on a visit
- Gives harsh commands to the animal
- Doesn't anticipate the animal's position or responses
- Is more focused on the tester than on the animal
- Responds to the animal instead of directing the animal's behavior
- Stands back and observes, rather than participates in interactions

Animal –

- Has to be guided or cajoled into position, requires multiple commands
- Is uncomfortable or restless, wants to move away or out of the situation
- Is more interested in the environment than in either the handler or tester
- Tolerates the interactions

Pass 2

A team will receive a score of Pass 2 with the following responses:

Handler –

- Is somewhat stiff or formal with tester
- Is able to pretend and role play at least half the time
- Gives forceful or clipped commands
- Is somewhat aware of animal and animal's responses to testing

Animal –

- Goes into position easily, without undue repositioning or extra commands

- Is neutral in response to the tester, showing neither interest nor anxiety

- Seeks out attention part of the time

- May be neutral to handler or may be focused on the handler and unaware of testers

Pass 3

A team will receive a score of Pass 3 with the following responses:

Handler –

- Is relaxed, confident, natural, and friendly

- Clearly treats interactions as a role play all the time

- Gives cues to animal in a gentle tone or with unobtrusive hand signals

- Is aware of animal's behavior and attentive to animal's well-being, while at the same time interacting socially with testers

- Praises appropriate animal behaviors

- Works together smoothly with animal and teamwork is evident at all times

Animal –

- Goes into position the first time

- Is clearly interested in testers, is very social and seeks out attention

- Appears happy and confident at all times

- A strong bond between the handler and animal is apparent

As you can see, both the handler and the animal are being evaluated in the PPST and PPAT. Teams receive one score for their teamwork together. There may be times when the handler and the animal are operating at different levels. For example, there may be a social, loving, calm cat handled by a woman who is unaware of possible dangers to the cat (she sets the cat in its basket down on a chair in the waiting area next to a dog straining on its leash to get to the cat while she rummages in her oversized bag to find and apply her lipstick).

Or there may be a skilled handler who has visited for many years, coming to be tested with a young dog who is inexperienced and has never visited. In cases where the two parts of the team could receive different scores (if scored separately), the Evaluator will give the *lower* score. A team is only as strong as its weakest member.

If you have questions about scores or comments, ask your Evaluator for clarification.

Pet Partners who wish to have an Advanced designation must be tested by Advanced Evaluators. Advanced Pet Partners are able to visit in environments which have high levels of distractions *and* have a low level of staff assistance. Distractions may come through client behaviors, staff activity, equipment noises, etc. Without staff help, the team is left to handle potentially difficult or challenging situations mostly by themselves. For more information, refer to the Matrix of Environmental Dynamics on page 23.

The Advanced Test asks the team to do four additional role-play exercises. To qualify for Advanced Testing, the team must first go through the PPST and PPAT on the same day as the Advanced Testing is performed. The team must have a minimum total score of 50, scoring a 2 or better on all aspects of the PPST, with 3's in:

- Exercise 1—Accepting a Friendly Stranger
- Exercise 3—Appearance and Grooming
- Exercise 4—Out for a Walk
- Exercise 5—Walking Through a Crowd

In addition, the team must have scored a 2 or better on all aspects of the PPAT with 3's in:

- Exercise A—Overall Exam
- Exercise B—Exuberant and Clumsy Petting
- Exercise C—Restraining Hug
- Exercise G—Crowded and Petted by Several People

 # Video

Video: *Pet Partners Aptitude Test.*

Passing and Passing with Qualifications

Some animals might be wonderful, great animals, but feel unsure in some areas. For example, a dog may pass the Skills and Aptitude Tests, but the Evaluators may feel it is just too exuberant to visit with very small children. In such cases, teams are "passed with qualifications." This means that the Evaluators will approve the team to visit with some types of people but not others.

An animal that is quiet may not be the right animal for a group of active, loud teenagers. Rather than force this animal to accept all people, the Evaluator will pass the team with the understanding that the animal should be safe from loud, active populations. We want animals to be in the best placements possible so people benefit and our animals are happy and comfortable.

The story about Sophie in the sidebar gives a description of a team that would be passed with qualifications.

Sophie

Sophie is a large, loving 3-year-old golden retriever. Sophie is very sociable and extremely people-oriented. Sophie is the first to reach the car or the door when its time to go for a walk. She has never met a person she didn't like. Even the mailman is her special friend. Everyday he brings her a biscuit, and he misses her if she is not home. Sophie loves to go for walks in the park where people stop to pet her, admire her big yellow eyes and tell her how wonderful she is. It seems as if everyone knows Sophie by name.

She has had obedience training, sits nicely, stays and comes when called. She can also do a few tricks.

However, Sophie has one problem—she loves children too much. Sophie gets overly excited and wants to play. She forgets how big she is and, as a result, has a tendency to knock things over.

Sophie would be a perfect AAA/AAT animal to visit nursing homes and programs for the elderly. She would also work nicely with teenagers and young adults but would not be suitable to work with small children.

by Mary Burch

Identifying Where Your Animal Fits In

Why We Evaluate Teams

It is very important to evaluate visiting animals to be sure that they are:

- People-oriented/sociable

- Comfortable being touched

- Suitable for visiting

- Able to enjoy visiting

- Predictable/reliable in a given situation

- Controllable at all times

- Able to cope with stressful situations

The Pet Partners screening process evaluates how the person and animal work together as a team. It helps the handler learn where the animal might need work, where the animal will best perform and where the animal is the most comfortable. Evaluating teams helps avoid problems related to liability for both you and the Pet Partners Program. Finally, a complete evaluation of teams that will be involved in AAA/AAT can provide their handlers with information about the best way to ensure that each animal has a successful experience.

What Kinds of Animals Are Involved in AAA/AAT?

Besides dogs and cats, there are a great many other species that make wonderful visiting animals and can form a strong human-animal bond. To name a few of the animals:

• Birds	• Rabbits	• Goats	• Hamsters
• Domestic rats	• Llamas	• Guinea pigs	• Ducks
• Horses	• Cows	• Miniature pigs	• Chickens

Note: Wild or exotic animals such as snakes, ferrets and lizards are not registered by Pet Partners. Wild or exotic animals are not legally acceptable as pets in many states. Without research documenting their predictability over time, we cannot evaluate their behavior and reaction to stress. Without research documenting diseases which can be transmitted between people and these animals, we cannot evaluate health risks to people or the animals.

What Makes a Team Appropriate?

Not all animals or people are suitable for doing AAA/AAT visits. Visiting animals must be in good health. One of the best ways to help your pet to good health is a proper pet food. Just as in human health, a high-quality, nutritionally balanced diet helps provide pets with a firm foundation to maintain good health and prevent problems later on.

Animals must have a basic level of training so that they are reliable and under control even in crowded situations and when there are loud noises. Pet Partners animals should convey the image that they are well-behaved and have good manners. Because we love our animals, it is important that animals who participate in AAA/AAT have an interest in people and enjoy visiting. Look at the following checklist about what makes an animal appropriate for AAA/AAT. How does your animal fit in?

1. Animal demonstrates behavior that:
   - ☐ Is reliable
   - ☐ Is controllable
   - ☐ Is predictable
   - ☐ Inspires confidence in the person s/he is interacting with

2. Animal actively solicits interactions with people and is accepting and forgiving of differences in people's reactions and behavior.

3. Animal demonstrates:
   - ☐ Relaxed body posture
   - ☐ Moments of sustained eye contact (dependent upon species and breed)
   - ☐ Relaxed facial expression

4. Animal is more people-oriented than animal-oriented.

5. Animal likes being:
   - ☐ Petted   ☐ Touched   ☐ Hugged

6. Animal is able to remain calm with:
   - ☐ People speaking loudly
   - ☐ Clumsy movements
   - ☐ Clapping

7. When approached from the rear, the animal may show curiosity, but does not:

   • Startle   • Bark   • Act shy   • Jump up

   • Growl   • Eliminate   • Act resentful

8. The animal can walk on various surfaces. The animal is comfortable walking on:

   ❏ Carpet   ❏ Tile   ❏ Rubber matting

   ❏ Concrete or asphalt   ❏ Linoleum   ❏ Wooden floors

Note:

> There should be no refusal to walk on safe surfaces. ***Do not*** attempt to walk your animal on a surface that you feel could be hazardous. When facilities have floors that are wet, handlers should take all necessary safety precautions.

9. Animal can be held by another person for several minutes while the handler goes out of sight. Animal should demonstrate good manners when left. There should be no:

   • Vocalizing   • Extreme nervousness

10. Animal is:

    ❏ Outgoing

    ❏ Friendly

    ❏ Confident in new settings

11. Handler is:

    • Relaxed, confident

    • Attentive to animal's well being

    • Interactive with animal

    • Social with strangers

    • Gives cues to animal in conversational tone of voice

Note:

> For more information refer to Unit 1.

Matching Animals to Facilities and Populations

In Unit 1, you learned about the Facility/Team Matrix. As you proceed through this course, continue to think about the Matrix and what the best match will be for you and your animal when it comes time to choose a facility and people to visit.

Do you like noisy, stimulating environments, or would you prefer to visit a quiet setting? What is your animal's preference in terms of noise and activity levels?

What kinds of people do you think you could visit with and feel comfortable? What about your animal?

If you have a dog, horse, or other animal that can be trained, what is the skill level of your animal?

Article

Before proceeding, turn to Appendix A and read,

Article #4:   "Helping Your Pet Work in New Environments."

Activity

As a final learning activity for Lesson 2.1, go on a field trip to observe animal behavior. Watch how animals behave in the settings you visit. Are they nervous? Do they seem to be enjoying the outing? Notice differences in the behavior of animals of different species and breeds. Assuming they were registered as Pet Partners, think about how you would handle some of these animals on an AAA/AAT visit. Watch how the animal and handler work as a team. Write your observations in your journal.

- Visit local obedience classes. Lists can be found in your local phone book or contact your local high school, park district, or humane society.

- Visit dog shows, cat shows, dog match shows, Pet Expo's, 4-H Club shows, and animal clubs. A list of local dog clubs and shows can be obtained from: The American Kennel Club, 51 Madison Ave., New York, NY 10010

- Go to public places such as parks, parades, or petting zoos to observe how animals behave.

 **Research**

1. To find a certified Animal Evaluator near you, contact the Delta Society office.

2. To find out more about animal behavior, look into the following resources:

    *   Information, literature, and video tapes on the Canine Good Citizen Program and Test can be obtained from The American Kennel Club's Public Education Department at the address listed above.

    *   Local libraries have books and videos on animal behavior and AAA/ AAT programs.

    *   Some humane society/animal welfare organizations have information on animal behavior.

    *   Universities with veterinary programs may be another source of information.

Lesson 2.2 Acting as Your Animal's Advocate

Lesson Overview:

The bond between animals and people is the primary reason the AAA/AAT team is present in the health care setting. So, it goes without saying that your animal is a very important part of this team. Its needs must be considered before, during, and after AAA/AAT visits. First and foremost, your animal must be a willing participant in the interactions and must be constantly monitored for signs of fatigue or stress during visits.

Lesson Objectives:

1. Identify what to do when an animal exhibits signs of stress.
   a. Identify the signs of stress in animals.
   b. Identify the causes of stress in animals.
   c. Identify techniques for preventing stress in animals.
   d. Identify techniques for reducing stress in animals.
   e. Identify training that prepares animals for AAA/AAT.

2. Identify methods to handle and modify the behavior of your animal during a visit.

3. Identify methods of protecting your pet from inappropriate actions.

4. Identify how to tell when your animal should retire or take a sabbatical from visiting.

Materials Required:

Video: *Animals Under Stress.*

Video: *One Method to Reduce Stress* (optional).

Video: *How to Protect Your Animal.*

Article #5:   "Recognizing and Managing Stress."

Article #6:   "Communication with Touch."

Reducing Stress in Animals

We strongly believe that for animals to do well at AAA/AAT, they must enjoy it. As your animal's handler, it is up to you to ensure that your animal maintains a happy attitude and is comfortable doing AAA/AAT. Even though you and your animal may be well suited for AAA/AAT, you should remember that the kind of work you will be doing can lead to burn out and stress in both humans and animals. To protect your animal and understand how you can reduce your animal's stress, you must first be able to recognize the signs of stress in animals.

Have you observed your animal when it is under stress? How does your animal behave in a new setting or on a trip to the veterinarian? Every animal is an individual, with unique capabilities and individual tolerances. Learn to recognize the signs of stress and fatigue that *your* animal exhibits.

Signs of Stress in Animals

Birds

Signs of stress in birds include:

- Depression
- Moodiness or irritability
- Excessive activity
- Increased pecking
- Increased elimination
- Inactivity or sluggishness
- Lack of desire to socialize
- Abnormal vocalization
- Ruffled feathers

Cats

Signs of stress in cats include:

- Restlessness, distraction, agitation
- Listlessness, unusual passivity
- Defensive vocalizations
- Excessive shedding
- Dilated pupils
- Clinging

Dogs

Signs of stress in dogs include:

- Shaking
- Panting and salivating
- Dilated pupils
- Excessive blinking
- Increased activity or pacing
- Loss of appetite
- Restlessness, distraction, agitation
- Sweating through the pads of the feet
- Inappropriate urination/ defecation
- "Shutting down" by turning away or avoiding eye contact

- Excessive shedding
- Diarrhea
- Yawning
- Whining, excessive vocalizing
- Licking lips
- Hiding behind the handler

Rabbits

Signs of stress in rabbits include:

- Eyes enlarge and show whites
- Body tenses with tail up
- Ears are laid back tightly
- Growling or squeaking
- Rabbit pushes hands away
- Lack of vitality or interest
- Flinches when touched
- Breathing becomes rapid

Causes of Stress in Animals

Every animal reacts differently to its environment. Some of the more common stressors for companion animals in AAA/AAT include:

- Unusual noises

- Unknown places

- Confusing or inconsistent training or handling

- Rough or unpredictable handling

- Crowding by people or other animals

- People exhibiting inappropriate or unusual behaviors

- Unusual smells

- Unusual emotional reactions of the handler

- Extreme temperatures (outside and inside)

 Video

Video: *Animals Under Stress.*

Techniques to Prevent Stress and Fatigue in Animals

Choosing the Environment

Be aware of the things that cause your animal stress. Avoid placing it in stressful situations. In many cases, this means carefully selecting the AAA/AAT setting that is best for you and your particular animal. Be aware of hot and cold outdoor surfaces on which your animal must walk to enter the facility. Carry small animals in a familiar, lined basket to reduce stress due to handling and to avoid overheating. Schedule visits at times consistently good for your animal. Take the animal's favorite toy or a familiar item on visits.

Taking Breaks

Provide short "time-outs" during all visits, *before* signs of stress or fatigue are seen. For dogs, this can be as simple as a short walk outside or play time away from people. For cats, quiet time in a lobby or away from people may be beneficial. Provide fresh, cool water.

During visits, consistently monitor your animal's behavior. If you notice signs of stress or fatigue, remove your animal from the setting and provide a "time-out." If necessary, end the visit and note the cause of the problem so you can avoid it in the future.

If your animal requires multiple "time-outs," you may need to reconsider whether that environment is a good match for you and your teammate.

After visits:

- Provide exercise/play with no mental stress.
- Use touch or massage to encourage relaxation.
- Give your animal regularly scheduled vacations from visiting.
- Give your animal a quiet, undisturbed area to rest.
- Give your animal at least eight to ten hours of rest before visiting again.

Staying Healthy

Make sure your teammate is eating well. Animals that are fed foods lacking the proper balance of nutrients such as sodium and phosphorus, may already have stress on their systems, which can be aggravated by a stressful external situation. An animal eating a nutritious formula that is precision-balanced will usually be healthier, have more vitality and be better able to handle environmental stress.

Preventing Stress and Fatigue

The setting you and your animal will be visiting should be thoroughly assessed and potential stressors identified prior to introducing your animal. Visit a new setting at least once before taking your animal with you.

Train your animal for the setting's stressors before making visits. A gradual system of desensitization can be used to familiarize animals with the new sights and sounds that will be encountered in that setting. Desensitization simply means getting the animal used to something gradually, by introducing it slowly. For example:

- Provide daily walks outside a crowded shopping area* to get the animal used to large numbers of people. Start by going at quieter times. When the animal shows confidence in the situation, begin going when it is crowded.

- Provide short and positive "petting periods" with new people. This acclimates the animal to being handled by strangers. Begin with short, positive visits. As the animal becomes comfortable with the facility, increase the length of visits.

- Gradually expose the animal to loud noises that are similar to those it will hear in the AAA/AAT setting.

- Gradually expose your animal to animals that will be seen in the AAA/AAT setting.

- Teach commands that will aid in control during visits. For example, you might tell a stressed dog to lie down until it becomes calmer.

 **Article**

Before proceeding, turn to Appendix A and read,

Article #5:   "Recognizing and Managing Stress."

CD Video

Video: *One Method to Reduce Stress.*
(Optional.)

Protecting Your Animal From Inappropriate Actions

In all situations, your animal's comfort, safety, and happiness are of utmost concern. Animals that are continually stressed or do not appear to be at ease in the AAA/AAT setting should be removed from the setting and re-evaluated. While many animals that show mild signs of stress when first introduced to AAA/AAT will adapt and begin to enjoy AAA/AAT, some are unable to do so. In these cases, it is in the best interest of the animal to discontinue involving it in visits.

---

* Remember that Pet Partners animals are not service animals and do not have access to all public places. You can train outside of a store, but should not train inside unless the animals of the general public are welcome (e.g., Pet Supermarket).

The active involvement of the facility's staff is an important con in protecting your animal's welfare. Staff should be involved in pr screening and selecting people to visit. People who may benefit from interactions with animals and who exhibit safe behavior around animals should be selected. Staff should provide appropriate information about the people you visit that will aid in establishing meaningful relationships with the animal. Staff should also be actively involved in monitoring interactions and helping to evaluate the outcome of visits.

Important:

If at any time a person behaves in such a manner that puts your animal in danger, immediately and quietly remove the animal from the environment. Before returning to that setting or visiting the person who put your animal in danger, ask to meet with the staff to share your concerns and resolve the problem.

 **Activity**

Most of our animal companions are not used to environments other than home. Many of us, on the other hand, go off to work away from home. We are used to coping with different environments. Think about what your animal is accustomed to.

There are 168 hours in a week. Estimate how much time you spend in the places listed below, and write down the number of hours. Then think about how many hours your animal companion spends in these locations.

Location	You	Animal
In a car (riding or staying)	_____	_____
In a park, or the neighborhood (walking)	_____	_____
In a friend's home	_____	_____
At the beauty/barber shop/groomer	_____	_____
At the veterinarian's	_____	_____
In a place of business (other than home)	_____	_____
In a building (shopping for groceries, etc.)	_____	_____
At home	_____	_____

This is your animal companion's life-style. When we ask them to go into a facility to visit, we are asking them to willingly and cheerfully accompany us into an unfamiliar environment where very few people understand their language.

 **Video**

Video: *How to Protect Your Animal.*

Identifying the Need for Change

Like people, animals can become bored, fatigued, or "burned out" with their activities. While some animals can visit the same facility for years and continue to enjoy visits, others may begin to show signs of stress or fatigue after only being involved in AAA/AAT for a short period of time.

Sabbaticals

A short-term break is often all that is needed for animals who are in their prime. Introducing a new activity or just taking a break from everything for a few months may be beneficial. In many cases, the animal can return to the AAA/AAT program after the sabbatical and may once again enjoy attending.

Retirement

As your animal ages, his/her ability to adapt quickly to new people or environments may decline. Elderly animals have reduced stamina and may become less tolerant of the demands of AAA/AAT. As animals age, it is important to be aware of these changes and to respect them when they occur. When it becomes necessary, retirement can be instituted in a gradual manner by decreasing the frequency or duration of visits. In many cases, older animals can continue to be involved in AAA/AAT on a reduced schedule or in less demanding settings. As always, continually assessing your animal's welfare and comfort is of utmost importance. Visits should be modified to fit your animal's changing needs.

Activity

- Visit the facility or facilities alone before taking your animal. Identify all potential stressors so that these can be addressed when you prepare your animal for visits.

- Set up an informational meeting with the facility's staff who will be involved in the visits. This meeting can be used to discuss methods of selecting people to visit and ways in which staff can help you attend to your animal's welfare during visits.

Article

Before proceeding, turn to Appendix A and read,

Article #6:   "Communicating with Touch."

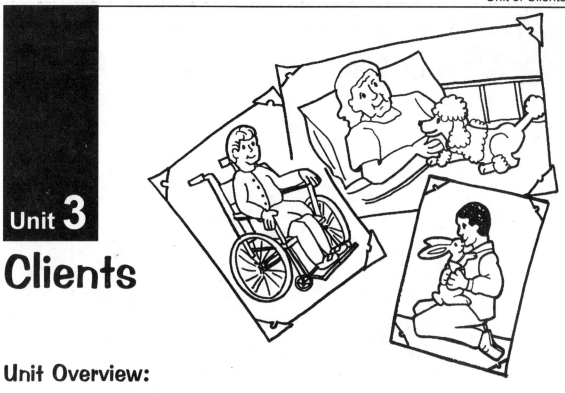

Unit 3
Clients

Unit Overview:

The people you will be visiting are the focus of this unit. You will learn terminology that puts *people* first. This unit also provides specific information to help you have successful visits with people who have certain characteristics.

Unit Map:

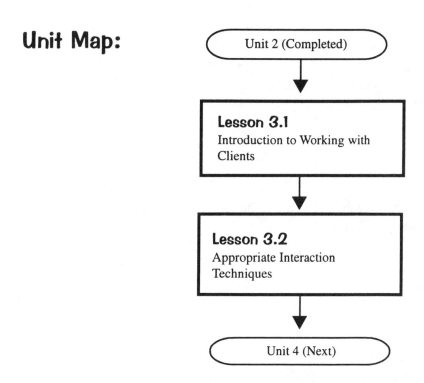

Unit 2 (Completed)

Lesson 3.1
Introduction to Working with Clients

Lesson 3.2
Appropriate Interaction Techniques

Unit 4 (Next)

Lesson 3.1 Introduction to Working with Clients

Lesson Overview:

This lesson provides a basic introduction to visiting with people who have specific medical conditions. There are some preferred terms that are used in health care settings and this lesson provides information on using the proper terms. In addition, since you and your animal may become a part of the facility team, this lesson describes the team approach.

Lesson Objectives:

1. Identify the appropriate terms to be used when referring to people with specific conditions.

2. Describe a "team approach."

Using the Proper Terms[4]

You will be visiting with people who have a variety of different conditions. The table that follows will help make sure that you are familiar with the appropriate terms to use when you meet/visit people. Notice that the appropriate terms put the emphasis on the person, not the condition. They are a person *with* a condition; not identified *as* the condition. Also, unless referring to people who are sick and in a hospital, the people you will visit with are "clients," not patients.

Using the correct terms, such as the ones presented below, shows sensitivity on your part. When you use the preferred terms, people will be more likely to think of you as a well-trained person and a valuable resource to the facility team.

Appropriate Terms	Inappropriate Terms
Person with a disability	Disabled person
Person who has mental or physical disabilities	Disabled victim, unfortunate victim, poor, pitiful, abnormal, deformed, invalid
Person who has a mobility impairment, or person who uses a wheelchair	Wheelchair bound, restricted to a wheelchair, or wheelchair victim
Person with quadriplegia, paraplegia, person who is paralyzed, or person who uses a wheelchair	Quad, quadriplegic, paraplegic
Person who uses crutches or cane	Cripple, gimp
Person who has, person who experienced, person with	Victim of, suffers from, afflicted with, stricken with
Person who has a disability resulting from or caused by	Invalid, victim, afflicted with
Person with a stroke characteristic, person who has had a stroke	Stroke victim, suffered from a stroke
Person with a congenital disability	Birth defect
Person with mental illness or disability, Psychiatric disability	Mental deviant, crazy, mentally deranged, insane, nut, former mental patient, wacko, one brick short of a load

---

[4] Adapted from, What's in a Name? 1990, December. *CONNECTIONS, Information Newsletter of Bridge Ministries for Disability Concerns*. Kirkland, WA.

Appropriate Terms	Inappropriate Terms
Person with brain injury	Brain-damaged
Person with traumatic brain injuries	Traumatically brain injured victim
Person with a closed-head injury	Closed-head injured victim
Person with arthritis	The arthritic
Person who has epilepsy	The epileptic
Person who is deaf, hearing-impaired, hard of hearing, has partial hearing loss	Deaf mute, deaf and dumb
Person who has a speech disorder, a person without speech, or a person with a speech impairment	Mute
Person of short stature	Midget, dwarf, little person
Person who is blind, vision-impaired, has partial vision, or loss of vision	Blink, blur, bluff, squint, or hard of seeing
Person with Down's syndrome	Mongoloid
Person with cerebral palsy	Palsied or spastic
Person with learning disabilities	Retard, lazy, stupid
Person with chemical or alcohol dependency	Drunk, addict, crack head, junkie, alcoholic
Person with developmental disabilities	Retard, moron, feebleminded, mentally deficient or defective, elevator doesn't go all the way to the top

The "Team Approach"

The health care and other staff of a facility use a "team approach" when providing treatment for clients. You and your animal may work with one or more members of this team. People from each discipline (PT, teacher, OT, nurse, social worker, RT or activity director, physician, etc.) work together to help the client reach his/her goals.

Team dynamics vary from facility to facility. You should be aware of your role and who you can turn to for guidance.

Being a Part of the Facility Team

As a volunteer, you will not be doing assessments or writing goals for clients. However, once you establish a working relationship with a facility professional, that person may want you to utilize your animal to address problems that have been identified for a particular client. For example, you might be asked to have someone pet and brush your animal. Petting and brushing requires that the person use his/her hands and fine motor (small muscle) skills. Improving fine motor skills might be a goal on the person's treatment plan and you may help him/her achieve this through AAA or AAT.

How A Treatment Team Works

The trend in health care is to use an approach that involves professionals working together toward common goals for a client. Usually, when people enter a facility they are given a complete assessment.

Staff members from each relevant department will evaluate each client using tests and assessment tools for their area. So, for example, Mrs. Jones is admitted to the XYZ Nursing Home. The doctors and nurses write reports of their initial assessments. The physical therapist does some tests and records the physical therapy needs of Mrs. Jones. The recreation therapist assesses Mrs. Jones in the area of leisure skills. The occupational therapist notes that Mrs. Jones needs a splint for her right hand.

Then they have a treatment team meeting. On a formal written document (which in nursing homes is often called the Nursing Care Plan), the team of professionals working with Mrs. Jones list some goals for her. The goals include:

- Will walk 50 feet each day.

- Will participate in a leisure activity in the day room.

- Will feed herself using a special spoon and splint on her right hand.

The same kind of team planning procedure is used for people with developmental disabilities and school children with special needs. People with developmental disabilities have a document called a Habilitation Plan and school children with special needs have Individualized Educational Plans (IEPs). These plans may have different names at individual facilities.

Other Team Interactions

In addition to being part of the facility's team, you may be a member of an AAA/AAT team at a facility or in your city. You may go on visits with a team. Belonging to an organized group of AAA/AAT volunteers has many benefits. A major benefit is having a support group of friends who understand your needs and problems and who can truly appreciate your successes.

Lesson 3.2 Interaction Techniques

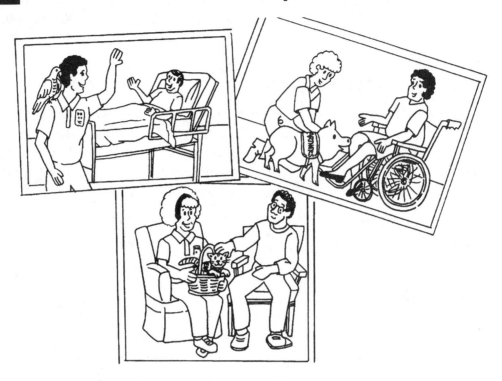

Lesson Overview:

During your visits, you will be visiting with people who have a variety of characteristics. This lesson describes characteristics you may recognize when you visit and lists some of the conditions they might be associated with. Most importantly, this lesson describes appropriate interaction techniques and guidelines that will help you and your animal visit successfully with specific populations.

Lesson Objectives:

1. Identify sources of information on common medical conditions.

2. Identify the characteristics of the following:

    - Confusion/dementias
    - Developmental disorders
    - Difficulty seeing
    - Difficulty speaking
    - Physical disabilities
    - Difficulty hearing
    - Psychiatric disorders
    - Elders

83   ©Delta Society

3. Given a set of symptoms:

    a. Identify guidelines for interacting with people who have certain symptoms

    b. Identify the conditions or diseases associated with certain symptoms

4. Identify special considerations for visiting people with suppressed immune systems.

5. Identify proper "wheelchair etiquette."

6. Identify the aptitude and skills animals need for given populations.

7. Identify special considerations for visiting children.

Materials Required:

Video:	*Visiting People With Confusion.*
Video:	*Visiting People Who Have Speech Difficulties.*
Video:	*Visiting People Who Are Blind.*
Video:	*Special Considerations For Visiting Children.*
Article #7:	"How to Help the Elderly Reminisce."
Article #8:	"Communicating with Older Adults."

Where to Find Terms and Definitions of Conditions

This lesson provides you with information on the symptoms of specific medical conditions that you are likely to encounter in your AAA/AAT setting. You might find that you want more detailed information about a particular condition. Try these sources:

- The Delta Society library. Contact Delta for assistance.

- Your local library.

- Your local hospital.

- Your local phone book and newspaper. Many groups have support group meetings and local resource rooms that provide information to anyone who is interested (e.g., the local Alzheimer's support group).

Interacting with Different Populations

You need to know about the people you will visit so you can have more enjoyable and effective visits. Please keep in mind, however, that it is not your responsibility to diagnose or treat the people you visit. This information will help you work with health and social service professionals to identify appropriate activities to use when visiting with people.

The information has been arranged by symptoms such as confusion, or hearing difficulties. During visits as a Pet Partners volunteer, your interactions with each person will be affected by the person's ability to interact with you. As you read through this section, think about what it would be like to experience these symptoms. How would you want a visitor to behave? How could a Pet Partners team enhance the visit?

People With Confusion

Description

You may visit a facility in which some or most of the residents are confused. The confusion may be temporary, or it may be long lasting and get progressively worse. Many diseases include confusion among their symptoms. Some of those diseases are:

- Alzheimer's Disease
- Multiple Sclerosis
- Dementias
- Schizophrenia

- Manic-Depression
  (Bi-Polar Disorder)

- Physical Abuse Survivors

- Depression

- Stroke

Visiting with This Population[5]

Perception

The most significant symptom for people with dementia is greatly distorted perception. What we see and hear is usually quite different from what they see and hear. Thus, what we think is going on can be radically different from their perception.

We show them our friendly animals, expecting them to see just that. And maybe they do see our best friends, but it's quite likely that they see something very different. The friendly smiling look that is so familiar to us could look like a snarling, raging monster to them. The animal that for a moment may have reminded them of a pet from long ago, can transform in an instant to a horrid and fearsome beast. Because their perceptive abilities can be so distorted and their perceptions change rapidly, they have very strong panic reactions.

Roger

Roger was a feisty older man, hospitalized in the Rehabilitation Unit. Staff tread softly around him at times, for Roger did not hold his tongue, and he was a man of strong opinions. Roger became quite frustrated with his decreased abilities, and staff members were handy to take the verbal brunt of his anger. When it was time for Jenny, the AAA volunteer, to make her visit, staff cautioned her about Roger, advising her that he had been irritable and impatient with staff, the hospital, and his treatment.

Undaunted, Jenny and her dog Poppi courageously entered Roger's room. If the nurses had not told Jenny that Roger was bad-tempered, she would never have known it. With Poppi in the room, Roger turned into a gentle, loving (but still opinionated) man. Poppi knew a challenge when she saw it, and soon was able to count another "love conquest," as Roger invited her onto his bed. Poppi and Roger got along famously.

Later, the staff saw evidence of the impact of Poppi's visit—Roger had drawn a picture of the event.

by Ann Howie

[5] Based on Baker, Carla. 1995, March. Senile Dementia. *St. Peter Hospital Animal-Assisted Activities/Therapy Program Newsletter.*

Remember:

> Their perception is their reality, and we must deal with them on that level.

As a precaution, you should have close control of your animal throughout the contact. You'll need to be able to respond immediately to any change in the person's behavior.

Maintain a calm environment. Be careful not to severely stimulate the person. Music that is too loud or too many people talking at once may increase confusion and anxiety.

Approach the person in an easy manner. Show confidence with slow easy movements and warm smiles. Follow a set routine. Keep changes to a minimum.

The Importance of Touching

For people who have dementia touching is very important. Often, the only perception that is still accurate is the sense of touch. Stroking our pet's fur is pleasant to us and it is especially enjoyable for people with confusion.

Tunnel Vision

By the time people with dementia enter a facility, they are already in the mid to late stage. Vision is primarily affected—there is no peripheral vision, no color perception, and the person sees the world in true tunnel vision. Even if the person can see color, they may be unable to interpret it. Sounds are distorted or lost. Also, many people with dementia have experienced a stroke, which both accelerates and complicates the process.

Always approach the person head on and slowly. If you approach from outside their visual tunnel, you can startle him/her.

Due to tunnel vision, the person may have trouble locating the animal with his/her hand and may need your gentle assistance.

During your approach, keep very close to your teammate so you will be perceived as a single visual item. During the initial contact, gently touching the person may help to orient his/her focus on you and your teammate. Ask him/her, or a staff member, for his/her name and use it frequently during any conservation. This also helps focus the person's attention and maintain concentration.

It is important to give the person extra time to adjust both visually and mentally. Try to move and speak more slowly than usual.

Positioning

Stand near the person. Avoid standing over the person. Make eye contact.

Many people use wheelchairs or geriatric chairs. For this and other reasons, they often cannot bend over or easily reach down to the animal.

- With smaller animals, you may need to pick up your teammate and carry him or her up to the person.

- Larger teammates don't have the advantage of being easily portable • and have the additional disadvantage of seeming more threatening during any perceptive dysfunction. You may want to try getting your teammate up in a chair, but be sure it doesn't seem to tower over the person. Otherwise, try sitting near the person with your teammate across your lap.

Communicating

People with dementia may have difficulty understanding you and may not welcome conversation.

- Quiet time is just as important as speaking. If you do talk, maintain a very calm and soothing tone of voice. People with dementia are especially sensitive to emotion. If they perceive any impatience or frustration in your voice or expression, they are likely to escalate that reality and over-react.

- Talk in short, simple, direct sentences. Use literal words, such as, "the sun is shining," instead of "the weather is beautiful." Ask them "yes" or "no" questions to clarify what they want.

When the person talks to you, s/he may go off on a tangent or may simply not make sense. If so, listen to his/her tone of voice and watch his/her facial expression for the meaning behind the message, instead of trying to understand the literal content. If you don't understand, it's okay to say so. Again, ask "yes" or "no" questions to clarify what s/he wants.

- Ask questions clearly and give ample time for the person to respond. Be patient and avoid speaking loudly to those persons with normal hearing.

- Avoid asking questions the person cannot answer. People find uncertainty and recognition of failure unsettling.

- Avoid baby talk, which decreases self-esteem and does little to help with understanding. Speak in clear, distinct tones on an adult level.

- Talk clearly. Keep sentences short. Be sure you have the person's attention before you speak. Touch the person on the shoulder and call the person by name to help him/her tune in to you. The intercom can create anxiety for someone who is confused and doesn't know where the voice is coming from.

- Give precise directions in simple, short statements. "This is the way to the bathroom."

- Repeat information when necessary.

- Remind persons of the time, date, etc. Use reality information in a conversational manner. Acquire the habit of announcing events. "It's time for your lunch, Mr. Smith."

- Refer to clocks and calendars and other reality props when appropriate.

- Don't encourage disorientation by allowing a rambling speech pattern. Ask questions that will bring the person back on the subject.

- Be kind but also be firm in pointing to the reality of the situation. "I'm a volunteer, not your wife. Do I remind you of your wife?"

- Avoid giving too many choices. Provide a choice between two alternatives, rather than three or four.

Don't be afraid to ask for assistance or advice from the staff. They have much more experience with this special kind of client and are an invaluable resource. With this condition and any other, you can approach facility staff for advice on dealing with a particular person's needs and behavior.

 Video

Video: *Visiting People With Confusion.*

People with Developmental Disorders

Description

Developmental disorders affect the person's reasoning and intellectual (cognitive) abilities and/or physical abilities. This is different from mental illness. Developmental disorders have many different names and forms. Some of the conditions that include developmental disorders are:

- Developmental Disability (formerly called Mental Retardation)
- Down's Syndrome (formerly called Mongolism)
- Fetal Alcohol Syndrome
- Cerebral Palsy
- Autism
- Attention Deficit Hyperactivity Disorder
- Learning Disorders
- Chemical Dependency (including drug-exposed children)

Visiting with this Population

When visiting with this population, you may be visiting with adults who act, think and respond like children. It is important to maintain a friendly, calm attitude and make and maintain eye contact.

Fear

When visiting children with autism, however, direct eye contact may be threatening. Also, many children with autism are extremely afraid of animals. You may need to work closely with staff to overcome this fear.

Never assume that the person knows how to appropriately touch or interact with your animal. It may be helpful to think of them like exuberant children who have the best of intentions but need help to remain safe. Some may even talk about or show behaviors that indicate extreme fearfulness. Their actions and emotions may be extreme because they have not learned the inhibitions necessary for "polite society."

Guidelines

You will need to use language and instructions that they can understand. Sometimes, they have not had a lot of experience around animals and you will need to watch carefully to make sure your animal stays safe. Give simple instructions and praise them for behaviors that you want to increase and maintain (e.g., "That is nice, gentle petting...the cat sure likes that.")

You should structure activities and give instructions in short, simple steps. Be clear, concise and very specific about what you are asking of the person. If the person is having a hard time understanding what you want him/her to do, you can model appropriate interactions with your animal. Actually show them what to do (e.g., "Watch me, hold the brush like this...").

It helps to have children with attention deficit disorder repeat the steps to a task or the rules out loud. You may need to keep visits short and gradually lengthen the time as the person is able to attend for longer periods. People with attention deficit disorder do best with activities that constantly change in some way, such as computer games. They get bored easily. For this reason, you may need to continuously change the activity during a visit.

Watch your animal closely for signs of stress when visiting people with unusual behaviors, such as shrieking or sudden, large movements.

People with Physical Disabilities

Description

People may become physically disabled through illness, accident, or genetic inheritance. People will have various degrees of disability, from what appears to be relatively minor difficulty walking, or relatively minor arm tremors, to paralysis and inability to move their arms and legs. Sometimes, the effects of the disability will vary from day to day for an individual. Physical disabilities may not always be noticeable (balance and loss of sensation, for example). People who are living with a physical disability must deal not only with their physical problems and limitations, but also with their feelings about needing to do things differently from the majority of the people in the world.

Some of the conditions which include physical disability are:

- Head, Brain, and Spinal Cord Injury
- Parkinson's Disease
- Muscular Dystrophy
- Cerebral Palsy
- Stroke
- Multiple Sclerosis
- Spina Bifida

Visiting with this Population

Some people with physical impairments may need to be physically guided in order to pet your animal. For example, you may need to gently take the person's hand, move his/her arm out to reach your animal, place his/her hand in the proper position, and guide his/her hand and arm down your animal's body to stroke from head to tail. Always move gently and slowly when working with a limb that does not work of its own accord.

Positioning for Petting

Sometimes, if people have limited control of their hands and arms, it is hard to present your animal for petting. In such cases, you might ask a staff person if the person could be placed on an exercise mat. AAA/AAT animals can lay beside a person for petting or just being close.

If you visit people in an orthopedic setting, it is important to know each person's special needs and what you can do with the person. *Do not* move an affected limb unless you have been trained and given permission to move the person. In some settings, volunteers *are not* permitted to move people with orthopedic problems or transfer them from beds to chairs, etc.

Communicate with the Client

Look into the person's eyes as you talk to him/her. Talk to the person, not to the staff or family member. S/he can hear you and wants to be treated as a person. Ask him/her questions directly, even if s/he cannot speak to answer you (the family or staff will answer for him/her).

Learn the person's name at the beginning of your interaction. If the person you are visiting loses concentration or becomes distracted, use his/her name to help him/her refocus on your animal and you.

The person may have some of the same characteristics as a person who is confused, so focus on reality. Use patience and speak clearly and distinctly.

Aggression

People with head injury might have problems with impulse control. This means that they might get extremely angry or aggressive with no warning. They might yell at you or say things they don't mean. Be aware of this and realize it is a symptom of brain injury; don't take it personally. If a person with a head-injury has a tendency to become aggressive, visits should only be done in the presence of a staff person. Never put yourself or your animal at risk of being injured.

Facial Expressions

For some people, difficulty showing emotions with facial expressions is part of their condition (which also affects physical ability). This may be disconcerting for you, but your animal probably won't notice. Don't become offended or think the person is emotionally cold or doesn't like you. Respond naturally to the content of the conversation. You may also need to become "invisible" as the person pets and relates to your animal without need of human interaction.

Emotions

Some people who have had a stroke are highly emotional. They may cry very easily when you and your animal are visiting. This does not necessarily mean that they are sad or depressed. Do not take the crying personally. Allow them to cry and *do not* say, "Everything's all right" (it's not), or "Don't cry" (they don't have control over the crying). Instead, talk to them; ask if they miss their animal; acknowledge that it must be difficult to be in the hospital/nursing home/etc. See if they will talk about their animal or family.

Muscular Control

Some people with physical disabilities may not have good control over their muscles. This means that they may think they are petting your animal gently, when in fact they are patting your animal too hard. Say the person's name and tell him/her clearly, calmly and firmly, "That's too rough for Barney. He likes gentle touches." You may need to verbally remind the person periodically to be gentle, and you may need to take his/her hand and show what a gentle touch is.

If you know that a person has trouble keeping control of the muscles in his/her hands, watch extra carefully to be certain that your animal does not get caught in a grasp that the person is unable to easily relinquish. Keep your hand between the collar and your animal, for example, so that the collar is not pulled too tightly without your knowledge.

Abilities

Some people who have had a stroke are impulsive and have poor judgement. Their brains are not processing their limitations after the stroke and they think they have the same abilities as they did before the stroke. For example, someone may think s/he can easily get up out of a chair and take your dog for a walk, when in reality s/he may fall in attempting to get out of the chair. The person may think s/he can walk for a long time, and instead will tire after a few steps. The person may go for a walk with you around the unit and get lost, not remembering where his/her room is. Remain alert to your surroundings. You may need to remember how to return the person to his/her room. Avoid areas with lots of obstacles to move around. Stay with your animal and keep your hand on its leash.

In addition, people with physical limitations may believe that they cannot do some things. It is true that they cannot do things in the same way they used to before their injury, but they are learning how to do things differently. You may ask someone if s/he wants to feed your dog a treat and hear him/her respond, "I can't do that." The person may not be able to reach into the packet to pick out a treat, but if you can hold out his/her hand, you can place a treat on his/her hand and your animal can lick it off. Thus, the person gets to experience success at feeding, and s/he gets to provide nurture to your animal at the same time.

People in a Coma

You may see people who are in a coma. People who seem to be non-responsive are just that—seemingly so. Always act as if they can hear. Talk to them and speak normally. Tell them who you are and what is the purpose of your visit. Describe your animal companion to them, using concrete terms (brown, long hair, big nose, etc.) as well as emotional descriptions ("He's my best buddy"). If you are allowed to place your animal on the bed, tell the person that you are going to do so, and tell them step-by-step as you do it. You may guide the person's hand over your animal, explaining as you go what you are doing. You may also want to describe how your animal is responding. "King is very interested in you. He is sniffing at your hand. Do you feel his cold nose? He feels very comfortable on the bed with you. Can you feel him snuggle against your side?"

If a person is going through a stage of recovery after a coma where agitation is predominant, it is best to avoid visits. If the person becomes agitated in the midst of a visit, you may need to end your visit. Ask the staff about the person's stage of recovery and whether or not it is beneficial for you to remain. If you are encouraged to stay, talk calmly to the person. See if you can redirect his/her attention to your animal by giving specific instructions: "David, would you like to pet Muffy?" You may use a firm (but non-restraining) touch to help the person pet your animal, but a light, feathery touch may make the person more agitated. Stay for a short period of time.

Your Animal

Keep a clear sense of what kinds of behaviors you will allow with your animal. For example, the physical tremors some people have may not be any trouble at all for a Labrador, but may be too much for a hamster. If you are uncertain about whether or not your animal likes something, then your animal probably does not like it. Your animal depends upon you to protect it from unpleasant touch. If the person is unable to stop, you may need to end your visit with that person for the day and move on to visit someone else.

Make certain your animal is accustomed to people who move differently so that your animal will not show fear or aggression at the "strange" behavior. A person's problems with balance, coordination, spasticity and tremors require that your animal be comfortable with unfamiliar movements.

Some people with physical difficulties have problems with bladder control. This may give them odors which are absolutely fascinating to many animals. This is a good instance where animals need to know and respond to instructions such as "Leave it" (meaning, stop doing what you're doing and focus on something else).

Keep Visits Short

Remember, it is important to prevent over-fatiguing the person. Visits should be short. The person should be able to set the physical pace of the interactions. If s/he appears to be getting tired, you should end the visit. Stay in close touch with your facility contact person to make sure that visits are continuing to be beneficial.

People with Difficulty Speaking

Description

There are many different kinds of difficulties with speaking. You may visit people who have trouble physically forming or articulating words. Their speech may be slurred or indistinct so that words are difficult to understand. You may also visit people who are physically able to speak but whose brain is not sending the right signals for them to speak the correct individual words or to string words together in an understandable sentence. Some people will have difficulty speaking, but can understand everything that is said to them. Some people will have difficulty understanding long sentences. In addition, some psychiatric conditions include refusal to speak or difficulty speaking because the person is withdrawn and has not spoken.

Some of the conditions that include speech difficulties (or apparent problems with speech) are:

- Multiple Sclerosis
- Head or Brain Injury
- Developmental Disabilities
- Stroke
- Hearing Disorders
- Depression
- Cerebral Palsy

Visiting with this Population

It is a common misconception in our culture to assume that if a person cannot speak "normally" then s/he also has an intellectual impairment. This is absolutely *not true!* A person's mental abilities may be completely intact with a speech difficulty. Inability to speak does not mean inability to think. You may be talking to a person with a Ph.D. in biophysics who has a body that works imperfectly.

Communicating

As you talk to a person with a speech difficulty, look into his/her eyes. Talk to the person, not to the staff or family member, even if the person is completely unable to speak. The person can hear you and wants to be treated as a person. Ask the person questions directly, even if s/he cannot speak to answer you (the family or staff will answer for him/her). Give him/her time to respond to you. S/he may be struggling to say one word, and if you rush over his/her effort in your discomfort with silence, that person may give up on you. Maintain eye contact and talk to him/her normally (speaking louder or speaking v-e-r-y-s-l-o-w-l-y doesn't help!).

If a person has a severe impairment, you may want to limit your conversation to questions that can be answered with a yes/no or a shake or nod of the head. On the other hand, staff may want you to ask open-ended questions to encourage the person to work at speaking more. Ask staff for guidance.

Understanding

If a person is having difficulty understanding your words, you may still engage in conversation. Speak in short sentences. Include concrete objects in the room. Use hand gestures to illustrate concrete subjects. Give choices between two options. "Do you have a dog at home? [person nods yes] Is your dog big [place your hand at big-dog level] or small [place your hand low to the floor]? Is your dog brown or black?" Listen carefully to the person's responses and be alert to his/her nonverbal communication, as well. Give the person time to answer you.

If you don't understand what a person is saying, it is okay to say so. Don't pretend you understand when you don't. "I'm sorry. I don't understand. Can you tell me again or in another way?" The person may have a picture board or book that s/he can point to, or may gesture or point to objects in the room which will help you understand. Repeat words or phrases the person says to help him/her know you are trying to understand. If you are wrong, the person will tell you. If s/he gets frustrated, it's okay to empathize. "It is frustrating, isn't it. I wish I understood better."

The Meaning Behind the Words

People who have had a stroke, for example, may have to learn to speak again in addition to relearning physical abilities. At times they may not say the words they mean. They know what they want to say in their mind, but their brain is not sending the right signals to the body to get the correct words out. For example, some people will say, "Yup!" to everything, even when they mean no. Some people will repeat the same phrase over and over, "The roses are pretty," even though it does not relate to the conversation. Some people will curse or swear easily and frequently, even though before the stroke they did not use that kind of language. Do not be shocked or offended or try to take the statements literally. Respond in a calm, flowing way to what you think was their intent.

 **Video**

Video: *Visiting People Who Have Speech Difficulties.*

People with Difficulty Hearing

Description

Hearing loss may come with age, a person may be born with a hearing loss, or a person may lose his/her hearing as a result of an accident or illness. Hearing loss may vary from day to day or situation to situation. Some people may wear hearing aids inconspicuously, and others may refuse to wear an aid at all. No aid can completely restore hearing. A person who loses his/her hearing may feel terribly isolated from the world around him. S/he may also feel fearful that s/he cannot keep him/herself safe or even be prepared for "ordinary" interruptions that others can hear coming. With some psychiatric conditions, a person may have the physical ability to hear, but has instead withdrawn from the world and does not respond to sound.

Some of the conditions that include hearing loss (or apparent problems with hearing) are:

- Deafness
- Schizophrenia
- Depression
- Physical Abuse Survivors
- Autism
- Multiple Sclerosis

Visiting with this Population

Communicating

Not all elderly people have difficulty hearing, so do not automatically speak louder when visiting with seniors. If you do need to speak louder, also lower (deepen) the tone of your voice to keep from screeching or shouting. Think about what you are saying and form each word clearly (but do not over-pronounce). You may also need to speak slower than your typical rate.

Speak in your normal voice and move close to the person's ear rather than shouting. You should avoid asking long questions or using complex sentences. Make sure that you give the person plenty of time to respond to your questions and requests. Do not change the subject abruptly. If an interpreter is present, speak to the person you are visiting, not to the interpreter. Maintain eye contact with that person, not the interpreter.

You may also want to carry an eraser board or a dark pen and writing paper with you on your visit. If it becomes too difficult to communicate with speech, you can write your communications. Never pretend to understand if you do not understand.

Use nonverbal communication including gestures, facial expression and touch. Offer things to see and touch as topics of conversation. Some people may like to do puzzles and play games such as checkers.

Remember, listening can be hard work. Don't tire the person. Be understanding when s/he does not seem to be listening very well.

Visibility

When visiting someone who has hearing loss, you may need to attract his/her attention first by touching his/her hand or shoulder lightly. Face him/her directly so s/he can see your face and mouth. Place yourself at his/her eye level, if possible, and look directly into his/her eyes. Be sure that lighting is adequate when you talk to people who are hearing-impaired so they can watch your lip movements and gestures. If s/he is facing an unshaded window and you place yourself between him/her and the window, you will be in shadow. You may need to turn the chair around so that you are facing the light (even if you have to squint during the visit).

Reduce Distractions

Reduce distractions. Move into another (quieter) room, turn down the radio or TV, etc. If you need to turn down a radio, ask permission first. "The music is too loud for my dog. I'd like to turn down the volume while we're here. Would that be all right?" Remember to be considerate as you leave, and ask if s/he would like the volume turned up again.

Visiting Groups

If there are several people together during the visit, make sure everyone is aware of and understands topic changes. Help everyone know what is being talked about by starting with a key word or phrase: "Speaking of horses . . ." If someone does not understand, use synonyms (words that have the same or nearly the same meaning) instead of repeating the same phrase: "What are you going to do this weekend?" becomes "What are your plans for Saturday?" If only one person in the group is hard of hearing, try to carry on your conversation with others in a way that the affected person can read your lips.

People with Difficulty Seeing

Description

People who have a vision impairment may have partial to total vision loss. People may have tunnel vision because they have lost their peripheral (outside the center) vision. Others may have lost central vision and still have peripheral vision. People may see clearly only things which are very close to them (near sighted) or very far away (far sighted). People may be considered "legally blind" and still have some ability to see. They may only see shadows however, or highly blurred images, which makes it impossible for them to drive safely and requires the use of assistive devices (e.g., a cane or guide dog), to help them walk safely. Some people are color blind. Some people's vision varies from day to day. Initially, you may not realize that a person has vision loss—his/her eyes, posture and manner may seem perfectly natural to you. In some psychiatric conditions, a person may have the physical ability to see, but be withdrawn into him/herself so that s/he appears not to see the world around him/her.

Some of the conditions that include difficulty with sight (or apparent sight loss) include:

- Blindness
- Developmental Disabilities
- Physical Abuse Survivors
- HIV/AIDS

- Schizophrenia
- Depression
- Multiple Sclerosis
- Head Injuries

Visiting with this Population

Coming and Going

While it may be true that some people who have lost one sense develop other senses more acutely to compensate, do not assume that this is so. You may startle someone if you come up on him/her unexpectedly. When you are visiting, ask a staff member if anyone has a vision impairment. If so, have that person pointed out to you. Then, as you approach him/her or enter his/her room, greet him/her casually so you don't startle him/her. Say something to announce your presence and your animal. Explain what is going on. As you give your name, explain that you have an animal companion with you and say what kind of animal it is. This helps avoid unsettling surprises. Identify yourself at each encounter until your voice becomes familiar to the person.

Make it clear when you are leaving. Never leave without excusing yourself or saying good-bye.

Communicating

Speak in a normal tone. There is no need to speak loudly. A person with difficulty seeing does not necessarily have difficulty hearing.

They cannot see your facial expressions, so use touch if you are both comfortable with it.

Don't be embarrassed if you happen to use an accepted, common expression such as "See you later."

Placement For Petting

You may need to help the person place his/her hand on your animal, since s/he cannot see where your animal is. If you have a small animal (under 15 pounds) or an animal in a basket, be sure to ask if it is all right before placing the animal on his/her lap.

You can use hand-over-hand guidance to help the person get to know your animal. Use descriptive words to enhance the interaction.

Verbalizing What You See

Help the person you are visiting share in everything that is going on. If your dog is wagging his tail vigorously and is eager to see the person, describe that to him/her. Tell him/her as your cat gets that special, contented look on its face that means it is thoroughly contented and relaxed. Describe the look—create a verbal illustration for his/her mind. Don't feel you have to make anything up to make him/her feel special; just explain what is going on that you can see. Develop your powers of observation and translate that into descriptive words.

Reading

When reading to a person who is vision-impaired, consult him/her about reading selections and make sure the material is of a nature that will hold his/her continued interest. Vary your vocal intonation to keep your voice interesting (a monotone puts people to sleep). If the person has some vision, they may be able to read large print.

◧▭ Video

Video: *Visiting People Who Are Blind.*

People with Psychiatric Disorders

Description

People with psychiatric disorders (mental illness) are ill in the same way people are physically ill—mental illness is just harder to see. The brain needs the right balance of chemicals in order to work correctly, just as the body needs the correct balance of fiber and protein, for example. Mental illness is not a matter of being "weak" or unable to "pull yourself up by your bootstraps." A chemical imbalance in the brain may be worsened by ineffective coping skills or traumatic life events. This is why many people with psychiatric conditions receive therapy as well as medications.

Psychiatric disorders may surface in childhood, adolescence, or adulthood. The disability may be mild to severe. It may come about as a result of prescription or recreational drug use, or be inherited (genetics). Psychiatric disorders are highly complex; they are not always easily diagnosed or treated. Many psychiatric disorders are safely controlled with medication, allowing people to live rich, active, "normal" lives. People with psychiatric disorders may be your neighbor or your best friend.

Some people with psychiatric disorders may have problems with *mood*: They may laugh or cry at odd times; feel extremes of anger, despair, or euphoria; or have rapidly changing moods. Some people have difficulty with *thought processes*: Their ideas fly from one topic to another, they are easily distracted, they put words together which don't make sense to you, or they cannot make up their mind. Some people have problems with *thought content*: They think constantly about suicide, they are convinced someone is out to get them (paranoid), they believe they are someone famous, or they believe they are worthless. Some people have difficulty with *perceptions*: They may have hallucinations (they see, hear, taste, or feel things that others don't). Some people have problems with *behavior*: They may be overly agitated, lethargic, or disoriented, or they may repeat a behavior (like rubbing their hands together), over and over and over.

Some psychiatric conditions include:

- Depression
- Schizophrenia
- Personality Disorders
- Substance Abuse
- Dementia
- Physical Abuse Survivors
- Suicide Attempt Survivors
- Bi-Polar Disorder (Manic Depression)
- Eating Disorders (Anorexia, Bulimia)

Visiting with this Population

Receiving training from staff and maintaining a close relationship with staff at the psychiatric facility you visit is probably more important for this population than for any other. Staff have a specific treatment plan for each client and should provide you with some guidance in what to do (and what not to do) with each person. What may seem unimportant to you in your conversation with someone may actually be a problem in that

Thomas

As Linda and Tank (Bearded Collie) were making their visit on the Psychiatric Unit one evening, they were—actually, *Tank* was—enthusiastically greeted by Thomas. In addition to whatever mental illness had necessitated Thomas' hospitalization, he seemed to have a physical palsy-type of condition which affected his coordination and ability to pet Tank smoothly. It was also very difficult for Thomas to speak clearly and evenly. Tank did not seem to mind any of these difficulties, much to Thomas' delight.

Tank and Linda allowed Thomas to have as much time with Tank as Thomas wanted. Thomas wanted to have as much physical contact with Tank as possible, so he was petting or hugging Tank almost constantly. Not very many words were exchanged, but words seemed unimportant.

Staff later told Linda that Thomas is usually quite reserved, keeping to himself and never showing his emotions. They were thrilled to see Thomas brighten and interact happily and at length with Tank.

by Ann Howie

person's treatment. In addition, reporting back to staff what you noticed during your visit is very valuable, no matter how small an event appears to you. For example, the fact that someone watched your visit from a distance of 20 feet may not seem important at first, but it may be the first time that person left his/her room that day.

The person you visit may be on medication. Medications may make it difficult for the person to focus on you or your animal. In some cases, medication may affect the person's speech. The person may be embarrassed about having difficulty speaking. Maintain an open, friendly attitude in your conversation with that person, and don't take it personally if the person abandons the conversation.

The staff may want you to ignore certain things a person talks about (e.g., "I'm so miserable," or "Jesus is coming!"). You can refocus discussion on your animal and your visit. A person may keep returning to the prior topic; it is not rude to continue to distract the person from their emotional pain by returning the conversation to your animal or something pleasant already mentioned in the conversation.

In some psychiatric disorders a person's brain is working so fast that his/her words cannot keep up, or the person may put words together which don't make sense to you (word salad). In this case, don't try to follow the conversation literally. Instead, respond to the tone of the conversation. You may also try to refocus that person's attention on your animal. ("You seem pretty excited. Would you like to pet my cat?") If the person calms down and pets your animal with concentration for only a few seconds, that may be longer attention than that person has had on anything else that day.

When a person is depressed, s/he may not be capable of maintaining a conversation with even the kindest visitor. However, the person may thrive on quiet physical contact with your animal. You may sit without talking for what seems like a l-o-n-g time simply allowing that person to be with and pet your animal. Being comfortable with silence is sometimes more important than keeping a conversation going.

Refer to the section on "People with Confusion" for further techniques in visiting with people who have psychiatric disorders.

Watch your animal closely for signs of stress when visiting people who have strong emotions and unusual behaviors.

The Pen

Nate was a patient on a mental health unit. He had been recently admitted and was under constant supervision. My dog Ham and I were introduced to Nate in his room, where he was relaxing after dinner. Nothing struck me as unusual about our introductions except, perhaps, for the large collection of pens that Nate wore in a pocket protector in his shirt pocket.

Nate and Ham hit it off well. Nate had grown up with dogs, one of whom was "just like" Ham. I was given a very precise description of how Nate had trained and cared for his dogs. Since there was no reason for Nate to remain in his room, I suggested that he might like to walk Ham around the hallway to help me fine tune Ham's heeling skills. The suggestion was readily accepted and preparations were put in motion. While I attached a second travel lead to Ham's harness, Nate methodically counted and adjusted his collection of pens.

Ham proudly escorted us along the halls. Our relative positions were significant to the process. I was on the right so that Ham would be in heel position, since I was really driving by means of a lead attached to his collar. Nate's position, on Ham's left, luckily accommodated his insistence to use his right hand to hold the travel lead hooked to the harness. Nate's left hand was kept free to hold onto his pens.

The events of the walk were routine. All of that changed as we rounded a corner. Nate fell behind a few paces and his line of sight was directed at the pen clipped to the knapsack I was wearing. Without hesitation, Nate took the pen from the knapsack and began a detailed and expert examination. Any interest in walking Ham was long gone.

I looked to the nurse to see if there was a problem that required intervention. I read the surprised look on the nurse's face as one of concern about my property rather than potential harm to her patient. I returned a reassuring gesture that the pen was of little concern; in fact, it was an inexpensive promotional give-away that I had gotten at a trade show. All the while, Nate was totally engrossed in the pen, to the exclusion of all else.

Eventually, Nate determined that my pen was very unique and he had none like it. He told me this at least three times as he put my pen in with the rest of his collection. There followed a few exchanges, between Nate and the accompanying nurse, about personal property and the need to return the pen. Nate, however, knew only that he had come upon a rare find and that it had to remain in his possession. I noted that without a pen I wouldn't be able to write things that were important to me. And, in consideration of Nate's already large collection of pens, I suggested that we work out an exchange. He would keep his newly treasured find and I would get something that I could use for writing in return.

Nate's concentration, as he reflected on my suggestion, was intense. He spent an indeterminate amount of time counting his pens before responding with a very positive "OK!" Then, with a decisive action, Nate removed a pen from his pocket and handed it to me. The pen I was handed was a simple stick pen that one finds in hotel rooms. Nate told me: "This is my best pen, I hope it works as well for you." We parted with the type of handshake associated with the successful conclusion of a major negotiation, and friendly salutations.

I still carry Nate's "best" pen. I suspect that Nate still has my pen.

by Wayne Sternberger

Well Elders

Description

Well elders are people who are senior citizens, have characteristics associated with aging, but have no serious health or physical problems. Some of the characteristics associated with aging include vision and hearing loss, decreased strength and speed, memory loss, and forgetfulness.

Visiting with this Population

When talking with people who are elderly, keep the following in mind:

Be Concrete

Some people may give answers that do not really relate to the question or comment. For example, when you say, "Mrs. Jones, I heard you went for a ride yesterday," and Mrs. Jones answers, "Yes, I always lived there as a child." Never laugh. The person will understand ridicule and disapproval.

Speaking about simple, concrete things helps. Compliment people on their dress or hair and touch the things to make it more obvious. Talk about plants, items in the room, or the view out of the window. Touch and point to the things to draw attention to them.

Don't humor a person by playing along with what they say. Say something realistic.

Forgetfulness

Though most older people do not have a problem with memory, some people become forgetful as they get older. Be patient when people say or ask you things over and over again.

A person may be upset about his/her forgetfulness. Reassure him/her. Let him/her know that you do not mind answering his/her questions. You can remind him/her that we all forget things sometimes, or mention your own forgetfulness.

Help a person by asking questions that are easy for him/her to answer. Some people may have a hard time responding to open-ended questions that require remembering all the possible answers. For example, "What dress do you want to wear?" is a more difficult question than, "Do you want to wear the red dress or the blue dress?" Some people may find it easier to remember and talk about things that happened long ago.

Frail Elders

Description

Frail elders are senior citizens who have no specific medical conditions, but are frail due to the aging process. They may have thin skin that is easy to tear and they may have an unsteady gait, requiring the use of a walker. Some frail elders will be in wheelchairs and, while they may have use of their hands, they lack strength. Some frail elders may have conditions that are associated with aging such as difficulty breathing, seeing, or hearing.

Visiting with this Population

Advice for visiting with well elders also applies to this population. Review information on people with difficulty hearing and seeing. If the person is in a wheelchair, bring yourself to eye level for communicating.

Your Animal

The proper selection of animals is very important with this group. Animals should be under excellent control and should not do anything that could scratch the skin or cause someone to lose their balance.

 **Articles**

Before you proceed, turn to Appendix A and read,

Article #7:   "How to Help the Elderly Reminisce."

Article #8:   "Communicating with Older Adults."

Terminally Ill

Description

People who are terminally ill are those who have an illness that will result in death, usually within a one-year period. Cancer can be a terminal illness, but it may not be. People with terminal illnesses may be cared for at home or in a hospital, nursing home, or hospice.

Visiting with this Population

You should take the lead from the person's family or professional staff involved as to how you should interact with the person. Frequency of visits may increase or decrease as s/he becomes more ill.

As the person grows closer to death, you may visit more with family, giving them a pleasant interlude from their crisis. (See Lesson 4.1 for information on dealing with the loss of a client.)

Families of Clients

Families will vary in the degree to which they would like to participate. You should recognize and respond to the preferences of the family and show respect for their feelings. Interaction with your animal may be a stress reliever for family members and it might improve the quality of life for the family during a very difficult time.

Special Considerations for Visiting People with Suppressed Immune Systems

People with suppressed immune systems have little or no ability to fight off infections and illnesses. This may be due to illnesses, such as AIDS, or from medical treatment, such as chemotherapy for cancer. When you are visiting people who have suppressed immune systems, you should:

• Follow the procedures of the facility (e.g., wearing masks or gowns).

• If masks or gowns are required you should visit *without* your animal (see Lesson 5.4, Universal Precautions).

• Follow all rules on washing hands (see Lesson 5.4).

• Be an active listener.

• Be sensitive to the fatigue level of the person you are visiting with.

Special Considerations for Visiting Children

We have recently described how to interact with people who are older. There are some considerations you should remember if you are going to do AAA/AAT with children:

- Gentle, quiet animals should be used around babies and toddlers.

- You can do many supplemental activities related to your animal. Children love funny stories about the animals. They also like to look at photos of animals.

- Children love to do even the most simple activities with an animal, such as learning to pet it the correct way.

Most severely emotionally disturbed children will be in a treatment program. In most cases, children will have a written "behavior plan," which should be followed by everyone who visits with the child. A staff person should teach you about each individual with whom you will visit. Many emotionally disturbed children are aggressive toward people and animals. Take precautions to ensure that you and your animal stay safe at all times.

Hair Today, Gone Tomorrow

During one of their visits to the pediatric oncology unit, Shari and her dog, Gandalf, visited with Jeff, a youngster about ten years old, and his family. Jeff looked, from all outward appearances, to have just gotten off the bus from school. He had on the requisite attire of a youth— tee shirt, baggy shorts, and sneakers. The only thing that distinguished him as a patient was the blue and white hospital wrist band. The whole crew was sprawled on the floor in the hallway, brushing Gandalf's fur and talking about his unique coloration. Jeff was obviously fascinated with Gandalf's long feathers and asked how difficult it was to keep him clean.

Jeff listened while Shari described the special dog bathtub, the myriad of shampoos and rinses, combs and brushes, and the industrial hair dryer. Jeff wondered how long the whole process would take. And, Shari explained, matter-of-factly, that each dog could take as long as an hour to complete.

Obviously, patience was not a virtue that Jeff could claim personally. He noted that an hour was a bit extreme. Shari countered by stating that the whole thing was no different that when Jeff washed his hair, totally unprepared for what followed. Jeff pulled off his wig and proudly said: "Not really, I just pull off my mop, wash it in the sink, and hang it out to dry."

by Wayne Sternberger

▭ Video

Video: *Special Considerations for Visiting Children.*

Proper "Wheelchair Etiquette"

You will meet many people who use wheelchairs. There are basic manners you should keep in mind:

- Remember that the wheelchair is a part of the person's body image. Respect this—do not move the chair without asking.

- Do not talk down to or over a person in a wheelchair.

- Do not lean on a person's wheelchair.

- For safety reasons, ask the person if the wheelchair is locked.

- When introduced to a person in a wheelchair, it is appropriate to offer to shake hands. Shake hands left-handed when necessary.

- Try to limit conversation while standing to introduction and greeting. Further conversation should be done while sitting or squatting.

✋ Activity

1. Think about the various kinds of populations just discussed and match your animal (behavior, size, personality) to the appropriate groups. Think back to the Matrix of Environmental Dynamics introduced in Lesson 1.3. Which people would you and your animal enjoy visiting with?

2. Attend a support group meeting to help you understand a particular condition. At the beginning of the meeting tell the group why you are there, and ask their permission to be there. Write your observations and feelings in your journal.

Unit 4
Visiting

Unit Overview:

This unit focuses on methods of interacting with the people you will visit. It provides tips for preparing for a visit. You will also read about the parts of a visit, from approaching with your animal to finding closure and saying goodbye.

Unit Map:

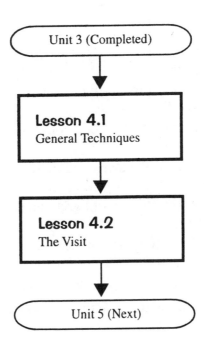

Unit 3 (Completed)

Lesson 4.1
General Techniques

Lesson 4.2
The Visit

Unit 5 (Next)

Lesson 4.1 General Techniques

Lesson Overview:

This lesson provides some basic ways to begin a conversation and to be a good listener. In addition, this lesson will show you how to avoid responses that block communication. It deals with specific situations that you may encounter when communicating with others.

Lesson Objectives:

1. Identify helpful hints for visiting.

2. Identify statements that are good conversation starters.

3. Identify responses that block communication.

4. Identify some characteristics of good listening skills.

5. Identify guidelines for communicating.

6. Identify how to handle the following situations:

    a. A person refusing to let another person interact with or pet your animal.

b. A family or staff member monopolizing your animal.

c. A person who is scared of your animal.

d. A parent who is visiting his/her child in hospital.

e. An uninformed staff person.

f. A person you have visited regularly but will not be visiting again.

7. Identify techniques of dealing with death and serious illness.

8. State additional interaction techniques.

Materials Required:

Video: *Conversation Starters.*

Video: *Characteristics of Good Listening.*

Video: *Active Listening.*

Video: *Conversation Blockers.*

Video: *Additional Interaction Techniques.*

Video: *Handling Difficult Situations.*

Helpful Hints for Visits

You will be meeting all kinds of interesting people in your setting(s) of choice. Remember that everyone you meet is a person just like you, with feelings and potential. Don't talk down to people. Be considerate and listen intently—you may become aware of a person's interests and talents which could be used to engage him/her.

Don't judge people or their families. As a volunteer, you are not there to play the role of social worker, nurse, pastor, medical doctor, or lawyer. Be yourself. If you have any problems, talk with a staff member.

When first meeting someone, comment on something concrete—something the person is wearing or using, or something in the room. If the person resists you, watch and listen carefully; s/he may just not know how to accept your friendship.

A person may be so involved in your visit that when you need to move on to someone else you may find it difficult. Say something like, "I have to be going because I need to visit with someone else." Your animal may provide a good "excuse" for leaving—"Spot needs to go to the bathroom now." If you use this as a technique for exiting, however, make sure you leave the building to follow through with your scenario.

No two visits will ever be alike. There is no "typical visit." This lesson provides general techniques you can use during a visit. The more tools you have, the better your visits will be.

Conversation Starters

Sometimes it can be difficult to start a conversation with the people you visit. Here are some examples of topics and phrases you may use during your AAA/AAT visits.

Your Animal

By calling attention to your animal, you can provide the person with something specific to talk about. You might say or do the following:

- "Hi. Would you like to see Peter, my dog?"
- "Hi. Look who I brought to visit you today."
- Allow the animal to lead. If eye contact is made, the person may call the animal. You follow from there.

- Talk for the animal. For example, "Kari wants to visit with you today. She wants to know if you will pet her."

- Interpret the animal's actions. "He likes you." "Look, he wants you to do that again."

- Ask the person to tell you about your animal. "How does he feel?" "What do you think he wants?"

The Past

To help a person remember past experiences, try these phrases:

- Where were you born?

- Name some of the places you've lived.

- Tell me about your school days. Where did you go to school?

- What kind of work (occupation) have you done?

- Tell me about how the world used to be (e.g., families, TV, movies, recreation).

- Did you have any pets? Tell me about them. Who was your favorite? Why?

- How did you spend your summers?

The Present

Conversations about the present could start with the following:

- What do you like to eat?

- What are your favorite shows on TV? Why?

- Tell me about your interests/hobbies.

- Do you enjoy reading? What kinds of books are you interested in?

- Do you have any pets?

- What kind of music/recreation do you like?

- Comment on something the person is wearing/using or something in the room.

- What have you done today?

- Can we visit you again?

You

Many of the conversation starters listed above involve asking the person questions. Be sensitive and don't over-do asking questions. In many facilities, it seems that the only kind of interaction people have is when people ask them questions such as, "Are you ready for lunch?" "Do you want to go outside?" Make yourself an interesting visitor. Tell the person some stories about yourself, your family, your hobbies, or your animal. Remember, you may have to tell a story to get a story. You may bring a small photo album to stimulate conversation.

 **Video**

Video: *Conversation Starters.*

Listening Skills

Characteristics of Good Listening

Proximity

It is important to be within three to five feet of the person.

Eye Contact

Look the person in the eye. Position yourself so s/he can comfortably look at you.

Body Language

Leaning forward, reaching out, and maintaining a soft, relaxed stance show you are interested. Fidgeting nervously, looking around and crossing your arms shows you are tense or preoccupied.

Facial Expressions

Appropriate facial expressions in response to what is being said help with good communication.

Appropriate Responses

Laugh or smile when the person is using humor; don't laugh when the person is describing his/her misfortune, even if it strikes you as humorous.

Video

Video: *Characteristics of Good Listening.*

Activity

- Observe several people talking in different situations (e.g., at the mall, in your home, at a club). Assess how they use the five characteristics of good listening. Make notes in your journal.

- Monitor yourself while you are listening to another person. Are you using good listening skills?

- When someone is talking to you, purposefully use poor listening skills. What happens? Use good listening skills. What happens? Make notes in your journal about your experiences.

Active Listening

Though our main focus is the animal's interaction with others, there will be times when people want to talk to you. They may want to tell you things that are really important to them. How can you encourage this?

One technique used by counselors and social workers is called "active listening." Active listening eliminates giving any judgments, advice, or opinions. As you practice, it will become more natural.

Listen for feeling

Client: I had a dog once.

Volunteer: **Your dog was special to you?**

Client: It got hit by a car.

Volunteer: **You must have been very sad.**

Here is a model to help you:

You feel _____ about _____ .
          (emotion)   *(event or situation)*

1. Listen and decide what *emotion* has been sent.

   - You feel *scared.*

   - You're feeling *really excited.*

   - You're feeling *worried.*

2. Determine what *event or situation* caused that emotion and put them together.

   - You feel scared *when you see a dog.*

   - You're feeling really excited that *you get to visit your children.*

   - You're feeling worried the *dog will scratch you.*

Other phrases to use:

- It sounds as if /
- You wish
- You think
- You mean

- It's disappointing that
- It sounds like
- You're feeling
- You're (name feeling)

Examples Of Active Listening Conversations

The examples of active listening are in bold.

Example #1

Client:	Ouch, that hurts.
Volunteer:	**It hurts you when the dog touches you?**
Client:	No, my chair.
Volunteer:	**You feel uncomfortable in your chair.**
Client:	I get tired sitting here all day.
Volunteer:	**The days really seem long?**
Client:	There is nothing to do.
Volunteer:	**You feel bored a lot of the time.**

Client:	I like it when the dogs come.
Volunteer:	**It's fun when the dogs come.**
Client:	I wish you would come more often.
Volunteer:	So do I!

Example #2

You don't have to use active listening format for every response.

Client:	I have a dog. I miss him.
Volunteer:	Tell me about him.
Client:	I had to give him to my son when I came here. I don't ever get to see him.
Volunteer:	**You must miss him a great deal.**
Client:	I do. I don't even think he would remember me now.
Volunteer:	**You feel he has forgotten you.**
Client:	Probably.
Volunteer:	You know, dogs remember very well. I'm sure he remembers you. (Here a supportive response is needed.) Tell me more about him, what kind of dog was he?
Client:	Black and white, like that dog.
Volunteer:	**This dog reminds you of your dog?**
Client:	Yes, except he was bigger. He would lick me like that.
Volunteer:	**You really like it when the dog licks you.** (Moves dog closer.)
Client:	I miss my dog.
Volunteer:	**You would really like to see your dog again.**

Using these listening skills assures the person you are communicating with that s/he is being heard. You are not making judgments, false promises, giving advice, or in any way blocking the conversation. It is very satisfying and therapeutic for people when someone really listens.

If you hear things you are bothered by or concerned about, report your concerns to the activity director or staff person in charge. Do not make promises to the person about what you will do to change things.

Appropriate and Inappropriate Responses

There are many kinds of responses. Some responses end or block "true communication" but they may not always be inappropriate. Some responses are never appropriate. Consider the following.

➤ Questioning

Asking questions can be effective, safe, and informative, especially if the questions show genuine interest. People may ask you questions. Answer as honestly and genuinely as possible. If a misunderstanding occurs because of hearing loss, or memory impairment, it is not important to correct it (a misunderstood name, for example).

➤ Praising, agreeing, evaluating positively, approving

Offering a positive evaluation or a compliment is always welcome.

➤ Reassuring, sympathizing, consoling, supporting

You can support the person by letting him/her know you hear him/her. It may help to restate the feeling s/he is expressing. For example, "That must have made you feel very sad."

Do not try to talk the person out of his/her feelings or deny the strength of his/her feelings. It is not possible to make someone's feelings disappear; you will only cause the person suppress them.

Hearing the person's feelings may trigger your own feelings. If you feel uncomfortable, it may be appropriate to let him/her know. For example, "It makes me very sad to talk about this because recently I..." You may not be comfortable continuing to talk about something that triggers painful feelings for you; being honest with yourself and the person you visit may make it less likely that s/he will feel that his/her feelings have been ignored or rejected.

➤ Advising, giving suggestions or solutions

Generally, it is not appropriate to tell the person how to solve a problem. Remember that many situations are beyond anyone's control. Avoid giving advice.

➤ Ordering, directing, commanding

It is inappropriate to tell the other person to do something, unless it is warranted by the situation, (e.g., "Go back inside now," "You're hurting the cat. Let go of its ear"). Sometimes, people who have memory impairments or developmental disabilities may need you to provide some direction. If you do, be clear and firm, but kind. If needed, get staff help.

➤ Persuading with logic, arguing, instructing, lecturing

Sometimes we need to instruct adults or children for the welfare of the animal and comfort of the visit. Never argue and always respect the other person's point of view. Avoid trying to influence the other person with facts, counter-arguments, logic, information, or your opinions.

➤ Interpreting, analyzing

Telling a person what his/her motives are or analyzing why s/he is doing or saying something is inappropriate. However, you might interpret what the animal is thinking or how it is responding to the person's actions (e.g., "Fluffy likes it when you rub his ears like that").

➤ Probing and interrogating to try to find reasons, or motives

Probing and interrogating is unpleasant and inappropriate for visits. There may be times when searching for more information is appropriate if it is related to the visit. If you have serious concerns, report them to the staff.

➤ Warning, admonishing, threatening

Threatening or alluding to the use of your power is never appropriate. However, sometimes it will be appropriate to warn someone about dog kisses or a cookie snatcher.

➤ Moralizing, preaching, obliging

Never tell another person what s/he should or ought to do.

➤ Judging negatively, criticizing, disagreeing, blaming

Never judge or criticize someone you visit, a fellow volunteer, a staff member, or the facility either directly or behind someone's back.

➤ Name-calling, ridiculing, shaming

Never try to make someone feel foolish. Don't stereotype or categorize a person or the care facility.

Guidelines for Good Communication

In any situation, whether you are visiting in an AAA/AAT facility or interacting with a co-worker, there are some basic guidelines for good communication.

Genuineness

Be yourself. Be friendly, courteous and sensitive to the needs of the other person. You might need to talk less and listen more. Your role is that of a supportive friend, not an expert or authority. If you don't know the answer to a question, say so.

Don't "Talk Down" to Another Person

Treat every person as you would wish to be treated. People are offended when spoken to in a childish manner. Treat everyone with respect.

Dependability

To people in a controlled environment with few distractions and little variety, it is essential that they can count on your visit. Never promise more than you can deliver. What may be a minor part of your week could be the single event that someone has been awaiting for days.

Listening

Always remember that your function is to try to meet the person's needs, rather than your own. It may mean listening non-judgmentally to the same stories over and over again. It may mean listening non-judgmentally to outbursts of anger, frustration and resentment. *Be a patient listener*.

Confidentiality

Information about an individual and his/her family is confidential. Trust is of the utmost importance. However, never promise that you will not tell anyone. Use your discretion as to whether information needs to be passed along to the facility supervisor or the volunteer coordinator.

Physical Contact

Some people like to touch and be touched. Be aware of the person's comfort zone and your own. Your comfort or discomfort will communicate itself, so it is important for you to be yourself.

Be aware that there are some "no-touch" facilities where under no circumstances should you touch a client. These facilities will provide you with training on their policies. The reason for the no-touch rule might be that the people in a given facility have been physically or sexually abused. They might misinterpret touching by another person. In some psychiatric settings, touching certain people can trigger aggressive responses. Staff will make you aware of these situations. In no-touch facilities, your animal can provide opportunities for the person to experience warmth and contact.

Meet Them Where They Are

Tune in to each person. Do not give unsolicited advice even if you strongly disagree with the facility or a family's way of dealing with their situation. Your responsibility is to visit in a helpful and harmonious manner.

Initiative

People will look to you to establish the relationship. Be open, honest, sensitive, and interested in the lives of your new friends.

Little Things Mean a Lot

Your personal grooming, a positive attitude, and just being there are all very special gifts.

Enjoy Yourself!

You can't make other people feel good unless you feel good about your visits and interactions. Enthusiasm is contagious.

 **Video**

Video: *Active Listening*.

Examples of Blocking Responses

The following conversations between Mrs. Smith and a volunteer provide examples of ineffective communication. The volunteer's responses block real communication.

Distracting

Volunteer: *Approaches Mrs. Smith with a white, domestic rabbit.* Mrs. Smith, would you like to see this rabbit today?

Mrs. Smith: *Begins to cry.*

Volunteer: Do you want to see him do tricks?

Consoling

Volunteer: Mrs. Smith, would you like to see this rabbit today?

Mrs. Smith: *Begins to cry.*

Volunteer: Come on now, don't cry.

Advising

Volunteer: Mrs. Smith, would you like to see this rabbit today?

Mrs. Smith: *Begins to cry.*

Volunteer: Mrs. Smith, rabbits won't hurt you!

Commanding

Volunteer: Mrs. Smith, would you like to see this rabbit today?

Mrs. Smith: *Begins to cry.*

Volunteer: Mrs. Smith, now pull yourself together and enjoy this little rabbit!

Analyzing

Volunteer: Mrs. Smith, would you like to see this rabbit today?

Mrs. Smith: *Begins to cry.*

Volunteer: That's okay. You know Mrs. Smith, sometimes when we visit, the animal brings back memories that elicit responses from the past. Generally, this is cathartic.

Example of Active Listening

Compare those you just read with the following conversation that uses active listening.

Volunteer: *Approaches Mrs. Smith with the rabbit.*
Mrs. Smith, would you like to see this rabbit today?

Mrs. Smith: *Begins to cry.*

Volunteer: **Mrs. Smith, do you feel sad when you see this rabbit?**

Mrs. Smith: Yes, my daughter had a white rabbit once.

Volunteer: **You are remembering your daughter and her rabbit.**

Mrs. Smith: My, that rabbit loved my daughter. It followed her everywhere.

Volunteer: **Sounds like they had a very special relationship.**

Mrs. Smith: Oh yes, I remember how sad she was when he died.

Volunteer: **You feel it's really hard to say good-bye to a good friend.**

Mrs. Smith: It seems like I'm saying good-bye to all my friends now.

Volunteer: **You feel it's hard to say good-bye.**

Mrs. Smith: *Cries a little harder.*

Oh, yes. The little rabbit lived a long time."

Volunteer: **The little rabbit had a good life.**

Mrs. Smith: *Nods yes.*

Volunteer: **You feel you've had a good life too.**

Mrs. Smith: *Looks at volunteer, hands touch, she nods yes.*

Volunteer: **Thanks for talking with me about this Mrs. Smith. I really care about you.**

 **Video**

Video: *Conversation Blockers.*

✋ Activity

Practice good listening skills by trying the following exercise. You will need someone to practice with.

- Have someone tell you a story about an important animal experience in his/her life. Use poor listening skills (e.g., file your nails, glance through a newspaper) while s/he talks for about a minute. Ask how s/he felt.

- Have the person continue the story, while you use good listening skills. After about a minute, have him/her stop and tell you how s/he felt.

Additional Interaction Techniques

Touch

Touch is another way of communicating with people we care about. A pat on the shoulder or a hug can show a person that they are cared for. In AAA/AAT settings, it is important that you use good judgment about how and when you touch other people. Some people are shy and do not like to be touched by people they do not know well.

One of the wonderful things about animals is that they provide a non-threatening opportunity for touching and hugging. There are many ways to encourage touch so it is comfortable and acceptable to both the person and the animal.

Guide or instruct the person to do any of the following:

Touch Can Be Feeling

"Feel the soft, warm fur; can you feel its nose?"

Touch Can Be Petting

"Here, let me help you pet him. He likes you to scratch him."

Touch Can Be Loving

"Tell her how you feel; pet her right here."

Touch Can Be Pleasing

"Let's find out what he likes; there, scratch him there. He loves it."

Touch Can Be Brushing

Carry a small brush or comb and let the person groom the animal. Make sure the brush is soft so people with a hard stroke will be less likely to hurt the animal.

No-Touch Facilities

Be aware that there are some "no-touch" facilities where you should never touch a client. In no-touch facilities, your animal can provide opportunities for the person to experience warmth and contact.

Giving

Giving can be therapeutic. Some people with low self-esteem have trouble giving to others. It is easier to give to an animal than a person. Just the act of giving can often make a person feel better, more worthwhile. Some ways to encourage giving with your animal are as follows:

- Allow the person to take care of the animal by getting it something to drink, giving it something to eat, or taking it out to relieve itself.

- Teaching is also a form of giving. Ask the person you visit to help you teach your animal a trick (whether the animal knows it already or not).

- The animal can be a motivator for giving to others. Have a child draw a picture of the animal for a special friend or take the animal to "show" someone else (e.g., parent, teacher).

- Let the person give a special goodie to the animal. However, if food disrupts your animal's focus while visiting, it may be best to wait until the end of the session.

Remember:

> The person's perception that s/he has given is more important than the gift itself.

Control

Self-directed control seems absent in the lives of some people. In contrast, the facility may seem to have total control over the person. There are many ways to visit with your animal that help the person feel in control:

- Have the person walk the animal on a leash. If the person is in a wheelchair, have him/her hold the leash while you push the wheelchair.

- Have the person throw a ball the animal can retrieve.

- Have the person ask the animal to respond to commands or tricks.

- Allow the animal to sleep on the floor or on the person's lap.

Feelings

Discussions of emotions can be focused on the animal or the person. Talking about feelings can be therapeutic. The person may identify with the feelings of the animal, transfer his/her feelings to the animal, or talk about his/her own feelings.

- Ask the person how the animal is feeling.

- Ask how the animal would feel if something happened or if it was in a certain situation.

- Talk about how the person feels about the animal.

Instruction

When lack of knowledge leaves a person feeling afraid or insecure, instruction can be therapeutic. For example, teaching a child to "read" an animal's language, how to approach and pet an animal, and how to know if an animal is going to bite or scratch, gives a child self-confidence and a sense of power or more control over his/her world. The child gains confidence and a greater sense of self-worth. Even simple instructions, "Here, pet him here. He likes that," gives a person confidence.

Presence

In some cases, just the animal's presence is enough to help people relax. They simply enjoy the animal being there. One study tells of a psychologist who worked in a juvenile detention home for teenage boys. She did entry interviews. In ten interviews, she had her dog present in the room. For the other ten, she did not. The interviews with the dog lasted longer, there was less hostility shown by the young men, and, in some of those interviews, rapport was established. In the interviews without the dog, the teenagers were all uncooperative.[6]

---

[6] Gonski, Y.A., C.A. Peacock and J. Rucker. 1986. The Role of the Therapist's Pet in Initial Psychotherapy Sessions with Adolescents. Presented at the Delta Society conference. Boston, MA.

Observation

Encourage the person to observe the animal; watch it play, sleep, or interact with another animal.

▄▄ Video

Video: *Additional Interaction Techniques.*

Handling Difficult Situations

Look through the situations that follow. Jot down or think through how you would handle the situation if it occurred. Compare your actions with those suggested.

➤ **A person refuses to let another person pet or interact with the animal**

Establish rules or guidelines for sharing so everyone knows they will get a turn. Assure people that they will have a turn and that you will come back to them. If you say you will come back, make sure you return.

➤ **The family or staff monopolizes the animal**

Firmly explain, "I know that you are enjoying my cat, but now it is time for Chris to visit with it."

Building Confidence

I once watched as a child learned to work with a dog, to teach it to heel, sit and come. She had been wary of all dogs, pulling back even from the friendliest ones.

At the beginning of the session, the child was disorganized and seemed unable to pay attention. As the child began to master the skills needed, she was proud and didn't want to stop. "Do I get to come back?" she asked.

In the sessions that followed the child approached confidently with her hand extended to greet the dog.

by Linda Nebbe

> ## A person is fearful of the animal

Many people express fears concerning animals. A few are highly afraid, or phobic. The person with a phobia will probably take care of him- or herself. Let him/her know that it is okay to feel that way. Offer to go to a "safe distance" or to another room. Assure him/her that the animal is not dangerous and will not hurt anyone. Often s/he will decide that at least "this dog" or "this cat" is okay and s/he will end up participating with the animal. When an extreme phobia is noted, the care facility personnel should be contacted and their suggestions followed.

Respect a person's right *not* to be visited by you and your animal. This allows the person to exercise control over his/her environment.

> ## A parent is with his/her child in hospital

Introduce yourself and explain what you are doing. Ask the parent for permission to proceed with his/her child. Then, although you may continue to talk to the parent, direct most of your conversation to the child. Let the child speak for him/herself. Don't talk over the child or about the child to the parent.

> ## Uninformed staff person questions whether you should be there

Be prepared with a brief explanation of your program, provide a brochure if you have one. Know the names of the administrators so you can say, "My visit has been authorized by_____."

> ## You are finishing/completing visits with a person who has been visited regularly

Be sure to bring each visit to closure. (See "Parts of a Visit—Closure" in Lesson 4.2.)

➤ **Your animal does not get along with another animal that visits when you do**

Take steps to avoid contact. Enter through a different door. Talk with the other animal's handler and make a plan so both animals will be comfortable.

➤ **You witness inhumane treatment of an animal or person**

If your animal is being mistreated, take the animal to a safe place and then contact a staff member. If a person is being harmed call on the staff to handle the situation. Report the action to the person in charge.

➤ **Your animal clearly does not like a particular person**

Once in a while this happens. Sometimes you can structure the visit so this is not evident. Perhaps someone else can visit that person.

➤ **A person wants to kiss you goodbye**

You may not be comfortable with such intimate contact. Instead, you may extend both hands in front of you to warmly clasp his/her hand(s) in yours. You may pat him/her on the back, or hug from the side. In addition to discomfort with intimacy, kissing is not recommended due to germ transmission.

➤ **The animal vomits, urinates or defecates in an inappropriate place**

Remain calm and clean it up. Use materials found in your pet pack (See "Preparing Yourself for a Visit—Equipment" in Lesson 4.2), and follow the facility procedures. Notify someone on the staff. If clothing or bedding was soiled, stay with the person until a staff member arrives to make changes.

Preventive measures are encouraged. Give animals an opportunity to relieve themselves outside before visiting and occasionally during the visit.

An accident may be a signal that the animal is stressed or does not feel well. Consider terminating the visit early. If the animal is sick, end the visit immediately.

 **Video**

Video: *Handling Difficult Situations.*

Dealing with Loss

As you spend more time visiting, the day might come when you have to deal with some difficult issues, such as the serious illness or death of someone whom you have grown to care about. While you are a Pet Partner, the day may also come when your animal becomes ill, needs to be retired, or dies. There are some ways that you can deal with the pain and grief that come with losing a friend or loved one, whether that loved one is a person or an animal.

When a Client Becomes Seriously Ill or Dies

This situation may present difficulties for you, and also for your animal, if you have visited the same person for a long time and a relationship has been established. Be aware of your feelings and your animal's feelings.

- You might want to talk to a facility staff person who knew the person and will understand your feelings.

- There are a number of excellent books on "saying good-bye" and death and dying. These can be found in the self-help section of bookstores.

- In the case of a person with a serious illness, it may get to the point that your animal provides too much stimulation for him/her. You may want to visit without the animal in some cases. On the other hand, some people who are terminally ill enjoy having a quiet animal beside them. Your role might be to sit quietly with them.

The Death of a Visiting Animal

Grief and the pain we feel when we lose a loved one can apply to the human and animal losses in our lives. Many of the techniques that help you manage grief related to clients can also be applied to your animal losses.

- You can talk with someone about your feelings or read some of the excellent books available on bereavement.

- You may want to plan a "farewell" for your pet. A picture of your team may be donated to the facility. Perhaps a memorial gift to a facility in the name of your pet would be appropriate.

As a volunteer, you will have to decide for yourself whether or not you feel comfortable visiting a facility after the death of your animal teammate. It is understandable and acceptable for you to take a break or discontinue visits. In either case, you *must* notify the facility of your situation and your decision.

If you feel comfortable visiting, handle the situation honestly and gently. Use statements such as, "I am feeling very sad because something very sad has happened. Lucky died last week." Spare people the details, but be honest and genuine. Death is a common situation we all face.

Connecting with Other Pet Partners

Whether you have lost an animal or a person who was special to you, remember that you have a network of colleagues who want to help. If you are having a hard time and need someone to talk to, call the Delta Society office for the name of a pet loss counselor or a support group.

Heather

Heather, a young girl about seven years old, was in the hospital because she had AIDS. The AIDS was very bad and had caused her to be blind.

Mom and I said hello at the side of the bed. Heather was very excited that I had come to visit her. Even though she couldn't see my tail wagging, she knew that I was happy to be there, too. Now, you have to remember that I am a veteran AAA dog and I work real fast. So, I was lying in bed with Heather within two minutes flat. I think Heather had something to do with it, considering that she said: "I want Hambone in bed" at least ten times.

Since she couldn't see with her eyes, she used her hands to get a "picture" of what I looked like. Mom described me from nose to tail while Heather felt every inch of my body.

She gave me some of the biggest hugs that could ever come from such a small person. My tail was in high gear. Just like my tail kept wagging, Heather kept talking. She talked about how big I was, how long and soft my fur was, how wet and cold my nose was, and lots of other thing that I can't remember. Heather grabbed my tongue, counted my teeth, and I'm sure that she would have tried to touch my tonsils if she had thought of it. Everyone was surprised how well behaved I was.

Heather and Mom were counting the toes on one of my feet and Heather couldn't understand why she could only find four toes. Mom explained that to keep me from getting hurt, I don't have dew claws, so I only have four toes on each foot. Without missing a beat Heather said: "That's OK, some people only have four fingers, too."

Before I knew it, we had to leave. Heather gave me a big hug good-bye and I made sure that I gave her a good ear sniff and a wet lick on the nose before leaving. Mom and I said good-bye to Heather's family and were about to leave when we noticed that Heather's room was full of doctors, nurses, and therapists who were watching us. Someone told Mom that Heather was hyperactive and that no one had ever seen her occupied for more than five minutes. It was a pleasant surprise that she had spent more than 30 minutes playing with me.

Unfortunately, my story isn't all happy. The next time we went to visit, Holly, the recreational therapist, told Mom that Heather had recently died. Mom was especially sad, because she knew how much Heather was looking forward to seeing me again. Holly told Mom that I had really made an impression on Heather and her whole family. They all talked about my visit until the day that Heather left to go home. After Heather died, her family held a memorial service at the facility. Part of the service included pictures of Heather's stay and all of the important people that made a difference in her care. And, you know, I was one of those important "people!" The family included a picture of me lying in bed with Heather.

by Hambone, as told to Wayne Sternberger

Lesson 4.2 The Visit

Lesson Overview:

Your participation as an AAA/AAT volunteer is as important as the animal you will share. Your friendly smile, gentle touch, and ability to be a good listener will be invaluable gifts to the people you visit. This lesson provides techniques and guidelines that will help you make visits effective and enjoyable.

Lesson Objectives:

1. Identify how to prepare for a visit.

   a. Identify what must be done to prepare an animal for a visit.

   b. Identify when an animal should not be taken on a visit.

   c. Identify when you should not go on a visit.

   d. Identify your responsibilities if the visit cannot occur.

2. Identify the supplies to take on a visit.

   a. Identify the items you should always take on a visit.

   b. Identify additional items you may take on a visit.

3. Identify the appropriate dress for a visit.

   a. Identify the appropriate dress for the volunteer.

   b. Identify the appropriate "dress" for the animal.

4. Identify the parts of a visit.

5. Identify actions to take after the visit.

Materials Required:

Video: *Parts of a Visit.*

Article #9:   "The Cat on A Visit."

Article #10:   "Taking Your Dog on A Visit."

Preparing for a Visit

The image that you and your animal portray is very important. Impressions do count and people will develop opinions about you, your animal, and AAA/AAT as a result of the way you present yourself. It is important that you and your animal are well-prepared for every visit. Both you and your animal should be healthy, clean and groomed. You should also be prepared with the equipment you may need, such as a water dish, brushes and cleaning supplies.

Being prepared and having everything you need will show that you are professional and well-organized. Good preparation will also result in you and your animal being comfortable and having a successful visit.

Preparing Your Animal

To prepare for each visit, you should make sure that your animal is clean and well-groomed.

Coat, Feathers and Skin

It may be too much to bathe your animal before every visit; it may not be practical or good for the animal. Still, the animal needs to be clean and groomed. Knots, snags and debris must be combed out of the coat. When shampooing your animal, use a shampoo that does not leave a residue or odor and does not make the animal's skin/coat dry or dull. Be sure you know your facility's policy on bathing.

Nails

The animal's nails must be reasonably clipped. They should not pose a danger to the person you visit, catch in clothing, or interfere with the animal's ability to walk on various surfaces (e.g., tile, or long fiber carpet). File any rough edges of the nail. If a cat is not declawed, the tips of the nails can be clipped so they are not sharp or hooked. Birds may need wing clipping.

Eyes and Ears

The drainage from the eyes must be cleaned. Ears should be clean and free of any odor.

Teeth

If the animal's breath is not agreeable, use toothpaste or oral rinse. Make sure you use a product specifically made for your species of animal.

If your pet's bad breath is a result of eating strong-smelling pet food, switch to a premium pet food. Users of premium pet foods notice that these foods usually have a more agreeable odor, which will make a significant difference in your pet's breath and stool odor.

Persistently bad breath could also be a sign of dental problems, which, left untreated, can contribute to a variety of additional health problems. Consult your veterinarian for proper diagnosis and treatment.

Paws

Make sure the animal's paws are clean. Clip back any excess hair.

Equipment

Disinfect or clean cages or crates before taking them to the facility. If you visit with your animal in a basket, disinfect the lining and provide clean bedding.

Necessary Equipment

Carry a backpack or shoulder-bag with you that can be available all the time and does not restrict the work you and your animal are doing. The following items should be included in that pet pack:

Identification and a Notebook

- Your animal's tag and your Pet Partners ID card.

- Notebook to document visits.

- Emergency phone numbers. Record contact names and phone numbers in the front of the notebook or somewhere you can easily get to them.

Cleaning Supplies

- Plastic bags for feces removal (a heavy duty one, in case a place to dispose of the refuse is not available).

- Paper towels—among other uses, sometimes people like to wipe their hands after being licked.

- Disinfectant cleaner. Know the policy of the facility you are visiting; some prefer you use their disinfectant. Do not use Lysol—it is toxic to cats.

- Bath towels — can be placed on a person's bed or lap for the animal to lie on. They can also be used to dry the animal if it's raining or snowing. Some facilities prefer that you use their towels and get a clean towel between rooms to avoid transmitting anything from one person to another.

Water and Food

- Water dish and water.

- Treats for the animal. Check with the facility about their rules or preferences about bringing in food.

Grooming Supplies

- Brush or grooming tools. Include a soft brush if people are going to groom your animal. An angry or very strong person may hurt or injure your animal with a wire bristle brush. A brush with a hand strap works well for people who can't grip a standard brush.

Toys

- Toys for the animal and client to play with.

Helpful Tip

Decide what your "goodie" policy will be. Check with the facility to verify that treats are permitted. For example, it would be inappropriate to bring treats when clients are on restricted diets or under treatment for eating disorders. Make sure clients understand that the treats are for the animal.

Sometimes, clients will want to feed your animal their own food. If you do not want this to happen, explain your "goodie policy" to the client. Food sharing can be a special experience. If you wish, take appropriate treats with you. Give them to the client and explain how they are to be shared.

Optional Equipment

- Deodorizer
- Baby wipes
- Crate (if the animal is crated)
- Newspapers (if needed for cages)
- Breed or species book to share

- Rubber gloves
- Nail clipper and file
- Photos of your animal

Appropriate Dress

For You

You need to be neat and clean. Wear *functional* and *washable* clothes. If you are part of a program, you might wear shirts or jackets with the program's logo/emblem. These look uniform, are recognizable, and have a professional appearance. If desired, you may wear the Pet Partners polo shirt. Wear shoes that will give you good traction and protect your feet.

For Your Animal

- Programs may use a particular leash, scarf, collar, or harness so the animals will be uniform and identifiable. Pet Partners has a vest and cape your animal may wear.

- All animals must wear a collar/harness and be under control at all times.

  —Dogs should wear a nylon, cloth or leather buckle collar, or a metal or nylon slip collar. If you use a slip collar, be aware of the potential for someone to harm the animal. Consider snapping the lead to the non-slip ring while visiting. The dog should be on a cloth, nylon, or leather leash that is no more than 6' long. Retractable leads, head halters, prong or pinch collars should not be used on a visit. In special situations, with a dog under control, it *may* be off-leash depending on the facility's rules. For example, working with an Occupational Therapist who asks the client to throw something for your dog to retrieve.

  —Cats, rabbits, guinea pigs, etc. shall be carried in a basket and/or on a towel. Birds visiting in their cage are not required to wear a harness.

- Hospitals and other specific environments may require that the animal's body be covered to prevent dispersal of dander from the coat. T-shirt uniforms can be made for the animal. You might create a gown that matches those worn by children in a hospital. However, Delta discourages "dressing up" the animals in costumes.

When You Can't Visit

If you cannot go on a visit, notify the appropriate parties as soon as possible. This includes your supervisor, the activity director, or a particular person you know will be waiting and watching for you.

Remember:

The people you visit, the facility, and your program are counting on you. You and your animal will be missed if you don't go.

Do Not Take Your Animal on a Visit:

- After the animal has had a stressful visit to the veterinarian or groomer. If an animal has had shots or an intrusive procedure, do not visit that day. Animals should not visit when they are on medication that would affect their behavior or the visit.

- If the animal is in heat, is pregnant, or is nursing young.

- If the animal is ill or injured. If the animal is a dog with a hot-spot (an irritated patch of skin that the dog has been licking or chewing; can be caused by an allergic reaction) that has started to heal, is no longer moist and can be covered, the dog may visit. Animals should not visit if they have stitches.

- If the animal has been emotionally stressed or appears to be behaving unusually.

- If there is an unusual odor from the ears, body, or mouth of the animal.

- If the animal has lesions, hair loss, atypical urine or stools, swelling or bloating, or has an abnormal temperature.

- If the animal has a change in appetite or fluid intake.

You Should Not Go on a Visit:

- If you are ill.

- If you are not emotionally competent to visit. This would be in an extreme situation, perhaps after a traumatic experience.

- If you have recently been exposed to a contagious childhood disease (such as Chicken Pox) or have an ill child at home.

Note:

Always be prepared to end a visit early if you or your animal are having problems while visiting.

During the Visit

Your Animal

- Be aware of your animal's need to relieve itself.
  - Allow the animal to relieve itself before the visit. Be sure to pick up refuse and dispose of it properly.
  - The stress of the visit may require breaks more frequently.
  - Give the animal a break and a chance to relieve itself every 20 or 30 minutes.

- Allow animals to greet one another or notice each other before the visit.

- Watch for signs of stress.

- Be cautious of the animal overheating.

- Provide water periodically.

- Keep the animal under control at all times.

Parts of a Visit

There are three parts of a visit: approach, process, and closure.

Approach

These are the steps to follow at the beginning of a visit.

- Approach the person from the front.

- Make visual and verbal contact with the person.

- Do not let the animal get too close before the person is aware that the animal is there. The sudden awareness of the animal could be very frightening.

- Present the animal at the person's waist-level or below, not from above or at their face level.

- Protect the animal by presenting it to the person in such a way that they are discouraged from poking its face. Turn it sideways or backward.

- Ask if the person wants to meet the animal.

- Encourage as much contact as possible.

- Move slowly. If the person does not reach out to touch the animal, carefully take his/her hand and move it slowly to the animal while asking if s/he wants to pet the animal. If the animal is small, ask if s/he would like to have the animal on his/her lap and proceed by putting the animal on the person's lap.

   —If the person resists in any way, stop. If the person refuses, respect that.

   —If there is no acceptance, but no resistance, continue to move toward as much contact as possible.

   —If there is open, active acceptance, you may need to encourage appropriate actions. For example, "She likes to be scratched here," or "Why don't we let her sit like this."

   —Listen to the person's *actions* and *words*. They may not always agree. The very person that resists you may be the one who would most benefit from a visitor. They may not know how to accept your friendship.

- If the person wants to hold the animal, always place it on the person's lap, never in his/her hands or arms.

- Use towel-lined baskets under guinea pigs, rabbits and cats. This protects the person from claws and accidents and gives the animal a familiar, comfortable surface.

- When talking for more than a few minutes with a person who is in a wheelchair or lying down, utilize a chair or squat down in order to place yourself at eye level.

- If an animal is jumpy or exhibits any unusual behavior, put the animal back in its carrier. Discontinue the visit and notify the supervisor.

- If someone handles an animal too roughly, take his/her hand and tactfully demonstrate the proper touch. Remove the animal from the person right away if this is ineffective.

- For the animal's safety, never leave an animal unattended with someone you visit.

Process

The process is what happens during the visit. Talking with the client was covered in Unit 3 and Lesson 4.1. Additional activities follow.

- The person may sit quietly and stroke or hold the animal. Actions or words are not always necessary.

- The person may groom the animal.

- The person may walk the animal. This can be a special treat for someone in a wheelchair.

- The person may feed the animal. (See "Equipment" earlier in this lesson about the proper use of treats.)

- The person may play with the animal and with toys you have brought.

- The person may observe the animal doing tricks or playing by itself.

- The animal might lie down at the person's feet and sleep while you visit. If your animal is able to do so safely and the person wants the animal to, the animal may climb onto the person's bed. Put a sheet on top of the bed first to keep fur off of the person and his/her bed.

- Watch the person you are visiting for signs of fatigue or loss of interest.

Closure

Closure is very important. It involves saying good-bye, letting the person know that you and your animal enjoyed the visit and perhaps telling the person what will happen next. For example, "We have to go now. Say good-bye to Kari (cat). We will be back to visit you again next week."

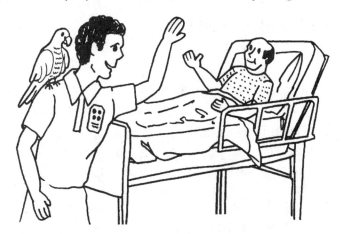

If you can't seem to break away from someone after a period of time, say something like, "I have to be going because I have other people to visit, too."

In situations where there are a lot of people, it may be very easy to move quickly from one to another without closure. When someone appears unresponsive you may find yourself simply getting up and leaving. Think about how you feel when someone is talking to you and suddenly walks away without warning. Even if the person appears to be unaware, always treat him/her with the respect you would give any person or that you would hope to receive yourself.

Video

Video: *Parts of a Visit.*

After the Visit

The Animal

- Allow the animal to relieve itself.

- Recognize that your animal is tired and needs some quiet time.

- Assess the animal's stress level.

- Praise the animal, offer water and a special treat.for a "job well done." (See Lesson 2.2, "Techniques to Prevent Stress," for ways to give your animal relaxation time after visits.)

- Clean and store your equipment.

The Volunteer

- Document your visit. If the facility or program has a method of documentation, complete that process. See Appendix B for an example of a Program Report form. We recommend that volunteers keep a small, informal diary about visits. List date and time and a simple description of the visit. Do not use people's names in your informal diary.

- Contemplate the visit; think of ways to improve the next visit. Talk to your facility contact person or AAA/AAT group leader (if you have one).

- Congratulate yourself for a job well done! Reward yourself too!

 **Articles**

Before you proceed, turn to Appendix A and read,

Article #9: "The Cat on A Visit."
Article #10: "Taking Your Dog on A Visit."

Documentation Can Be Easy

The following are some samples from volunteer documentation.

"We visited one patient in her room after she'd stalked out of the common area, saying she didn't want a visit. Roscoe [Golden Retriever] decided to follow her, and we ended up having a lovely visit with lots of petting, crying, and dog tricks."

"The staff were glad to see Tank [Bearded Collie]. One lady spoke of a recent visit by Baxter [dog] and how she wouldn't visit with Baxter because he had the name of her abuser."

"At first Miriam didn't want to meet Roscoe, but he reminded her of the pets she had years ago, which reminded her of her children. This began a conversation about parts of her memory which seemed to be just coming back. So, she petted Roscoe and cried and talked about her kids— names, birthdays, etc.—details she said she couldn't remember this morning. Fun visit—we shared this with her nurse."

"Karen is still here. She remembered our visit from two weeks ago and described in detail how Roscoe snuggled on the bed. Her behavior with other people was unusual—arms flailing in the air and crying 'boo,' but with the dog she was calm, focused, and quite articulate."

St. Peter Hospital, Dec. '94.

Unit 5
Facilities

Unit Overview:

The facilities you will visit are the focus for this unit. Given that you will visit various types of facilities, you need to understand how they typically operate, their policies, and the staff members you will encounter. This unit also covers extremely important infection control procedures and the steps to follow in case of an injury.

Unit Map:

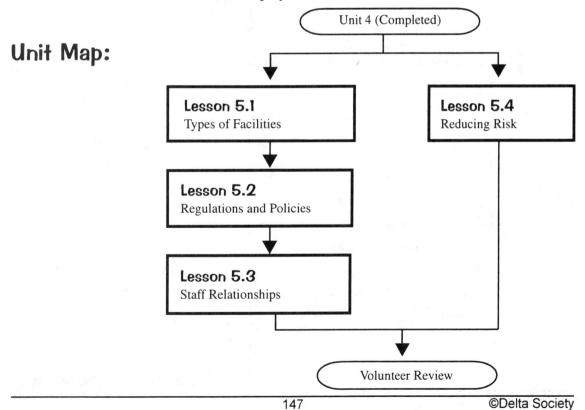

Unit 4 (Completed)

Lesson 5.1
Types of Facilities

Lesson 5.4
Reducing Risk

Lesson 5.2
Regulations and Policies

Lesson 5.3
Staff Relationships

Volunteer Review

Lesson 5.1 Types of Facilities

Lesson Overview:

As an AAA/AAT volunteer, you can choose to visit at a variety of facilities. This lesson will describe some of them. You will learn how to assess a site and accommodate its undesirable features.

Lesson Objectives:

1. Identify the different facilities where AAA/AAT may take place.

2. Identify the conditions and populations you might encounter in each facility.

3. Identify how to assess a site.
    a. Note site features to be surveyed.
    b. List desirable characteristics.
    c. Explain how to accommodate undesirable characteristics.

Conditions You Might Encounter

There are numerous facilities that you can visit. Some are publicly owned, such as state hospitals or schools. Others are privately owned, such as many nursing homes. At residential facilities, people live there 24 hours a day. Other facilities have day programs, and people go home at the end of the day. Specialized programs, such as hospice programs, provide services to people in their own homes.

Although there are exceptions, private facilities tend to be clean, well-maintained, and have adequate staff available. Public facilities may not be as clean, or maintained as well, and staff shortages are common.

Depending on the type of treatment provided at the facility, you may encounter locked wards and/or specific protocols to follow (e.g., no gum chewing when visiting people with eating disorders).

Facilities

Nursing Homes (or Skilled Nursing Facilities)

Nursing homes tend to be quiet, low-activity facilities. Often, nursing homes adhere to set schedules that include pre-planned activities for the residents. To make your visits successful, be aware of meal times, bed times, and other scheduled activities.

Frail elders, well elders, young people, and people with Alzheimer's disease all can be found in nursing homes. Keep in mind that people in nursing homes may have the need for physical rehabilitation, or psychiatric care.

Rehabilitation Centers

Rehabilitation centers provide therapy following an accident, injury, or stroke. Rehabilitation centers generally have a high level of activity during the day as people move to and from appointments and therapy sessions. This setting is very structured. Clients are encouraged to do as much for themselves as possible. The facility has easy access. Evenings and weekends tend to have a slower pace.

People in rehabilitation centers need acute care and/or physical rehabilitation. They may have head injuries and brain trauma.

Hospitals

Hospitals usually have three shifts of staff per day. The size of the hospital, and whether or not it is a community or university hospital, will determine if there is a set schedule with many activities planned. Larger hospitals are generally busier. You will have to schedule your visits around medical procedures.

People with AIDS are sometimes treated in hospitals. Frail elders might be hospitalized. People with eating disorders can receive treatment in a hospital, and hospitals have pediatric units for treating sick children. Many have an oncology (cancer) unit in addition to surgical and general medical units.

Schools

Schools are normally very structured. Class sizes can vary from a small group of five to a gymnasium full of students. The age of students will greatly affect the conditions that you will encounter. Very young children have short attention spans, and you will need to keep visits shorter.

Schools provide educational programs for children who are in pre-kindergarten through 12th grade. School programs now provide services to school-aged children with developmental disabilities, autism, and cerebral palsy. Children with epilepsy attend school programs unless seizures are not managed effectively with medication.

Half-Way Homes/Group Homes

Half-way homes provide a home-like environment. Most often, they are homes in a neighborhood. A small number of people live in a half-way house and staff are scheduled throughout the day. Half-way houses are usually transition programs from larger settings; the "half-way" mark before someone is ready to live independently in the community. They provide people with the skills they need to become more independent. The facility can operate at a very demanding pace for animal/handler teams.

Group homes are different from half-way homes in that people who live in a group home may live there permanently.

Half-way homes and group homes exist for people with AIDS, frail elders, adults with psychiatric problems or developmental disabilities, and people who need a transition placement from a prison program back into the community. Also, in cases of substance abuse, people who were homeless may live in half-way houses as they begin gainful employment.

Hospices

Hospice care is provided to people with terminal illnesses who have an approximate life expectancy of six months or less. Hospices provide care in the patient's home or in an in-patient setting. Hospices are designed to meet people's medical needs in a home-like environment. There are hospices for people with AIDS. There are also hospice programs for people of all ages who are terminally ill with diseases such as cancer.

How to Assess a Site

It is important that you assess the sites to identify potential problems for you and your animal. Go without your animal. Take paper, a pencil, tape measure and a camera (if permitted). Draw a floor plan of the facility. As you survey the facility, take note of the following details:

- Is there a safe, outside location for walking your animal?

- Where is the trash receptacle for waste disposal?

- Where are the clean linens kept?

- Where is the restroom?

- Where will you sign in and out?

- Who will participate in the program? Who will not?

- Where will your visits be conducted?

- Who will accompany you on the first few visits?

- Who will evaluate the visits?

- Where are the food preparation and sterile supply areas?

- Are there any additional facility requirements that you should be aware of?

- Where are the telephones?

- Where are the emergency buzzers/phones for contacting staff?

Features to be Evaluated

Consider the following features as you complete an assessment of the site you will be visiting. Check off the areas that might be potential problems for you and your animal.

❑ **Location**

How long is it going to take you to get to the facility of your choice? Does your vehicle have good temperature control? Can your animal tolerate that length of ride?

Keep in mind that travel time needs to be included in your plans. One-way trips of 30 to 45 minutes could shorten the time available for the actual visit.

❑ **Size**

Is the size of the facility appropriate for the activity level expected when you visit? Depending on your comfort level, and your animal's, you will need to assess which setting is the best for both of you.

❑ **Grounds**

There should be an area for your animal to eliminate and an accessible trash can to place waste in. If this area has not been identified, talk to staff and make arrangements before you bring your animal. Large, open grassy areas are great for animals to relieve themselves and to unwind after the visit is over. How much concrete/asphalt is there? In the summertime, it could get too hot for the animals to walk on. Is there an open parking area or a multi-level garage and is it well maintained? Glass, trash, and motor oil can all affect your animal.

❑ **Entrance**

What type of doors does the facility have? Automatic doors that slide open permit easy access. Do you need a key or security card to enter the facility? Is there easy access to the facility or is it congested?

❑ **Flooring**

Carpeted areas seem to provide the best footing for animals. If floors are slick, find ways to accommodate your animal.

❑ **Lighting**

Soft, adequate lighting is preferred.

❑ **Furnishings**

Well-maintained furniture is best, preferably in an arrangement that facilitates visiting.

❑ **Sound Level**

Depending on you and your animal's sensitivity to noise, the sound level can be a big factor when choosing a facility. Does the background noise interfere with your activity?

❑ **Maintenance**

Clean floors are a must! The facility should be in good condition. There should not be broken furniture or equipment, poorly maintained stairwells, hallways or elevators. Electrical cords should be in good condition and out of the way.

❑ **Rooms**

The general arrangement of the rooms, including any medical equipment, should permit safe access to the person you are visiting. If the room is shared, there should be privacy curtains (as required).

❑ **Common Areas**

Common areas should be bright, open and spacious so that many people can be there for your visit.

❑ **Layout**

Review the overall facility layout. How does the traffic within the facility flow? When are the shift changes? How large are the rooms, stairwells, elevators, hallways?

❑ **Security**

What is the facility's security system? Are guards available during evening hours for escort, if needed? Does the parking garage have cameras for security? Are parking garages well lit? Is there help available if your car breaks down?

❑ **Bathrooms**

Is your animal permitted to enter the bathroom with you if you need to use it? Is the bathroom well-maintained?

❑ **Staff**

Does the staff want you there? What feelings are they expressing? Friendly, supportive staff can be an asset to you and your animal.

How to Accommodate Undesirable Characteristics

Sometimes, a facility will have some undesirable characteristics. You may not be able to fix them, but you might be able to do something to improve the situation. Use common sense.

For example, imagine you are visiting in the day room and the TV is blaring. Everyone has just finished their lunch, there are crumbs all over the floor, and someone has spilled a beverage. You could ask a staff member to turn down/off the TV and have the floor cleaned.

Staff members may be unaware of your needs. Expressing your concerns in a positive manner will often resolve the problem. However, if a situation cannot be corrected and it will affect the quality and/or safety of your visit, then you will have to make a judgment call. If the situation continues, you may want to reconsider visiting that facility.

Activity

Go on a field trip without your pet, to the sites you plan to visit. Go to at least two facilities even if you intend to visit only one facility.

1. Call the activity director and explain that you are in training for visiting care centers with your animal.

2. Ask if you can meet and have a tour to learn about the facility.

3. Make observations at each site. Record them in your journal.

4. Observe the features of each site and draw floor plans. Highlight three good features, three unacceptable features, and three features that you could work around or easily improve.

5. Write a thank you letter.

Lesson 5.2 Regulations and Policies

Lesson Overview:

There are a number of laws and policies that apply to AAA/AAT. This lesson will familiarize you with public health policies, confidentiality, patient rights, and situations that require reporting.

Lesson Objectives:

1. Demonstrate understanding of the need for specific administrative procedures for any visit.

2. Identify specific institution regulations or where to find them.

3. State the general public health guidelines that apply to AAA/AAT.

4. Identify the health codes/laws for your state.

5. State the general policy on patient rights.

6. Identify confidentiality policies.

   a. Identify reasons for confidentiality.

   b. Identify situations that require confidentiality.

7. Identify situations that require reporting.

©Delta Society

Administrative Procedures

It is important that you follow the administrative policies and procedures of each facility you visit. Each facility will have specific policies and procedures to guide staff and volunteers in the safest way to do their work. There are some general administrative guidelines for you to follow in any facility, however:

- When you start volunteering at the facility, you should get the name of a facility contact person.

- Most often, you will be provided with a general orientation of the facility. The orientation will usually include a tour of the facility and a packet of information about the facility's guidelines and policies. Often, volunteers are simply given the same orientation materials that are given to new employees.

- The written orientation materials should describe policies that will pertain to you and your animal. If there are no such materials, ask your contact person for information that is relevant to you. To help you develop AAA/AAT policies, you may use the Facility Policy Agreement found in Appendix B under "Forms."

- If you belong to a local organized AAA/AAT group, your group will most likely provide you with policies and laws that apply to you.

Public Health Policies

You will need to comply with guidelines for health care facilities in your state. The public health guidelines, policies, and laws that apply to AAA/AAT will vary widely from state to state.

 # Research

Your Facility

Talk with the volunteer coordinator of the facility you will visit to identify policies that apply to AAA/AAT. Remember that this person may be busy. Give him/her plenty of time to get the materials you ask for. Often you will work with the facility to develop policies. Contact Delta Society for guidance.

Local Guidelines

Find out the specific guidelines, policies, and laws that apply to your local situation. You can start by asking your facility contact person for this information. If the contact person cannot provide it, call your local Board of Health and ask for the guidelines, policies, etc. that affect the type of facility you are visiting (e.g., nursing homes).

State and National Guidelines

You can also ask your contact person for any national or state regulations for the facility. For example, many people with developmental disabilities live in Intermediate Care Facilities for Mentally Retarded (ICF/MR). These are residential programs that are federally funded. ICF/MR's and other programs have national standards that are very detailed. Many states require that volunteers be tested for TB. Be sure to ask.

Documentation

It is important that you document each visit. Documentation involves signing in and out for each visit and completing facility paperwork on client participation and progress.

Sign In and Out

As a minimum, a sign in/out sheet is important for documenting all visits. Signing in and out proves you were present at a given time. If a question arises as to whether or not you visited as scheduled, signing in and out consistently will provide verification of your visit.

Facilities are required to document all volunteer contact with clients and the sign in/out forms can be used to meet this need.

Document the Visit

Information such as the date, time, length of visit, staff in charge, floor visited, clients visited, brief description of visit, and unusual occurrences should all be documented.

In some cases, facilities will ask that you document the specifics of your visit (e.g., which clients attended, who participated, what the response to your animal was). This information can be used to justify continuing or expanding the AAA/AAT program at the facility.

General Policy on Patient Rights

Clients have the right to refuse visits with animals if they so desire. This may be the only control they have.

Everyone has a right to privacy. The fact that you know that a particular individual is a client of a facility is privileged information. Similarly, an individual's medical condition is privileged information. Do not discuss clients or their conditions.

General Confidentiality Policies

Every facility you visit will have a basic confidentiality policy. Most facilities require that you read and sign a statement that you will follow their policy. Confidentiality is an ethical necessity for continued, proper treatment and therapy. Clients in health care and human service programs need an emotionally safe environment that will protect their privacy.

If it is necessary to talk about a client to your AAA/AAT group to get advice, do not identify the client by name. Do not use information that is specific enough that other people can identify the client. Use general terms such as, "I'm visiting with a man in a nursing home who is afraid of my dog."

If you recognize a client in public, do not approach the client and start engaging in conversation about the facility. You should give no indication that you know the client. If the client chooses to initiate contact, you can return the greeting.

Do not take photos or video tape without release forms signed by the people involved. Do not give stories or pictures to the media without written clearance from the facility's public relations department.

Situations That Require Reporting

Some situations may arise that require you to report to the facility you are visiting *and* to Delta Society. The facility may call these situations Unusual Incidents or Unusual Occurrences. These situations include:

- When a person or animal is injured

- When the potential was great that an injury could occur to either a person or an animal, even though no one was hurt at that time

- When something happens which may be *perceived* to cause an accident or injury

For example, imagine that you are visiting a facility with your dog. In the midst of your visit, your dog is startled and becomes frightened by something. It backs out of its collar and bolts from the room. You catch your dog, calm it, and end the visit. No one was hurt, but your heart is beating rapidly and you feel a mixture of emotions about the incident. Do you need to report this? **YES**, to *both* Delta and the facility. Someone might complain that a dog was running loose. Without a report and documentation, people in authority don't know what happened.

The process to follow for reporting any of these situations is the same process described in Section 5.4 and listed on the Pet Partners Volunteer Policies and Procedures form found in the Registration Packet in Appendix D. If a Pet Partner is found to have neglected to report an incident, s/he may be suspended or dropped from the Pet Partners Program.

Some situations require that you report to the facility only, and not to Delta Society. These situations include information you discover during your visit about a person's medical or emotional condition. Information about something that could compromise the person's health and well-being or someone's safety should be reported to the staff. In addition, if the person says something or acts in a way that you feel the staff may need to know about, it is best to inform a staff member. Most volunteers are not trained in the proper methods of responding to a person's medical condition. You are not asked to diagnose or treat. The information you report will often help in the client's overall treatment/therapy.

Lesson 5.3 | Staff Relationships

Lesson Overview:

For you to have successful AAA/AAT experiences, you will need to be able to get along well with facility staff members. This lesson will identify key staff participants. This lesson will also make you aware of common staff concerns that pertain to AAA/AAT. It is important for you to understand how staff relate to various other people in the facility. This lesson will identify the nature of staff relationships with clients, administrators and volunteers. Finally, this lesson will describe some methods for dealing with uncooperative staff members.

Lesson Objectives:

1. Identify the key participants in AAA/AAT programs and their responsibilities.

2. Identify common staff concerns regarding AAA/AAT programs.

3. Identify differences between staff/patient, administration/staff and staff/volunteer relationships.

4. Identify methods for dealing with uncooperative staff members.

Materials Required:

Article #11: "Sharlow Learns Art of Persuading Administrators."

Article #12: "Getting in the Door: Convincing Facilities to Welcome Pet Partners Teams."

Key Participants in AAA/AAT and Their Responsibilities

The following table lists some key staff members in AAA/AAT facilities and describes their main responsibilities as they relate to the AAA/AAT program.

All of these people (and perhaps more) may be involved in the AAA/AAT program at the facility. Their concerns should be addressed before beginning a program. If you are having problems getting staff acceptance of a program, review this checklist for help identifying what their concerns might be. If you have any questions about the role of various staff members, ask your facility contact person for information.

Participants	Responsibilities
Nurses	take care of patients may facilitate AAA/AAT
Physicians	take care of patients may prescribe AAT
Administrative Staff	determine and carry out hospital policy
Janitorial/Housekeeping Staff	keep facility clean and well-maintained
Dietary Staff	supply clients and visitors with food
Security	provides protection
Volunteer Coordinator	assists in facility's programs interfaces between facility and volunteers assures compliance with policies
Activity Coordinator	plans activities may facilitate AAA/AAT
OT, PT, RT, etc.	provide therapy may facilitate AAA/AAT
Immunologist/Infection Control	provides in-service training studies immune system and diseases

Common Staff Concerns Regarding AAA/AAT Programs

The staff at the facilities you visit will usually have questions and concerns about you bringing an animal into their facility and interacting with their clients. The answers to most of their questions are in this *Team Training Course*. If the staff has questions you don't feel comfortable answering, call Delta Society for advice. The following questions are typical of those asked by facility staff.

- How much staff time will this involve?

- Will the staff be required to change hours in order to be available during visits?

- How will I know that these animals are appropriate for visits?

- Are the animals current on all vaccinations and health requirements?

- Are the animals trained? Will the dogs jump on people?

- Will the animals bring fleas, ticks, or other insects into the facility?

- Can people get any diseases from the animals?

- Will the animal urinate/defecate in the facility?

- Will the team show up at the scheduled time and on the correct day, or advise me if they cannot come?

- Will the team come if the handler is ill?

- Will the team respect our administrative policies?

- Will the team respect the fact that some people may not want to visit with the animals?

- Are the animal/handler teams educated in how to interact with our clients?

- Will the animals be clean?

- How will the staff communicate with the handler that the visits are going well or need improvement?

- Will there be a charge for this service?

Relationships

A good working relationship between all levels of staff at the facility will result in an effective treatment program in which people are satisfied and happy.

Staff/Client

In any facility, the relationship between the staff and clients is very important. The staff meets the basic needs of the clients. People are often dependent on the staff for their care. When you are visiting with a particular person, determine if you need to be dealing with a certain staff member. A direct-care staff member could ensure that the person is ready when you arrive.

If you have a problem with someone or notice something out of the ordinary, a staff member who is familiar with the person can provide invaluable information to help you understand him/her.

Often, people (including clients) forget to thank staff members for the hard work they do. Share the person's progress with the staff members who take care of them. Be sure to thank staff members for having people ready when you come and for supporting your AAA/AAT activities.

Hospital Staff

Staff turnover in Rehabilitation and Pediatrics has reinforced the need for adequate staff preparation in order for an AAA/AAT Program to run efficiently and be utilized effectively.

Psychiatry staff's response to (Wheaten Terrier) Spirit's burnout has been poignant. All who know him have expressed concern for his well being, and many have asked that Ann, the AAA/AAT Coordinator, take documentation to administration. If *even* the animals experience stress working in the Psychiatric Unit, so do the humans who work there.

St. Peter Hospital, Dec. '94

Administration/Staff

The administrators are responsible for supervising staff members. They can help you with any problems you might have related to the staff. Make sure you also take time to tell them when their staff is doing a great job.

The administrator can help you if you have problems with anyone regarding the AAA/AAT program. One way to prevent problems is to prepare a short presentation on AAA/AAT for an in-service program. Having the administrator attend this presentation shows that the administration of the facility supports AAA/AAT.

Staff/Volunteer

Your relationship with the staff is very important. Some staff members will welcome you with open arms. On the other hand, staff members may feel jealous of the relationship you develop with "their" clients. Some may be sensitive to volunteers calling their visits "therapy" without being a licensed therapist.

Remember:

There is a difference between therapy and something that is therapeutic.

If staff members are not happy with you or your visits, they can undermine the entire AAA/AAT program. Volunteers count on the staff to have people ready when they come, to help schedule visits, to provide relevant information about the people they visit, and to assist as needed in facilitating the AAA/AAT program. Make sure you thank them for being helpful.

Methods of Dealing with Uncooperative Staff

Unfortunately, no matter how hard you try to have good social skills and be an excellent volunteer, sometimes problems arise involving uncooperative staff members. Resolve the problem as soon as possible.

If you have a problem with a staff member, it is best not to create a scene while people are watching. Ask if you can follow up with the staff member at a later time. Listen to his/her concerns using *active listening* (see Lesson 4.1), then suggest ways to improve the situation. If you are emotionally caught up in the situation, wait until you can be calm. Put your concerns in writing, but don't use a letter to let off steam. That will only make things worse. Make it short, and let him/her know you want to find a solution that will satisfy you both. As a last resort, if the person is still uncooperative, talk to his/her immediate supervisor.

Be sensitive to the fact that this person can sabotage the AAA/AAT program. Always try to have other staff members present to help verify your visit. If you feel uncomfortable, you may want to ask your facility contact person to accompany you a few times.

 **Activity**

Turn to Appendix B and look over the forms and articles that will help you introduce yourself to new facilities.

 **Articles**

The following articles show how, with adequate groundwork and persistence, you can win over even the most difficult staff members. Turn to Appendix A and read,

Article #11: "Sharlow Learns Art of Persuading Administrators."

Article #12: "Getting in the Door: Convincing Facilities to Welcome Pet Partner Teams."

Reducing Risk

Lesson Overview:

As you visit in AAA/AAT settings, you need to take precautions to protect yourself, your animal, and the people you visit from getting infections or illnesses. This lesson describes some infection control procedures and provides precautions for preventing zoonotic diseases. Zoonosis is an "infection or infectious disease transmittable under natural conditions from vertebrate animals to man"[7] or people to animals. This lesson also provides you with the Pet Partners policy for reporting an injury during a visit and the basic provisions of Pet Partners Insurance.

Lesson Objectives:

1. List/define Universal Precautions.

2. Identify infection control procedures.

3. Identify precautions to follow to prevent zoonotic diseases.
   a. Define zoonosis.
   b. Identify the common causes of zoonosis in companion animals.

---

[7] Benenson, Abram S. Ed. 1990. *Control of Communicable Diseases in Man.* Washington, DC: American Public Health Association.

4. Identify techniques for preventing injuries.

5. State the Pet Partners policy for reporting an injury.

6. Identify fire/safety procedures for your local facility.

7. Identify your legal responsibilities and how you are protected.

   a. State the insurance provisions of Pet Partners if your animal injures someone.

   b. State the insurance provisions if you are injured at the facility.

Materials Required:

Video: *Congratulations.*

Article #13: "Volunteer Insurance Program."
Article #14: "How to Handle a Mishap."

Infection Control

While volunteering in various human service/health care facilities, you may be exposed to a number of diseases. To avoid contracting or spreading diseases, you will need to follow infection control procedures. With some people, you must follow Universal Precautions, which require you to wear gloves and other protective clothing. Even if this is not required, you should treat the blood or body fluids of *any* person as potentially infectious.

Universal Precautions

The American Public Health Association says,

> "...blood and certain body fluids (any visibly bloody body secretion, semen, vaginal secretions, cerebrospinal fluid and synovial, pleural, peritoneal, pericardial and amniotic fluids) of all patients are considered potentially infectious for HIV, HBV and other blood-borne pathogens. Universal precautions are intended to prevent parenteral, mucous membrane, and non-intact skin exposures of health care workers to blood-borne pathogens. Protective barriers include gloves, gowns, masks and protective eyewear or face shields." [8]

Important:

It would be very difficult to dress an animal in gloves, mask, gown, or booties to protect it from contact with body fluids. If you have to wear protective barriers to visit a patient, don't visit with your animal.

---

[8] Center for Disease Control. MMWR. 37:42.

Infection Control Procedures

You need to follow certain guidelines to prevent the spread of any infection or disease, including the common cold.

- Do not visit if you or your animal is sick.

- People should be screened by staff before you visit them to help prevent infection. Check at the front desk or with your contact person at the beginning of each visit.

- Hand washing between clients is critical. You should also make sure that people wash their hands before and after they've finished visiting with you and your animal.

Important:

The secret to hand washing is *friction*. All rings should be removed when going on visits, except for a wedding band. The hands should be lathered and vigorously rubbed together. Rinse under comfortably hot water, dry with a paper towel and use the towel to turn the faucet off.

- Find out where you should dispose of used rubber gloves, masks, etc. There is usually a specific location for contaminated items.

- If someone becomes ill or body fluids suddenly present themselves, *do not panic*. Call for help as soon as reasonably possible. Remove your animal and clean up according to the hospital's infection control policies.

The Animal

You must remember that your animal is able to transmit disease from one person to another person. Theoretically, no visiting animal should be in contact with any discharge from anyone. Otherwise, the coat of the animal (or footpads, etc.) will become contaminated and the infection can be spread to subsequent "petters."

It is crucial that Pet Partners and site staff members assess the potential for infection before visiting someone. If people with low immune response will be visited, they should be visited *first* to reduce the hazard of cross-contamination.

If the animal does end up with blood or other body fluids on its coat or feathers, the animal should be cleaned before leaving the facility. Otherwise, you risk spreading the infection by taking the contaminated animal into your car, home, and/or yard before cleaning it.

The Client

Important:

> Make sure clients wash their hands *before* handling the animal, as well as after.

Why? People can transfer germs via saliva or mucus on their hands to the animal's fur or feathers. The next person may then be exposed to these germs when they pet the animal.

The Volunteer

Important:

> Consider blood and body fluids of all clients as potentially infectious to you. Different facilities will have different policies about hand washing. Some facilities will require you to wash your hands thoroughly *before* and *after* contact with each client. Other facilities will require hand washing only after visiting someone. Hand washing is *the* biggest factor in infection control.

Common sense will be your best guide. Think about the interaction that you are about to have with the person. If s/he has just had a chemotherapy treatment and feels nauseous, or needs to vomit, a bed visit would not be appropriate. Placing your animal on a chair next to the bed gives you room to maneuver. The same holds true if the person has open wounds. Be especially careful of people who have broken skin or mouth lesions. A "doggie" kiss may not be appropriate.

Objects

Poor hand washing remains the #1 cause of infections within hospitals. Since it is clear that good hand washing (before and after client contact) greatly reduces the risk, it makes sense to apply sanitary guidelines to objects with which multiple people have contact (e.g., toys, brushes, etc.).

Preventing Zoonotic Diseases[9]

"One of the risks of bringing people together with other members of the animal kingdom is that we can share not only warmth and companionship with each other, but also the parasites, bacteria and fungi which live in, on, and around our bodies. Some of these microscopic life forms can, under some circumstances, cause disease. Diseases which can be exchanged between people and other animals are called *zoonoses*. An example is rabies, a disease transmitted from animals to humans. Most of these diseases are easily prevented.

Keep your animal on routine vaccination and parasite prevention schedules. Make sure that your animal does not have an opportunity to come in contact with wild animals (e.g., raccoons) or run at large.

There are no good health reasons why dogs and other animals who are properly cared for should not be allowed into schools and nursing homes. The benefits of cavorting with animals far outweigh the small, easily preventable risks involved. The existence of zoonotic diseases should be seen as a cause for celebration; they are a clear sign that we are all part of one extended family of animals.

Anyone reading the medical and veterinary literature might come away with the impression that there are hundreds of diseases that people could pick up from dogs, cats, birds and turtles. This is true. Most of these

[9] Walter-Toews, D. and A. Ellis. 1994. *Good For Your Animals, Good For You.* Distributed by Delta Society. Ontario, Canada: University of Guelph.

diseases, however, are not very common. Furthermore, there are really only a few ways that diseases can be transmitted from other animals to people. We can pick up some diseases from our animal friends through direct contact, not only through biting and scratching, which we hope to avoid altogether, but also through those kinds of contact, such as petting, which we are trying to promote.

Animals may contaminate the environment we live in, including the air. This can happen if their excrement is not properly cleaned up, if they shed hair or dander, haven't been cleaned and groomed properly, or are not well and are shedding bacteria or parasites onto the carpet or bedding. By paying some attention to these ways of transmitting diseases, we can prevent pretty well everything that we might be concerned about.

Hopefully, we haven't given you the impression that animals are nothing more than flea-bitten, parasite-ridden, bacterial-spewing things that bite, a threat to life and limb. On the contrary, you are much more likely to catch something from another person than from an animal—and that shouldn't stop you from getting close to other people. Get close, but be careful!

In fact, in some rare cases, sickness in people can rub off on pets. This could happen if you had a bacterial infection, such as tuberculosis, and coughed it into the dog's face, or if you had the plague and kissed a cat, or, more likely, if you had a case of diarrhea caused by Salmonella and you didn't wash your hands after [using the bathroom]. In general, if a person has an infection that is highly transmissible to other people through casual contact, then it may be passed to animals as well."

In Summary

The benefits of AAA and AAT far outweigh the risks of zoonotic diseases. By following the suggestions listed below, you can help to ensure safe interaction between the species:

1. Ensure that animals have a specific place to defecate and urinate, and that they are cleaned up after.

2. Establish a written set of rules for animals entering the facility. These rules about feeding, watering, grooming, and going to the bathroom, should be clear for all to see. Any abnormal behavior or signs of diarrhea, coughing, scratching and the like, should be noted and the animal should not visit.

3. Run your fingers and thumbs through the animal's coat, looking for fleas, ticks, mites, and other skin problems. Make sure that all the animals you work with have been thoroughly checked over prior to a visit.

4. Animals' coats (and feathers) should be regularly groomed and their nails clipped. Fresh drinking water should be provided; drinking from toilets is, for an AAA/AAT animal, a definite social and health *faux pas*.

5. Visiting animals should have their mouths checked and teeth brushed prior to a visit.

Techniques for Preventing Injuries

Preparation is a major part of injury prevention. These guidelines can help you be prepared:

- One animal per handler.

- Only you should handle or correct your animal.

- Animals should never be left unattended with the people you visit.

- Know your animal and its limitations.

- Know yourself and your limitations.

Unusual Incidents

In the first three years of the AAA/AAT program at St. Peter Hospital, there were two incidents of an animal injuring someone. In the first instance, an elderly patient's hand was grazed by a dog's tooth during a game, requiring antiseptic and a Band-Aid. This incident reinforced the rule that tug games are *never* to be allowed, no matter how much fun the patient seems to be having. The dog was retested for temperament, and for three months his visits were scrupulously monitored. There was no indication of a problem, so the dog remained an active member of the program until he retired. The problem was entirely with the handler, who learned her lesson.

In the second instance, a visitor's child was playing with one of the visiting dogs. The dog had been on a down stay, and as the volunteer team prepared to leave, the dog began to sit up. The child was leaning over the dog and their heads collided, making the child bite his own lip. Unfortunately, the child's mother thought the dog had bitten her child. Staff who witnessed the incident knew the animal was not at fault, but the mother was not mollified.

Staff did their job well by dealing with the visitors (mother and child) and attempting to debrief the volunteer. Sadly, the volunteer was so traumatized by the incident that she quit the program. This incident reinforced that it is not necessarily what actually happens during an incident, but what the *perceptions* are of the people involved (staff, visitors, patients, and volunteers).

by Ann Howie

- Abide by the policies, procedures and precautions of the facility you are visiting.

- Don't be afraid to say "no" to the staff or the person you are visiting, if necessary, to prevent injury to people or animals.

- Get to know the population you will be interacting with and adapt your visits to fit that population and their environment.

- Understand the layout of the facility and potential dangers to you, your animal, and the people you visit.

- People who have potential for harming animals in any way should *not* be included in AAA/AAT programs.

- Visits should *only* be conducted when staff members are present.

Techniques for Handling an Injury

At the Facility

Volunteers who are well-trained and have animals that have been adequately trained and screened will, for the most part, have successful AAA/AAT experiences. Unfortunately, accidents do happen. In the event of an injury to any person or animal at the facility, including you, these are the procedures you should follow:

1. Immediately secure your animal so that you can manage the situation. Do not tie your animal to furniture. Put your animal in the car (if weather permits), carrier, or in the office.

2. If the person you are visiting is injured, assist him/her in any way that is appropriate. If your dog jumps on the person and s/he is falling, intervene to stop the fall if possible. If someone is injured by the animal and is sitting or is stable (e.g., your cat has scratched someone seated in a wheelchair), then get help for the person. Get the nearest staff person and report what has happened.

3. Facility staff should provide medical treatment to clients, even if it is as simple as cleaning a wound and applying a Band-Aid. It is never appropriate for you to give medical aid to the injured client.

4. End the visit. Before leaving, report the incident in writing to your facility contact person. Some facilities have Accident or Unusual Incident Report forms. You will need to fill out all required

paperwork.

After You Leave the Facility

5. If applicable, you will need to contact the organization that sponsored your visit. This would be your local volunteer group if you belong to one, such as the ABC Therapy Dog Group of your city.

6. The day of the incident, or on the first business day after the incident if you visited on a weekend, you **must** notify Delta Society. This is very important since any accident can result in an insurance claim.

    Even if you think everything will be fine, you must notify Delta Society if there is an injury while you are visiting as a Pet Partner. Follow all procedures described under "Pet Partners Policies and Procedures" in Lesson 1.4.

7. Delta will provide help in troubleshooting whatever went wrong. We may even learn from your experience and feel we need to add a specific kind of information to volunteer training.

The Insurance Provisions of Pet Partners

As a Pet Partner, you will be covered on the Pet Partners insurance policy when you are doing volunteer work as a Pet Partner. In cases where professionals are using animals in the context of their jobs, Pet Partners insurance for volunteers does not provide coverage. It is important that you understand your coverage in case of an accident.

Fire/Safety Procedures For Your Local Facility

When visiting at a facility, be aware of the fire and safety procedures and policies for that facility. Make mental notes of alternate exits in case you need them.

 **Article**

Before proceeding, turn to Appendix A and read,

Article #13:   "Do State Liability Laws Leave Volunteers Unprotected?"

Article #14:   "Volunteer Insurance Program."

Article #15:   "How to Handle a Mishap."

Research

1. Research your homeowners or renters insurance policy and determine how you and your animal would be covered if an accident occurred. It is important for you to do this because some policies may change your liability coverage depending on the kinds of activities you are involved in. Pet Partners insurance will provide you with liability coverage secondary to your homeowners or the facility's insurance.

2. Ask the volunteer coordinator at each facility you visit for the fire and safety procedures for his/her facility.

Video

Video: *Congratulations.*

 Activity

Congratulations—you are almost there!

Now it's time to turn again to Appendix D. The first page will guide you through the process to follow to become a registered Pet Partner. This will be your first registration. You will need to renew your registration every two years. Renewing is a very simple process.

Contact the Delta Society office for a certified Animal Evaluator in your area.

Appendix A

Articles

Historical Perspectives on Human-Animal Interactions

Chief Seattle Didn't Say It

"What is a man without beasts?"

This quote has been widely published and quoted in ecological and human—animal bond articles in Europe and America as part of a speech delivered by Chief Sealth (Seattle) in the 1850s.

However, in a paper by Professor Rudolf Kaiser in West Germany, delivered at the European Association for American Studies, Rome, Italy, 1984, he offers convincing evidence that this "speech" or "letter" was written by Ted Perry of the University of Texas in the early seventies as a script for a film, based on ideas from a speech by Chief Seattle given in the 1850s. Ted Perry's name

was wrongfully omitted and the piece was attributed to Chief Seattle and extensively published as such. Professor Kaiser writes:

This text does not represent the mind of the old Chief, but the mind of a sensitive Euro-American, worried about our ecological situation and the general dualism in our culture. Not that the text of the speech is, therefore, spurious, but the headline which names Chief Seattle as the author.

Professor Kaiser's article will be published in Christian F. Fest, Indians and Europe, Gottingen FRG (Edition Heodot).

People-Animals-Environment. (1986).

Over 11 years ago, a native American of the Duwamish Tribe in what is now Washington State, Chief Sealth, expressed ideas now prominent in articles by psychologists, sociologists, and anthropologists:

The white man must treat the beasts of this land as his brothers. What is man without the beasts? If all the beasts were gone, man would die from great loneliness of spirit, for whatever happens to the beasts also happens to the man. All things are connected. Whatever befalls the earth befalls the sons of the earth.

Three themes from this excerpt of Chief Sealth's address provide valuable perspective on the interactions of people and animals:

1. The connection between humans and beasts is deep and long-standing.

2. Human physical and psychological health are affected by interactions with

animals—without them "loneliness of spirit" and other ills can result.

3. Animals and people are part of the same family—"brothers" and "sons of the earth." [We would add "sisters" and "daughters of the earth."]

The deep psychological as well as historical ties between people and animals were vividly described by Dr. Boris Levinson in his pioneering book *Pets and Human Development* in 1972. His ideas were reiterated just before his death in 1984 in a foreword to *Dynamic Relationships in Practice: Animals in the Helping Professions* (Ed. Phil Arkow).

In the universe of primitive people, animals were integral—as equals, partners, or even superiors. An animal ancestor was the tribe's totem: animal spirits accompanied human souls to the land of the dead; people talked to animals and, in the time before people, animals could talk and were like people. The first gods of humans were animals symbolizing elemental forces of nature. Sacred dogs in China, sacred cats in Egypt, and animal imagery in the Judeo-Christian tradition are all a part of our heritage. In our century it seems only children regard animals as equals, as Freud observed in 1913:

Children show no trace of arrogance which urges adult civilized men to draw a hard-and-fast line between their own nature and that of all other animals. Children have no scruples over allowing animals to rank as their full equals.

One of the most intense human—animal bonds is described by Dr. Calvin W. Schwabe in The Pet Connection as the drinking of cow's milk:

During that period between about 8,000 and 5,000 years ago when the precursors of civilization began to emerge in several parts of the world, adult man—of his own volition—did the biologically and culturally very, very strange, we might even say unnatural, thing of deliberately adopting for his foster-mother the female of a totally different species of mammal, the cow.

From at least 6,000 B.C. the domestication of cattle and the rise of cattle cultures were motivated by religious practices, as well as the need for a source of sustenance. Margaret Sery Young explains Zeuner's stages of domestication (see Veterinary Clinics of North America):

1. Loose contacts with free breeding;

2. Confinement to human environment with breeding in captivity;

3. Selective breeding to obtain certain characteristics with occasional crossing with wild forms;

4. Planned development of breeds, especially for economic reasons;

5. Related wild animals persecuted or exterminated.

In addition to domestication, as Schwabe points out, the religious ceremonies involving cattle led priests to perform some of the first surgical operations—e.g., dehorning and castration. The operations were a key to acquisition of power greater than human muscle—a prerequisite to intense and remarkable grain production, necessary for city life and, ultimately, "civilization." Religious sacrifices and dissections also allowed priest to acquire factual biomedical knowledge.

Predating the rise of cattle cultures (from at least 12,000 B.C. and maybe earlier), another of the closest relationships between two higher species—man and dog—developed. Dogs and men hunted together, shared dens, and ultimately were buried together. With domestication of sheep and goats, as a partial result of man—dog cooperation, a sheep-culture people arose with qualities of gentleness, caring, compassion, responsibility, nonviolence, and contemplation.

Some have hypothesized that the need for companionship motivated domestication of animals as pets, and that pet keeping might have been a model for domestication of certain species for economic reasons later.

From earliest times, for primitive people, animals were central, either as food or in hunting food or in religious ceremonial systems or as companions, often at deep metaphysical and psychological levels. More recently, authors have contemplated the importance of companion animals and the living environment in different ways.

In his book "New Perspectives on Our Lives with Companion Animals," Aaron Katcher speculates that they help us preserve our mental and physical equilibrium by providing safety, kinship, intimacy, and constancy. (See Aaron Katcher, "People and Companion Animal Dialogue: Style and Physiological Response.") Of course, animals have always functioned in these ways to a greater or lesser degree.

The second theme of Chief Sealth emphasizes the necessity for beasts in human wholeness and wellness. The historical perspective showing the closeness of animals to people has led to a concern that as we become separated and alienated from other animals and the environment, as the bond is broken, we suffer psychologically and physically. Other articles on this issue address the role of animals in human health.

Historically animals have long been part of programs to help people. The early Greeks gave horseback rides to raise the spirits of persons who were incurably ill. From the seventeenth century the medical literature contains occasional references to horseback riding as beneficial for gout, neurological disorders, and low morale. In 1859 in *Notes on Nursing*, Florence Nightingale wrote:

A small pet animal is often an excellent companion for the sick, for long chronic cases especially. A pet bird in a cage is sometimes the only pleasure of an invalid confined for years to the same room. If he can feed and clean the animal himself, he ought always to be encouraged to do so.

In the twentieth century, programs have been established to make the horse a partner in the treatment and rehabilitation of persons with a wide range of disabilities. Beginning in Europe, the programs spread to the United States in the 1960s, and now over 500 North American programs feature riding for the handicapped for recreation, sport, and/or therapy.

Indications are that animals were involved in helping handicapped people in Gheel, Belgium, when this community encouraged their residents to accept them into their homes starting in 800-900 A.D. In the late eighteenth century the York Retreat in England included animals in the facility in which mentally disturbed persons lived.

About 75 years later, at Bethel in Bielefeld, Germany, animals were an integral part of the community for disadvantaged and disabled persons. In the 1940s at the Pawling New York Convalescent Hospital, the American Red Cross and the army air corps set up a program for recuperating patients which involved association with a wide variety of animals in a farm situation.

But it wasn't until the publication of Boris Levinson's "Pet-Oriented Child Psychotherapy" in 1969 that anyone made a serious plea for careful investigation of the healing power of association with animals, based on extensive records of his experiences in his own practice. Levinson's studies were soon followed by further case reports of patients in a psychiatric hospital and residents of a nursing home in Ohio who were given carefully selected companion animals by Dr. Samuel Corson and his wife, Elizabeth.

The idea that human interactions with companion animals can result in physiological changes and psychological benefits is gradually being accepted. The possibility that this is a legitimate area of scientific inquiry and a legitimate addition to curricula at universities was explored for the first time in a systematic manner by an international, interdisciplinary group convened in May 1984 by the Delta Society, a national nonprofit organization with research, educational, and public service activities in the area of human-animal interaction.

Three international conferences have been held on this subject, with a fourth scheduled in August 1986. The resultant published conference proceedings contain key articles in the field. Some research funds are now available through the Delta Society to universities for study of the role of pets in normal human development. It is hoped that this research will fill a great gap in our knowledge. More funds are needed to investigate the efficacy of pets in institutions and therapy programs.

But the universities are really latecomers in taking notice of the potential of this field. Community programs bringing animals and people together for companionship and therapy began in the seventies and are growing rapidly, according to the national database at the Delta Society office.

Some prisons allow animals as part of vocational training programs and also as pets for individual inmates as an integral part of their rehabilitation. Nursing homes are encouraging visiting, mascot, and individual therapy animals. Some hospitals are opening selected wards to pets as part of programs to benefit patients. Specialized programs train animals to aid disabled persons. A federal law makes it illegal to forbid pets in subsidized housing for the elderly and handicapped, and several model programs are providing support services for elderly pet owners.

The success of all such public service programs depends upon selecting activities that meet the specific needs of an institution or community, building upon the excellent models already established elsewhere, and planning and implementing the programs carefully.

Boris Levinson provided an important perspective to such programs in the prologue to "Pets and Human Development" when he said that pets are not—

a panacea for all the ills of society or for the pain involved in growing up and growing old....However, pets are both an aid to and a sign of the re-humanization of society. They are an aid in that they help to fill needs which are not being met in other, perhaps better ways, because society makes inadequate provision for meeting them....In the meantime, animals can provide some relief, give much pleasure, and remind us of our origins.

As Aaron Katcher has explained, companion animals are something to decrease loneliness, to care for, to keep us busy, to touch and fondle, to watch, to make us feel safe, and to provide a stimulus for exercise. As we have often observed, they can be a source of unconditional love and concentrated attention.

The third theme so eloquently expressed by Chief Sealth is that animals are our brothers and together we are children of the earth. It is not surprising that recent research reveals that in the majority of households with companion animals (now over 50 percent), the animals are considered members of the family. They give and return love, and family members are grieved when they die.

But just as family bonds are too frequently broken by a 50 percent divorce rate, and just as lives are shattered by child abuse and neglect, similarly the human—animal bond is often fractured. Unfortunately, for too many people, companion animals are throwaway items, as witnessed by the euthanasia of millions of animals each year.

One benefit of the serious scientific study that is now beginning of human—animal interactions, of the increasing inclusion of this subject in schools, of the attention the topic is receiving in the media, and of the proliferation of well-planned programs involving animals can be an awakening of the commitment we must give to the care of our "brothers" and of our mutual environment.

Our survival as a species may well hinge upon our ability to develop compassion— for each other and for the animals that share our earth and help make us whole persons. As Chief Sealth said, "All things are connected. Whatever befalls the earth, befalls the sons of earth."

The wisdom of these words is perhaps even more apparent in the sometime despair of the twentieth century than when they were uttered in sadness in the nineteenth. If heeded, they promise hope and wholeness.

by Linda M. Hines and Leo K. Bustad

Hines, L.M., and L.K. Bustad. (1986). Historical Perspectives on Human-Animal Interactions. *National Forum* 66: 4-6.

2

How Animals are Used in Therapy

The ways animals are incorporated into therapeutic situations are varied. New ways and new methods continue to develop.

Animals are being used increasingly with geriatric patients in residential and treatment centers and with individuals with special needs. Programs vary from live-in animals to visiting animals provided by individuals or by the Humane Society. (State laws limit what can be done, though many are leaning toward modified use.)

Animals have also been and are being increasingly used with physically limited patients in both physical and mental therapy. Specific uses include cases of multiple-handicaps, including brain-damage; perceptual impairment, blindness, polio, CP, deafness, leprosy and accident victims including veterans and paraplegics. Additionally people who are emotionally disturbed are being helped through private therapists and in family therapy which may include family pets. Children in institutions benefit from contact with animals and in some areas programs have been initiated for college students. Foster homes and orphanages are using programs that include animals to varying degrees. Animals have been introduced into rehabilitation centers, including alcohol and drug treatment centers; deterrent programs for juvenile delinquents; programs for mentally retarded individuals; and correctional institutions such as prisons and homes for the criminally insane (Arkow, 1982).

Animal-assisted therapy is indicated for patients who are non-verbal, inhibited, autistic, withdrawn, obsessive-compulsive, and culturally disadvantaged. Animal-assisted therapy is also a treatment for patients lacking self-esteem or exhibiting infantile helplessness and dependence, and for individuals in times of bereavement (Arkow, 1982). Children with ego center problems can also be treated with pet therapy (Levinson, 1969).

The list of possibilities is as long as a list of human needs. According to a variety of authors, animals can be included within the therapeutic process in many ways.

- A pet can provide fulfillment of the client's emotional needs (Wallin, 1978).

- The therapist may use an animal as an ice breaker (Wallin, 1978).

- An animal may greatly aid problem assessment (Levinson, 1969).

- An animal offers an opportunity for multi-dimensional communication. With an animal, the need for language is low. Patients often can communicate, or believe they are communicating, with an animal and do not feel threatened (Levinson, 1969).

- An animal can provide a non-threatening relationship and can easily establish trust (especially with those who have not learned to trust). This trust is projected onto the human therapist (Levinson, 1969).

- An animal can offer a safe and easy way for the client to participate in giving (Levinson, 1969).

- An animal provides a stimulus for other types of therapy, i.e. walking the animal, playing with the animal, caring for the animal (Levinson, 1969).

- An animal helps interpret a client's thoughts and feelings, especially children. Observations of the animal's behavior can often be transferred into a setting the client is striving to understand, i.e. some children become interested in the dog's phallus. Why does the dog perpetually lick itself? Is the dog dirty? Does the dog like it? Are people that way too? A natural jumping off point is then provided for a realistic discussion of dog or human sex activities. Another example: Why does the dog fight with other dogs. This might help the child patient think in terms of sibling rivalry and jealousy (Levinson, 1962).

- A pet can help differentiate reality vs. fantasy. Though a child can play fantasy games with a pet, the pet is real, it has needs, and the child must recognize them (Wallin, 1978).

- A pet can provide motivation for learning and living (Levinson, 1969).

- A pet provides an excellent tool for sex education (Levinson, 1972).

- A pet allows for role playing opportunities (Levinson, 1969).

- A pet provides a way to set "natural limits" for the client (Levinson, 1969).

- A pet can be used as a guide or role model.

- A pet provides stimulus for social interaction (Levinson, 1969).

- A pet may teach life function, roles, and responsibilities (Arkow, 1982).

- A pet may provide preparation for coping with death (Levinson, 1972).

- A pet may become a pseudo-sibling for a child (Levinson, 1969).

- A pet may provide hours of companionship, particularly for those who are lonely or restless (Levinson, 1961).

- A pet may offer an indication of progressive healing. Changes in the client's relationship to the pet generally coincide with the client's increasing ability to handle other problems (Levinson, 1969).

- A pet can provide someone to talk with who will listen (Ruckert, 1987).

- Pets can provide acceptance.

- Pets provide nurturing touch experiences.

- Pets, and common interests in pets, help individuals develop an interest in people (Levinson, 1969).

However vital a pet may be in a therapy role, pets are not for everyone. A professional working with animal-assisted therapy must be sensitive to the client. In some situations the client may not like animals, but the pet may still play an important role in therapy. For example, persons living in an institution have very little control over what happens in their lives. The opportunity to say, "I hate dogs. Get that dog out of here," may give those people something they can control.

by Linda Lloyd Nebbe

Nebbe, L.L. 1991. from *Nature as a Guide*. Minneapolis, MN: Educational Media Corp.

3

Plain Talk About Handling Stress

You *need* stress in your life! Does that surprise you? Perhaps so, but it is quite true. Without stress, life would be dull and unexciting. Stress adds flavor, challenge, and opportunity to life. Too much stress, however, can seriously affect your physical and mental well-being. A major challenge in this stress-filled world of today is to make the stress in your life work *for* you instead of against you.

Stress is with us all the time. It comes from mental or emotional activity and physical activity. It is unique and personal to each of us. So personal, in fact, that what may be relaxing to one person may be stressful to another. For example, if you're a busy executive who likes to keep busy all the time, "taking it easy" at the beach on a beautiful day may feel extremely frustrating, nonproductive, and upsetting. You may be emotionally distressed from "doing nothing." Too much emotional stress can cause physical illness such as high blood pressure, ulcers, or even heart disease; physical stress from work or exercise is not likely to cause such ailments. The truth is that physical exercise can help you to relax and to handle your mental or emotional stress.

Hans Selye, M.D., a recognized expert in the field, has defined stress as a "non-specific response of the body to a demand." The important issue is learning how our bodies respond to these demands. When stress becomes prolonged or particularly frustrating, it can become harmful—causing *distress* or "bad stress." Recognizing the early signs of distress and then doing something about them can make an important difference in the quality of your life, and may actually influence your survival.

Reacting to Stress

To use stress in a positive way and prevent it from becoming distress, you should become aware of your own reactions to stressful events. The body responds to stress by going through three stages: (1) alarm, (2) resistance, and (3) exhaustion.

Let's take the example of a typical commuter in rush-hour traffic. If a car suddenly pulls out in front of him, his initial alarm reaction may include fear of an accident, anger at the driver who committed the action, and general frustration. His body may respond in the alarm stage by releasing hormones into the bloodstream which cause his face to flush, perspiration to form, his stomach to have a sinking feeling, and his arms and legs to tighten.

The next stage is resistance, in which the body repairs damage caused by the stress. If the stress of driving continues with repeated close calls or traffic jams, however, his body will not have time to make repairs. He may become so conditioned to expect potential problems when he drives that he tightens up at the beginning of each commuting day. Eventually, he may even develop one of the diseases of stress, such as migraine headaches, high blood pressure, backaches, or insomnia.

While it is impossible to live completely free of stress and distress, it is possible to prevent some distress as well as to minimize its impact when it can't be avoided.

by Ruth Hay

Hay, R. (Ed.). Plain Talk About Handling Stress. *Plain Talk Series*. National Institute of Mental Health—Division of Scientific and Public Information.

Helping Your Pet Work in New Environments

Hey, what happened to the Personality Kid?

You may have asked yourself this question about your pet if the two of you are part of a visiting program that goes to more than one type of facility. You may have seen your star attraction at one site become clearly unhappy at another location.

Why is this?

A variety of factors could be involved when an animal has such difficulties, says Linda Case. Case teaches Companion Animal Science at the University of Illinois at Champaign-Urbana, owns the Autumn Gold Dog Training Center, and coordinates the Paw-to-Paw Visitation Program of Bloomington, Illinois.

These factors include:

- **Socialization**. How much have you socialized your pet? Is it familiar with a variety of settings, people and noises? If an animal's environment is not varied a great deal, it will be more difficult to switch from one type of visiting site to another.

- **Personality**. Certain dogs and cats will habituate only to one or two environments and that's all you can expect of them. Others are social butterflies and will be comfortable in all settings.

- **Reactions to patient/client body language**. The animal could be reacting to cues from the people being visited. Dogs communicate by body language, relying on body posture, facial expressions and eye contact to understand how a person is feeling. They could also respond to scent. Picking up on any of these could trigger a negative response in a dog, resulting in avoidance, barking and possibly showing fear. With socialization, some pets can get used to these new cues—others cannot.

Case suggests that volunteers socialize their pets from an early age and, before they begin visiting, have their animals temperament tested to learn what kinds of facilities and people they are best suited to visit. Such testing will reveal how an animal reacts to the noises, equipment and other stimuli found in facilities.

An animal's breed or age can be significant. Case says that high energy breeds of dogs, such as Golden Retrievers, Labrador Retrievers and Boxers, and cats such as Siamese and Abyssinians are often excellent with children.

Lower energy dogs and cats such as Newfoundlands, St. Bernards or Persians (and elderly animals) often do well with nursing home residents.

Case says it's also a good idea to know and respect your pet's time tolerance. Some animals can visit 15 people in an hour and others burn out after three visits.

Before they were associated with Pet Partners and participated in screening procedures, Joan Loeffler of Franklin, PA., and other volunteers in the Love in a Box visiting program of the Venango County Humane Society experienced problems with pets crossing over into new environments. Love in a Box will soon be a screening site for Pet Partners. Loeffler is chairperson of the Venango County Humane Society Board of Directors.

As the program developed, its volunteers had begun visiting a variety of sites, including nursing homes, classes for children with severe developmental delays, hospitals, and facilities for those with mental, emotional or substance abuse problems.

"My malamute, Juneau, did beautifully with children in the classroom environment, but at the facility for those with emotional and mental problems, her disposition changed—she would growl. She was dear with everybody else, but with patients who were seated on the floor in bean bag chairs, she was a different dog," says Loeffler.

After two unsuccessful visits to the facility, she decided it was in everyone's best interest (including Juneau's) to discontinue her visits at that particular site.

"An animal should not be required to do more that it's comfortable with. If an animal is not an active participant in a visit, it's not good for the animal and it's not good for the person it's visiting either," agrees Case.

Delta Society. 1993. Helping Your Pet Work in New Environments. *Pet Partners Program, A Delta Society Newsletter*. Vol. 3, No. 1.

Recognizing and Managing Stress

Ann Howie is a social worker, Pet Partner and recipient of this year's Spirit of Jingles award for her AAA/AAT work. She visits St. Peter Hospital in Olympia, WA with her team mate, Spirit, a Wheaten Terrier. At the Delta Society Conference this past October, Howie presented a workshop on recognizing and managing stress. We felt those of you who were unable to attend would find it helpful.

Negative stress causes destructive physical symptoms and behaviors in both us and our animals. We need to learn to recognize these symptoms and take steps to alleviate the stress that causes them.

Howie says the most important action you can take is to stop and listen to what he/she is telling you. Things your pet may normally do can be signs of stress, such as panting or yawning. Shyness, dilated pupils, lack of desire to socialize, or reluctance to get in or out of the car may be less obvious signals. Signs of prolonged stress may be a disruption of eating habits, moodiness, or excessive sleeping.

Sometimes stress is as simple as needing to go to the bathroom. Don't forget that AAA/AAT visits are more stimulating than sleeping on the couch for 10 hours!

Many times we contribute to our animal's stress. Are your expectations unrealistic?

Must your dog perform perfectly every moment? Are your thoughts elsewhere? Are you upset because of a close call in the parking lot or worried about making your next appointment on time? Our emotions travel right down the leash and are picked up by our animals.

They may think your stress is directed at them, become anxious and start exhibiting stress-related behaviors. Assess your animal's state of mind before you even go on the visit. Stop and listen. Are you willing to cut the day's activities short if you need to for your pet's well-being?

Sit down and realistically examine your goals and motivations for participating in AAA/AAT. Are you doing it to have fun with your dog, to help people, to make friends? If you are clear about your own needs, you will be able to better select activities which will meet your expectations. Are you visiting the right facilities for you and your animal's skills and aptitude? Constant negative experiences can wear out the most well-meaning team. Be willing to stop for a few weeks to head off a case of burn-out. Is there further training or socialization that would help? Don't forget that proper diet and exercise help keep you both in top condition and fight off stress.

Don't assume that you and your animal teammate must automatically enjoy what you're doing. Accept that animals are individuals too—some like going out, some prefer to stay home, some like to fetch, some like to chase. Some like to be petted, some prefer to be left alone. The same is true for you. Some people enjoy working with children, some prefer adults or senior citizens. Some enjoy visiting schools, but can't take the emotional burden of a rehabilitation center.

Once you recognize signs of stress in yourself or your animal, take steps to provide relief. Evaluate the time you spend with your animal. Is it only AAA/AAT time? Howie suggests participating in other activities together. Play time: tag, fetch, Frisbee, walks; these cement the bond between you and cure a lot of ills. Try some activities your dog was bred for: herding, lure coursing, field trials. Use new training methods or teach new skills such as agility, flyball or scent hurdles. Visit places where your animal meets people in an undemanding atmosphere such as parks or friends' homes.

Build communication with your animal through massage or TTeam work, before, during and after visits, or while watching TV.

Jennifer Wilk of Chicago's People & Pets and a member of the Pet Partners National Committee visits developmentally disabled clients and a nursing home for children. She takes her guinea pig Poppy or her dog, Dancer, with her. Because she is doing AAA/AAT visits three times a week, she schedules breaks by planning some activities with no Pet Partner at all. She finds even the people with the most limited level of ability understand when Dancer is tired and needs to rest. She incorporates this into their discussion groups. Wilk structures her visits so that activities vary and they don't become monotonous for her or her animals.

She has observed higher stress levels when a volunteer is going into a facility for the first time. Even with the most careful planning there is an adjustment period. Staff changes also cause disruption to the routine.

Knowing which situations are likely to be stressful prepares you to manage them effectively.

by Terry Albert

Albert, T. 1994. Recognizing and Managing Stress. *Pet Partners Program, A Delta Society Newsletter*. Vol. 4, No. 1, 1994.

The Soothing Touch

Imagine that through touch, you could make permanent and profound changes in your dog's behavior, performance and even his appearance. Imagine using your touch to deepen the communication, trust and partnership between you and your dogs. Such a touch exists, and can be learned by anyone. It is known as the Tellington Touch.

Broad Usage

Developed by Linda Tellington-Jones, an internationally known horse trainer and teacher of riding instructors and horse trainers, the TTouch is an integral part of a system of animal training known as TT.E.A.M. (The Tellington-Jones Every Animal Method). Originally developed for use with horses, this method was organized into a teachable concept in 1978. TT.E.A.M. is now taught and used in 32 countries by people ranging from pet lovers to Olympic riders and zookeepers, and with animals both wild and domestic, from giant pythons and elephants to horses and dogs. Whether your involvement with dogs (or other animals) consists of breeding, training, showing, grooming, handling or just loving dogs, the Tellington Touch is a useful tool.

Basic Method

Although Tellington-Jones has developed a wide variety of touches (see sidebar, "Methods of TTouch"), the basic TTouch is a simple circle and a quarter (see Figure I).

Use your three middle fingertips to make the circle, with the thumb and little finger resting on the animal as supports for the hand (Figure II). The hand and fingers should be softly curved, and all movement of the fingers should come from the joints in the hand, without engaging the larger muscles of the arm and shoulder. Imagining a clock face, the circle begins at 6, moves upwards around the clock, passing 6 again to end at 8. At the completion of each circle, quietly move your hand at random to another spot and begin again. The circle always begins at 6 so that it is initiated with a lifting of the skin; starting a 12 results in the skin being pulled downwards and tightened.

Pressure used can vary from extremely light (no more pressure that would be needed to move the skin on your eyelid in a circle) to firmer, though still quite comfortable, pressure. Let your intuition, your dog's response and the part of the body being touched guide you to an appropriate pressure. Like humans, some dogs are extremely sensitive, and appreciate a lighter touch, while others, especially heavily muscled breeds, may respond to a firmer touch. Remember that you are only working to move the skin, not the underlying muscle.

The TTouch is not massage, but an activation of the neural pathways and brain cells. The purpose of massage is to affect and relax the muscles, and massage is sometimes painful when muscles are tight. The intent of the TTouch is to activate the function of the cells, a delicate connection that does not require force. Unlike massage, the TTouch should never be painful. Painful or extremely tense areas are worked only with a pressure that is acceptable and causes the dog no pain.

Experiment on yourself. Varying the pressure, try a few circles on some part of your body that you give little thought or attention to, like the back of your neck or the underside of your knee. As you experiment, is important to experience the difference between the one-and-a-quarter circle (which begins at 6, moves around the clock past 6 and ends at 8) and repeated circling on the same area. The one-and-a-quarter circle is complete, and easily understood by the brain. Repeated circles on one spot soon become annoying, and your ability to focus your attention on that area of your body diminishes rapidly.

After making a few random TTouches, notice that even after you have stopped, you can "feel" the area you were touching. You have increased your awareness of this part of yourself. Experiment on other areas of your body—you will probably discover areas that are tense, painful or sensitive, though you may have had no conscious awareness that you were holding tension or pain in these areas.

Our dogs also hold tension and pain in their bodies. While this sometimes means nothing more than a dog dislikes having his nails clipped, it can be the cause of severe behavior problems.

Rudy was a 14-month-old Siberian Husky who had developed an aggression problem as a result of poor socialization and learned misbehavior. Nervous, intelligent and quick to react, he had bitten several people, including his owners, and threatened many others. In public, he had lunged at passersby and other dogs. Euthanasia had been recommended, but his tearful owners couldn't bring themselves to choose that solution.

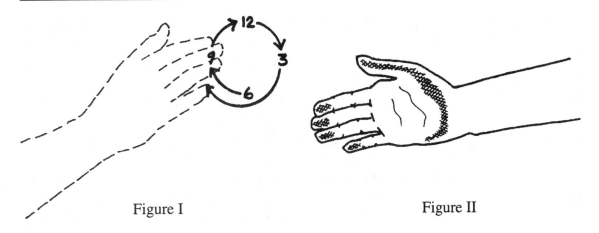

Figure I   Figure II

When Rudy felt threatened, which was often, his tail became rigid, he held his breath, and most of the muscles in his body tensed. Anything that he perceived as a threat triggered an unconscious pattern of bodily discomfort due to muscular tension and fear, and Rudy reacted with aggressive behavior.

Using a variety of Tellington TTouches to bring new feelings to the tense areas in his body helped break the pattern, which allowed Rudy to behave in new ways. In just two sessions, Rudy lay quietly in my lap as I worked in his mouth, touching his gums, teeth and tongue. Two months later, Rudy graduated from a beginner's obedience course. Was this a miracle? Although his grateful owners thought so, what had happened was a break in the cycle of fear and pain that Rudy had experienced most of his life. (It's important to note that dogs with aggression problems should only be worked on by qualified TT.E.A.M. practitioners.)

Ears and Mouth

Another TTouch called the ear stroke is enjoyed by nearly all dogs, and is especially useful during whelping, and in situations of stress, shock, bloat, injury or trauma. Throughout the ear are acupuncture points that relate to the entire body, so working the ears can affect the whole animal. Around the base of the ear is an important acupuncture meridian which affects breathing, digestion and reproduction. At the very tip of the ear is the acupuncture point for shock.

To "stroke" an ear, gently hold the ear leather starting at the base between your thumb and first finger. Regardless of your dog's ear type, stroke the ear between the fingers in an upward fashion, applying moderate pressure all the way to the outer edge of the ear. Work in overlapping sections, being sure to cover the entire ear.

Using the Tellington Touch in and around the dog's mouth will allow you to make changes in the dog's emotional state. This area is associated with the limbic system, that part of the nervous system connected to emotional response. Tension or stress in dogs (and many other animals, including humans) is revealed in tightly drawn lips, clenched jaws and a rigid chin. Releasing the tension in these area is crucial to changing behavior — the biggest breakthrough with Rudy came when I was able to work in his mouth. Mouth work is also useful during the puppyhood periods

Methods of TTouch

The various Tellington Touches are named after animals. This means of naming touches was devised to help attach a memorable visual image with each touch, and to add a little humor. These are just some of the Tellington Touches.

- Clouded Leopard describes the basic TTouch position with the fingers lightly curved. Using the pads of the fingers...keep all three knuckle joints soft and moving as you make each circle.

- Lying Leopard is a less invasive TTouch using the fingerprint part of the finger and also the first knuckle joint to push the skin in a circle. It spreads the pressure over a larger area, and is useful when the animal is too sensitive for a deeper touch.

- Raccoon Touch is done using the tips of the fingers just behind the nail. Raccoon circles are used with very light pressure around areas of injury or swelling.

- Python Lift requires that the whole hand be place on the body or around the leg with enough pressure to gently lift the skin and support the muscle. The lift is only one-half to one inch. (If you lift too much, it often causes the animal to hold his breath.) Hold for about four seconds, then *slowly* return the skin to the starting point and then release.

- Flick of the Bear's Paw is the name for the cupping stroke which is used randomly over the body. These can be done lightly as in feathering, using gentle sweeping movements with your fingers going in the direction of the hair. This is used for animals who object to being touched, especially in areas like the legs or under the belly. The fast random flicks are usually effective for quieting a nervous animal or to wake up a very relaxed one after using the TTouch.

- Noah's March calls for long, firm strokes of the hand all over the body of the animal, which reintegrates the whole body after using the circular touch. It brings the body back together after bringing new feeling to individual parts.

of excessive chewing. The unique stimulation and sensory input of the Tellington Touch is the mouth often relieves the need to chew.

When working in or around the mouth, be sure to control the dog's head to avoid being bitten accidentally when your fingers are in the mouth. Although some dogs will not object, it is usually easier to get to the muzzle if you prepare the dog by working on other "safer" areas of his body first, gradually moving your touch toward his head. If the dog objects, move back to a safe area for a few moments before trying a few circles near the head. Patience and gentle persistence are the key to working with a reluctant dog.

Restraining the head lightly, gently work the lips, chin and nose, noting any tight areas. Using the circles and firm strokes, work the gums and inner lips. If the dog's mouth is very dry, moisten you hand with warm water. Use only as many fingers as comfortably fit—for smaller dogs, perhaps only one finger will be needed. Gently holding the mouth open, also work with the tongue, moving your fingers across it as if playing the piano.

A frequently asked question is "How long do I need to do this?" Tellington-Jones believes that "less is more," and stresses short sessions of maybe 5-20 minutes depending on the dog. She notes that is not necessary to work the entire body at each session. How many sessions are needed depends on the animal and the problem. While amazing results can sometimes be seen after just one session, some animals need more. Some dogs respond immediately to the TTouch, happily accepting the new sensations and relaxing quickly. Other dogs,

especially spoiled or fearful dogs, may resist your attempts to work with them. The problems may be an issue of trust, so be patient—it takes time to establish a trusting relationship.

by Suzanne Clothier

Clothier, S. 1991, February. The Soothing Touch. *Purebred Dogs/American Kennel Gazette.*

How to Help the Elderly Reminisce

Listening to the reminiscences of older people can help them keep their minds alert, therapists say. But the reminiscing will have a lot more value if the listener follows a few simple guidelines:

Remember that the process and the feelings that surface are the important part of reminiscing. If the person's memories aren't objective or factual, don't try to set the record straight or you might stop the flow of memories. Try not to interrupt.

Give yourself plenty of time to listen. Show by your tone of voice, body posture and facial expressions that you're interested, not bored. Be patient when the stories are repetitious. Sometimes it helps to ask about the feelings behind the memories when the elderly person keeps repeating a story.

Allow emotions to run their course. If sad memories cause tears, they can be healing. If the elderly person becomes unduly depressed, however, ask about events you know were happy.

Draw the individual back to the present from time to time by connecting past events with present ones. If an elderly man tells you what his first home cost, ask him what he thinks it would be worth today.

Before sitting down to hear reminiscences, it can help to prepare a list of questions. But be willing to let the session follow its own course, even if it gets away from the original subject. You might bring along a box of props: family pictures, old clothing, travel souvenirs or music.

Questioning older people in the family can serve a double purpose. Not only does it stimulate thinking and communication, but it can serve as research for an oral or videotaped family history.

Experts say the questioner has to be comfortable with what is asked or the elderly person won't be. Some possible questions:

- Were you ever very sick as a child? Who took care of you?
- How did you celebrate Halloween as a child?
- Do you remember your first day of school?
- What did you like to do as a child: play sports, read books, play games?
- What did you want to be when you grew up?
- Was there a teacher or a neighbor who influenced your early life?
- How did your parents meet?
- Tell me about the pets you had as a child.
- What do you remember about your first boyfriend/girlfriend?
- Tell me about your first job.

Sources: Tacoma gerontologist Doris Weaver; Diane Lee of the Seattle Day Center for Adults; "How to Tape Instant Oral Biographies," published by Guarionex; "Reminiscence," by Carmel Sheridan.

Seattle Post Intelligencer. 1991, January 26. How to Help the Elderly Reminisce. *Seattle P.I.* Seattle, WA: Seattle Post Intelligencer.

8

Communicating with Older Adults

At any age, people need other people to talk to, people with whom they can share their ideas and feelings. But communication patterns may change as a person ages and hearing or vision changes. These changes may cause older people to feel cut off from others and may cause others to feel uncertain and uncomfortable when communicating with them. This is a shame because older adults are the living link that connects the past, present and future, and they have so much to share.

As the new Denali Center opens, we want to share some listening and talking tips you can use to make communication with older adults more effective and enjoyable.

When listening to older adults, try the following:

- When they are talking, show that you are interested by sitting down, keeping good eye contact, nodding, and saying a few words in agreement. ("Yes, I see...")

- Encourage them to talk about the past.

- Allow them to repeat a story you've already heard. They think it is important or they wouldn't repeat it.

When talking to older adults, remember:

- Speak clearly; avoid mumbling or talking too rapidly.

- Allow extra time for them to hear your words, interpret the meaning, and respond. The aging process can slow the hearing process. Be patient when waiting for an answer.

- If they do not hear what you say, repeat it using different words. You also may try to lower the pitch of your voice. Speaking louder seldom helps.

- Many older adults depend on lip-reading to help them understand. Wearing bright lipstick might be helpful. Men should keep in mind that a beard or mustache can make lip-reading difficult. Keep your hands or objects such as pencils away from your mouth when speaking.

- Nonverbal communication, especially touch and facial expressions, show that you care.

Keep the following in mind when talking with older adults who are upset:

- Remember, older adults experience the same emotions as younger people. Be accepting; everyone feels anger, doubt, and fear, regardless of age.

- Older adults need ways to express their emotions just as you do. Talking about painful experiences such as loss, death, or fear can be useful.

- Use good listening skills. Listen carefully and repeat your understanding of the conversation to double-check that you've heard what the person is saying.

- Speak in a calm, gentle, non-judgmental manner.

- Communicate your concern and acceptance nonverbally as well as in words. Often a touch or hug will send the message that you care.

Illness can sometimes prevent older adults from expressing themselves clearly, or understanding what you are saying. This is when nonverbal communication becomes even more important. Keep in mind that only a fraction of the meaning of any conversation is conveyed by the words you use; most of the meaning comes through your non-verbal messages and the tone of your voice.

Communicating with some older adults may take more thought and time, but the rewards can be immeasurable.

by Sally De Witt

DeWitt, S. Ed. '94, Spring. Communicating with Older Adults. *Health Report.* Fairbanks, Alaska: Denali Center Fairbanks Memorial Hospital.

9

The Cat on a Visit

Here are some things you need to know when taking your cat on a visit:

1. Transport your cat in a crate. It is the safest method of transportation for both you and your cat.

2. Have a small meat tray with litter in it, or a disposable diaper in the crate for elimination purposes. If the cat becomes irritable during the visit, he can be put back into the crate and perhaps solve his irritability problem!

3. Use a collar and leash with your cat. This can make handling much safer and easier.

4. Carry your cat in a secure and comfortable position. Cat experts suggest a "burping baby" position, close to your body. Some cats may find another position more to their liking.

5. Don't hand your cat to a stranger. Allow the resident to pet your cat while you hold it. If the cat initiates going to the person, let him.

6. Always encourage residents to pet the animal from the shoulders to the end of the tail. They also like petting or scratching under chin. Many cats do not like people touching their heads.

7. Some cats tire rapidly. Be sensitive to their condition.

8. Cats resist a tight hold on them.

9. Be aware that cats instinctively grab with the nails if they think they are falling.

10. Carry a large bath towel so you can cover the cat if it becomes frightened and tries to bolt. Wrap it up and cuddle it as you would a baby and talk to it soothingly. Return it as quietly as possible to the carrier.

11. Always stay near your cat. *Do not* leave the room or leave it with a resident. Always keep your eye on your cat. If an unexpected situation should arise, your cat needs you there and you need to be there!

12. A traumatic experience for a cat may be difficult to reverse, so keep everything positive. Accept the fact that the cat may have a bad day or it may just change its mind about being a social/therapy cat! If it becomes irritable, stop. Give the cat some time to recover. Try again another day. If the behavior is repeated, you may be dealing with "burnout." You know as well as anyone that cats have definite thoughts about things. It's OK if it doesn't want to go anymore.

13. Don't forget a special treat on the way home to make the occasion really special.

P.E.T. P.A.L.S. The Cat on a Visit. Waterloo, IA.: Black Hawk Humane Society.

10

Taking a Dog on a Visit

Before the visit:

• bathe dog

• clean the ears

• check the animal's breath (if not agreeable, put toothpaste on your fingers and rub across the pet's teeth)

• brush coat (removing mats)

• cut nails and file rough edges (especially dew claws)

• clean matter out of eyes

• assess the overall health and attitude of the animal

Equipment:

• collar and lead or carrier

• Pet Partners identification tag and card

• treats

• water bowl

• clean-up kit

• toys or retrieving items

• brush or comb

• towel

• crate (if the animal is crated)

During the visit:

- allow animals to greet one another or be aware of others present before the visit

- be cautious of the animal overheating, especially if the building is not air conditioned

- be aware of the animal's need to relieve itself. (Under the stress of the visit or in a territory of new smells, this may be more frequent.)

- watch for stress symptoms

- provide water periodically

- keep the animal in control at all times

- learn to read the dog's body language (ready to pounce, distressed, uncomfortable, etc.)

After the visit:

- recognize that most dogs are tired and need some quiet time

- avoid feeding for a couple of hours to let stomach recover from "goodies" received on visit

- offer water

- put away and care for the equipment

- praise the animal and offer a special treat as a reward for a "job well done"

- assess the dog's stress level

- think of ways to improve the next visit (shorter time frame, fewer persons to visit, more treats, more verbal reinforcements, breaks, etc.)

P.E.T. P.A.L.S. Taking a Dog on a Visit. Waterloo, IA.: Black Hawk Humane Society.

11

Sharlow Learns Art of Persuading Administrators

Neva Sharlow believed that she and her five-year-old golden retriever, Honey, had cleared the main hurdle to entering a health care facility when they were finally registered as Pet Partners. To her dismay, Sharlow soon discovered that being well-qualified isn't always enough to gain entry into health-care facilities. In some cases, in fact, registered Pet Partners volunteers find that their greatest obstacle is selling the very concept of patient or resident-animal contact to administrative decision-makers.

Sharlow, a registered nurse, thought other health-care workers would quickly see the value that patients could derive from animal contact, particularly from contact with a temperament-screened animal handled by a trained volunteer. She began contacting local hospitals in the suburbs south of Detroit, Michigan. According to Sharlow, administrators at these hospitals showed complete disinterest in patient-animal contact.

"My first problem with these hospitals was fighting my way through the secretarial level to reach someone who was empowered to make a decision," Sharlow recalls. "After I finally got through to an administrator, their response would typically be, 'I need to run this through our infection control people' or 'I can't tell you anything without first asking my boss.'"

Inevitably, Sharlow says, administrators resisted her request with a stock, "I'll get back to you"—which, of course, they never did. Follow-up calls to these facilities yielded no improvement.

Finally a friend encouraged Sharlow to contact Children's Hospital of Michigan, a large teaching hospital in Detroit that is associated with Wayne State University's medical school. Although Sharlow again had to work her way past the secretarial gatekeepers, her request eventually reached an enthusiastic director of rehabilitation services, who helped speed Sharlow's proposal through all internal red tape to ultimately win approval. Sharlow and Honey have since begun a regular visiting schedule and the hospital has expressed interest in formally involving Honey in patients' physical therapy.

How did Sharlow's successful approach to Children's Hospital differ from her earlier unsuccessful approaches to other hospitals? It didn't, which underscores the importance of the first and most obvious of several lessons Sharlow shares:

- Don't give up. Just because some facilities respond negatively, it doesn't mean all facilities will.

- Don't assume larger, more prestigious facilities will be harder to persuade. Children's Hospital is such a facility. As Sharlow discovered, however, administrators there have progressive attitudes.

- A request mailed to a facility should include a cover letter and support materials. The presentation should seem professional. Avoid misspellings, typos and poor use of language—all of which can discredit you. In addition to providing evidence of your team's general qualifications (including documentation of your Pet Partners registration, the animal's temperament- and disease-screened status, and proof of liability insurance coverage), demonstrate awareness of the particular needs of the patient population you propose serving. Sharlow accomplished this by furnishing administrators copies of AAT Population Worksheets (from Section 4 of the Pet Partners Training Manual) pertinent to the facilities' respective populations.

- If the press release announcing your team's Pet Partners registration has been published in your local newspaper, provide administrators with a copy of the published article.

- Give some thought to follow-up materials you might share with administrators who express interest in your proposal. To an interested director of rehabilitative services at Children's Hospital, Sharlow provided "AAT in the Hospital Setting," a video Sharlow rented from the Delta Society. Delta Society makes available other helpful resources as well, including a "Pets in Hospitals" resource packet.

- Assume administrators are interested until you have reason to believe otherwise. From Children's Hospital, for example, Sharlow initially received what she feared was an ominous silence to her mailed request and support materials. Upon further inquiry, however, she learned the administrator had merely been temporarily swamped with other work which prevented her from immediately responding.

- Dress professionally for any face-to-face meetings with administrators. Likewise, if the administrator asks to meet your animal, make sure the animal is well-groomed.

- Network with any other Pet Partners volunteers and/or members of Delta Society Chapters or Networks in your area. If you are having trouble obtaining suitable contacts at local facilities, other people involved in area people—animal programs may have helpful suggestions. The Delta Society office can help you locate these people.

Delta Society. 1992. Sharlow Learns Art of Persuading Administrators. *Pet Partners Program, A Delta Society Newsletter*. Vol. 2, No. 2. Renton, WA: Delta Society.

12

Getting in the Door: Convincing Facilities to Welcome Pet Partner Teams

With thorough groundwork on your part, you can set the stage for a successful working relationship with the facility you plan to visit with your animal teammate.

For two years, Karen Corbin has made weekly visits to Sand Lake Hospital in Orlando, Florida with her four collies and two shelties. She works with Lynn Prange, CTRS (Certified Therapeutic Recreational Therapist) and Dr. Victor Roberts, Medical Director for the BIRC (Brain Injured Rehabilitation Center) ward. Their experiences suggest some tips on surviving the approval process and point out some of the obstacles you will encounter when you approach a facility.

Begin by contacting the Volunteer Services or Recreational Therapy departments (the official name may be different). Try to find someone who will guide you through the red tape and be your advocate while the facility develops its guidelines for your visits.

Your association with the Pet Partners program will add credibility to your visiting plans. Delta Society has sample policies and procedures to assist you. Packets are also available with articles and letters of reference you can copy and give to the facility.

Risk Management departments often express concerns over possible mishaps. Each patient or their guardian at Sand Lake Hospital signs a consent form in advance indicating that they are willing to allow the pets to visit. Delta can help you explain your Pet Partners liability policy. Be prepared to also address questions about infection control, fleas or allergies.

Therapists, nurses, and physicians are under tremendous time pressures, and could initially anticipate your visits as an interruption to their busy schedules. Corbin and Prange find that an informal approach works very well. Corbin comes at the same time every week, so there is no need to constantly discuss scheduling. She visits most of the patients on the floor, and is flexible in the amount of time spent with each one. She works primarily with Prange, thus minimizing schedule disruptions for other staff.

The Medical Director or treating physician may be skeptical. Schedule a visit between your animal teammate and the facility staff, where you can put to rest concerns about behavior, cleanliness, and suitability for visits. Explain the Pet Partners registration process, and that your teammate has been screened for health, temperament, and obedience. Demonstrate your animal's special skills. For example, Dr. Roberts is not an animal lover so he was initially apathetic to the Pet Partners program. "But these animals are awesome," he now comments, "I would invite skeptics to visit the hospital when the dogs are here. They are so calm, you could do anything with them."

Dr. Roberts has seen the most dramatic results in young people or long-term patients who have not responded to human interaction. One example cited by Corbin occurred when a nurse placed a comatose teenage accident victim's hand on the collie's head and told the girl what she was doing. Over a period of weeks, the girl gradually responded by moving her fingers to pet the dog, then moving her eyes toward the dog. A breakthrough came when the girl lifted her other hand over her body and placed it on the dog's head, so both hands could now pet him. "It was a miracle," states Corbin. Today the teenager is at home and able to dress and feed herself. Dr. Roberts feels that although the results are hard to quantify scientifically, once physicians see the interaction, they will be persuaded to try the program.

The initial approval process is a necessary evil. If you are well-prepared and make it easy for the facility you are approaching, your chances for success are much greater. The professionalism you convey adds to your credibility as a meaningful member of their treatment team.

Delta Society. 1993. Getting in the Door: Convincing Facilities to Welcome Pet Partner Teams. *Pet Partners Program, A Delta Society Newsletter*. Vol. 3, No. 4. Renton, WA: Delta Society.

13

Delta Society Pet Partners Volunteer Insurance

When acting as a volunteer for Delta Society ("Delta") within the scope of their duties as a Delta volunteer, a Pet Partners Team is insured by Delta's liability insurance. That means that if either member of a Team causes a covered loss at a location where the Team is visiting, and that covered loss results in a claim for which Delta is legally liable, Delta's liability insurance carrier will defend and pay expenses of the claim.

Furthermore, Delta Society's liability insurance will be primary, i.e. it will provide coverage first. However, if the amount of any covered loss exceeds the limits of Delta Society's liability insurance, then the Pet Partner Animal Handler may be personally liable. And one notable exclusion to Delta Society's liability insurance pertains to losses suffered by one Pet Partner Team as a result of the acts of another Pet Partner Team. Those losses are not covered.

As of January 1, 2000, Delta Society's liability insurance has a $2,000,000 total limit and a $1,000,000 limit per incident. That includes a medical expense limit of $5,000 for any one person. These limits may change.

The preceding is a general overview only, and is for informational purposes only. It does not create a contract or other legal obligation of Delta, and may not be relied upon for this purpose. The details and precise language of the insurance policy must be examined to understand the extent of and limits upon insurance coverage. Many of those details, some of which may be important or relevant - or which may give rise to exceptions to the general statements above - are not referenced in this overview.

If you have any questions regarding volunteer insurance, please contact Delta Society.

14

How to Handle a Mishap

What would you do if your pet injured a client during a visit? An incident can be something as simple as an unintentional scratch. Or perhaps a dog takes a treat from someone's hand just a little too quickly and the person thinks they've been bitten. Real or perceived, mishaps can happen to the most experienced and best-trained teams.

For example, Ann Howie's great Dane/boxer cross, Falstaff, accidentally broke the skin on a patient's hand during a visit at the psychiatric unit of St. Peter Hospital, Olympia, Washington. Howie and Falstaff were the first registered Pet Partners team and Howie is director of the Animal-Assisted Activities and Therapy Program at St. Peter Hospital.

On the day of the incident, several patients wanted to be actively involved in playing with Falstaff and Howie engaged them in tossing a rope that the dog likes to fetch. One patient started to play tug-of-war with Falstaff, something that Howie usually discourages. At the end of the session, Howie saw blood on the patient's hand. Neither she nor the man had noticed the broken skin during the activity, and the man had not experienced any pain. Howie assumes the dog grazed the patient's hand with a tooth.

"I never expected anything like this to happen to me. It always seemed like it would happen to somebody else. I felt embarrassed, but it was a good experience for me, because I direct the program and my volunteers can learn from me. It showed we had good procedures already in place [to deal with incidents]. I was fortunate to have support from the staff."

You should be sure the facility you visit has written general procedural guidelines in case mishaps occur. Howie offers these suggestions:

- Remain calm. Don't act upset "even if inside you're quaking." This will help others not to blow the incident out of proportion.

- As soon as you notice there's a problem, stop the activity and, if possible, take the patient to a staff person. If the patient is not ambulatory, get a staff person immediately. Explain what happened to the staff person and let them provide first aid, if necessary.

- If appropriate, stop the animal's visit for that day. You or your pet might be upset and you could communicate the wrong message to your animal or to clients. There's no shame in saying, "Let's stop for the day."

- Explain what happened to your contact person at the facility. He or she will need to hear about the mishap from both the volunteer and the staff.

- If you visit as part of a program that does not originate at the facility, inform your program director of the incident.

- Write up a report of the mishap on the day it happens for your own records. Give a copy to the activity director or your contact person. Pet Partners must report the incident to Delta within 48 hours.

- Wait for the decision of the AAA/AAT program and/or facility. They may require your animal to be re-evaluated for temperament. Or you and your animal may have to undergo a probationary period during which you are observed during visits. Some directors will ask an animal to leave the program. Howie says that many incidents can be prevented by doing the following:

  - Don't break your own rules. Ever. Don't do things you don't feel comfortable with or that could be perceived as a problem.

  - Know your animal. Temperament screening is an important tool to help you learn how to work with your animal.

  - Know your clients. To protect them, know the activities in which they can participate safely. If in spite of these precautions you should experience a mishap while working with your pet and find that your confidence is shaken, Howie offers the following advice:

  "Do take a good long look at yourself and your animal and be honest about what went wrong. If these are things that can be changed and you're serious about it [AAA/AAT], find ways to get back into it. Find supportive people who will help you deal with it and figure out what happened. "It's serious, but it doesn't have to be the end of the world."

Delta Society. 1993. How to Handle a Mishap. *Pet Partners Program, A Delta Society Newsletter.* Vol. 3, No. 2. Renton, WA: Delta Society.

Appendix B

Resources

A Glossary of Terms

Abuse Survivors

People who have experienced physical, emotional, or sexual abuse during their life.

Active Listening

Involves listening with full attention to someone without making judgements, giving advice or sharing your opinions. It is intended to help someone share and to let him/her know s/he is being heard.

Activity Director

The person responsible for planning recreational activities for people at a facility. S/he has formal education but may not measure or document progress like a CTRS does. May also be called a Recreation Therapist.

Acquired Immune Deficiency Syndrome (AIDS)

A severe disorder characterized by an inability to fight off infection. It is spread primarily by contact with contaminated blood and sexual contact.

Allergy, Allergies

Extreme sensitivity to certain substances which may result in itching or sneezing. A person may be allergic to: pollen, certain foods, or animal dander (dander is dry skin like dandruff in people), etc.

Alzheimer's Disease

A form of dementia or impairment of mental ability. It may include loss of memory, orientation, speech and language. It is a progressive, irreversible brain disorder, and affects over 2,000,000 American adults. The disease has a significant effect on the person's family and friends and is the fourth leading cause of death in adults.

Ambulatory

Having the ability to walk independently.

Animal-Assisted Activities (AAA)

Activities that involve animals visiting people. The same activity can be repeated with different people, unlike a therapy program that is tailored to a particular person or medical condition.

Animal-Assisted Therapy (AAT)

Animal-assisted therapy involves a health or human service professional who uses an animal as part of his/her job. S/he will have decided on specific goals for each individual and will measure and record any progress made.

Anorexic

Someone who has anorexia nervosa—a disorder of the mind, behavior and body. It usually occurs in teenage women and is characterized by extreme fear of being overweight, distorted self-image, aversion to food, and severe weight loss.

Aphasia

Impairment of the ability to use or understand language. It is caused by a disturbance in certain parts of the brain.

Arthritis

A form of joint inflammation or degeneration experienced by people of all ages, but especially in older adults. Pain and stiffness may occur and seriously affect functioning.

Assessment

The act of determining the extent or significance of something. An evaluation.

Asthma

A recurring respiratory (breathing) disease, often triggered by allergies. It involves difficulty breathing and sometimes coughing.

Attention Deficit Hyperactivity Disorder

A disorder that occurs in children involving impulsiveness, hyperactivity, and a short attention span. It may lead to learning disorders or behavioral problems.

Autism

A severely disabling condition, marked by an extensive withdrawal from reality. Bizarre behavior, aggression, repetition and little use of language are also characteristic.

Bulimic

An eating disorder, usually in young women of normal or close to normal weight, involving uncontrolled binge eating followed by feelings of guilt and depression. Often associated with dieting, fasting and self-induced vomiting.

Caregiver

Someone, such as a physician, or social worker, who helps identify, prevent or treat an illness or disability. A caregiver may also be a family member or friend providing care to a person at home.

Catheter Bag

Used to collect the fluid, particularly urine, drawn from a person's body by a catheter tube.

Cerebral Palsy

A disability resulting from damage to the brain before or during birth. Symptoms may include muscular incoordination and speech disturbances. Wide individual variations in symptoms.

Certified Evaluators

People who have been specially trained and certified by Delta Society to perform the animal skills (PPST) and aptitude (PPAT) screenings required to register as a Pet Partners team.

Certified Therapeutic Recreation Specialist (CTRS)

Provides therapeutic recreation training for clients. S/he sets specific goals for clients and measures their progress. A CTRS has specialized training and national certification in therapeutic recreation.

Chemical Dependency

A physical and psychological addiction to a drug such as alcohol or cocaine.

Client

The person using professional or social services. A customer.

Cognitive

Involving thinking (e.g., perception, awareness, judgement).

Compulsive Behavior

A disorder characterized by behavior repeated over and over. The person cannot control the behavior.

Confusion

A mental state in which thought, memory and orientation may fluctuate or are disordered. May be the result of physical or psychological conditions.

Cross-Contamination

When germs are passed from one person to another within a facility.

Dementia

The loss of intellectual abilities so severe that it interferes with social or occupational functioning. It may be treatable, depending on the cause. It may be drug related, emotional, metabolic, nutritional, or caused by tumor or infection. Alzheimer's disease is the cause of 50 to 60 percent of all dementia. The term "senility" was once used to describe all forms of dementia.

Depression

A mental state or disorder marked by sadness, loneliness, inactivity, difficulty in thinking and concentration, and feelings of hopelessness. May be brought on by biological, psychological or social factors.

Developmental Disorders

A mental or physical disability that begins before adulthood and usually continues throughout a person's life.

DHLPP

A vaccination for dogs that protects against common, preventable disorders: Distemper, Hepatitis, Leptospirosis, Para-Influenza and Parvo Virus. It is required for dogs being registered as Pet Partners.

Down's Syndrome

A disorder existing at birth that is characterized by mild to moderate developmental delay, short stature and a flattened profile.

Eating Disorder

A potentially life-threatening disorder of eating habits (e.g., anorexia, or bulimia).

Empathy

Identifying with, and understanding the feelings and motives of another.

Facility

The building or location where you take your animal for AAA or AAT. It may be a nursing home, hospital, or school, etc.

Far-Sighted

Ability to see things at a distance better than things that are close.

Fetal Alcohol Syndrome

A condition, present at birth, involving a wide range of abnormalities to the heart, skull, face or nerves, and developmental disorders. It is caused by excessive consumption of alcohol by the mother during pregnancy.

Frail

The result of a normal decline in the senses or in physical strength which may accompany aging or illness. A frail individual may be "at risk" of being institutionalized and in need of a variety of supports to live independently.

FVRLP

A vaccination that protects against common, preventable diseases: Feline Viral Rhinotracheitis, Leukemia and/or Calici Virus, and Panleucopenia (distemper). It is a health requirement for cats being registered as Pet Partners.

Habilitation Plans

Documents used in facilities for people with developmental disabilities to record a person's goals.

Hepatitis B Virus (HBV)

Hepatitis B is a disease that affects the liver. It is spread by contact with infected body fluids. It is not the form of Hepatitis spread when someone doesn't wash his/her hands after using the bathroom.

Hospice

Health care for people with a life expectancy of six months or less. The focus is on relief of symptoms rather than cure. Physical, emotional and spiritual support is provided to people who are terminally ill and their loved ones.

Immunologist

A specially trained person who deals with people's ability to resist infection.

Incontinence

The inability to control one's bladder or bowel functions. May be the result of a variety of conditions; may be treatable; can be managed with proper care.

Individualized Education Plans   (IEPs)

Documents used in educational settings to record the goals and progress of school-aged children.

Infection Control

Procedures set in place to avoid the spread of disease.

I.V.

Short for intravenous, which is the introduction of something into the veins, such as fluid.

Learning Disorder

A disorder in one or more of the basic psychological processes involved in understanding or using language (spoken or written), which may manifest itself in the imperfect ability to listen, think, speak, read, write, spell or do math. The term includes such conditions as perceptual handicaps, brain injury, dyslexia, developmental aphasia and minimal brain dysfunctions.

Legally Blind

When someone has 20/200 vision or less in their best eye with glasses, or they have tunnel vision with a 20 degree range of field or less. Someone with 20/200 vision may still be able to read very large print. A person with tunnel vision may read small print within their field of vision. Most people who are legally blind still have some vision.

Manic-Depressive /Bi-Polar Disorder

A form of mental illness characterized by alternating extremes of hyperactivity and depression.

Multiple Sclerosis

A disease of the central nervous system causing muscular weakness, loss of coordination, and speech and visual disturbances.

Muscular Dystrophy

A disorder that affects a person's ability to control his/her muscles. It gets worse over time.

Nearsighted

Unable to see things at a distance clearly.

"No-Touch" Rule

In some facilities or with some people, no one may touch a client under any circumstances. This rule will often apply in facilities that provide psychiatric care and for people who are survivors of physical or sexual abuse. Pet Partners animals can provide positive opportunities for touch.

Nursing Care Plans

Documents used in nursing homes to record the goals of clients.

Nurturing

Promoting the growth and development of another living thing.

Occupational Therapist (OT)

Works on physical, social, and cognitive (thinking) skills with people. This may include daily living skills (e.g., eating, meal preparation, cleaning), and vocational skills. OTs also help people regain the use of their hands and upper body, and increase range of motion (how much someone can move a particular body part).

Orthopedic

Having to do with the spinal cord or bones.

Panic or Phobia Disorders

A psychological disorder involving intense attacks of anxiety in certain situations and resulting in extreme fear of that situation.

Parkinson's Disease

A disease, usually beginning after age 50, and becoming progressively worse with time. Characteristics include tremors, slowed movement, and weakness.

Pathogen

Bacteria, fungus or other microorganism that causes disease.

Peripheral Vision

The field of view outside of center, at the boundaries or outer edges.

Personality Disorder

When a person's personality traits significantly impair the person's social or occupational life.

Pet Partners ID Card

A picture identification card provided to registered Pet Partners. It indicates the areas the team is qualified to visit.

Physical Therapist (PT)

Works on improving movement that uses the larger muscle groups. S/he may help someone strengthen his/her legs and walk.

Physiological

The basic functioning of the body (e.g., heart rate and blood pressure).

PPAT

The Pet Partners Aptitude Test determines your animal's ability and potential for being a Pet Partner. It also evaluates the aptitude of the animal/handler team (see Lesson 2.1 for more information).

PPST

The Pet Partners Skills Test is similar to the American Kennel Club's Canine Good Citizen Test. It evaluates the animal and handler as a team (see Lesson 2.1 for more information).

Protective Barriers

Items used to prevent spreading germs. These may include: bandages, gloves, masks, sheets, towels, or gowns.

Psychosis

A severe psychiatric condition in which there is a departure from normal patterns of thinking, feeling and acting. Chronic and generalized personality deterioration may occur. One of the two main categories of mental illness. May require treatment in a mental institution.

Psychiatry

The medical science of the treatment, diagnosis, and prevention of mental and emotional disorders. A psychiatrist is a physician (M.D.) who specializes in psychiatry and may prescribe medication.

Psychology

The science of behavior and mental processes. A psychologist is educated to perform psychological testing, research and therapy. A psychologist may not prescribe medication.

Psychotherapy

A method of treating mental and emotional disorders by encouraging communication of conflicts. The goal is personal growth and positive change in behavior.

Recreational Therapist (RT)

See "Activity Director."

Rehabilitation

A program of treatment to restore physical, mental and/or emotional balance.

Schizophrenia

A psychotic, complex brain disorder affecting feeling, thought and conduct. It often appears in late adolescence or early adulthood and may have a variety of symptoms, such as: delusions (false beliefs), hallucinations (false perceptions), disturbances of thinking, odd habits or deterioration in daily functioning.

Senility

A word associated with mental degeneration and decline. Although "senile" has been commonly used to refer to a host of disorders such as confusion or lack of self-care (especially among elders), the term has no medical legitimacy. There are over 100 conditions that can lead to such symptoms.

Sensory Loss

An impairment of any of the senses (sight, touch, taste, smell, hearing).

Social Workers

Provide psychological counseling and assistance in efforts to improve human welfare.

Spina Bifida

A condition that is present at birth in which the spinal column is not closed properly and the spinal cord bulges out, resulting in disorders of the nervous system.

Stroke

A cerebro-vascular accident (CVA) resulting in cerebral (in the brain) bleeding or an obstruction to parts of the brain. It is sometimes fatal. One may be left with paralysis of the limbs and impaired speech. Rehabilitation therapy is often helpful in restoring abilities. The third leading cause of death in adults after heart disease and cancer.

Suppressed Immune System

The inability of the body's natural defense system to fully fight off disease.

Terminally Ill

To be in the last stages of a fatal illness.

Therapeutic

Providing cure, comfort or relief from illness or distress.

Therapy

Therapeutic treatment provided by a licensed therapist. It is reimbursable through insurance carriers, has measurable goals, is documented, and is evaluated.

Treatment Team

A variety of health care providers who work with a client to provide complete treatment services. This team may include, among others, an OT, physician, and social worker.

TTouch/TT.E.A.M.

TTouch is part of a system of animal training called TT.E.A.M. (The Tellington-Jones Every Animal Method). Developed by Linda Tellington-Jones, who sees a connection between behavior and tension, TTouch involves a variety of touches to relieve an animal's tension, and develop trust and communication between handler and animal. TT.E.A.M. involves learning exercises that teach self-control, balance and attention to the handler.

Tunnel Vision

When a person's field of view is constricted or limited, as if s/he is looking out through a tube or tunnel.

Universal Precautions

These are steps to take to avoid spreading infection. Consider body fluids to be able to cause infection. To prevent exposure, protective barriers such as gloves, gowns, masks and protective eye-wear should be worn when there is the possibility of coming in contact with blood or other body fluids. (See Lesson 5.4 for more information.)

Unusual Incident/Unusual Occurrence

A situation where a person or animal is injured; when the potential was great that an injury could occur to either a person or an animal, even though no one was hurt at that time; or when something happens which may be perceived to cause an accident or injury to a person or animal.

Zoonotic Disease/Zoonoses

Diseases that can be passed from animals to people and from people to animals (e.g., rabies).

Additional Reading

The following is an extensive list of suggested readings. This combination of books, magazines, and organizations will help broaden your general knowledge. Explore the list and take what works best for you and your situation.

We suggest that you start your own personal library. Books on grooming, training, health and veterinary care and breed-specific books are the basic building blocks for working with your animal.

The Delta Society Resource Center sells Action Guides, manuals, and guidelines on AAT, Service Dogs, and related subjects. You may also rent videos and audio-visual materials from Delta Society.

General Books

Beck, A. and A. Katcher. 1983. *Between Pets and People*. New York, NY: G.P. Putnam's.

Levinson, B. 1969. *Pet-Oriented Child Psycho-Therapy*. Ed. Charles C. Thomas. Springfield, IL.

Allen, K. 1985. *The Human Animal Bond: An Annotated Bibliography*. NJ: The Scarecrow Press, Inc.

1990. *Control of Communicable Diseases in Man*. The American Public Health Association.

1986. *Pet Therapy: A Study and Resource Guide for the Use of Companion Animals in Selected Therapies*. Colorado Springs: Humane Society of the Pikes Peak Region.

Ruckert, Janet. 1987. *The Four-Footed Therapist: How Your Pet Can Help to Solve Your Problems*. Berkeley: Ten Speed Press.

Shari Bernard, OTR. *Animal Assisted Therapy - A Guide for Health Care Professional and Volunteers*. Whitehouse, TX: Therapet. (Therapet L.L.C., P.O. Box 1696, Whitehouse, TX 75791.)

Walter-Toews, D. and A. Ellis. 1994. *Good For Your Animals, Good For You*. Distributed by Delta Society. Ontario, Canada: University of Guelph.

Tellington-Jones, L. and S. Taylor. 1992. *The Tellington TTouch*. Viking Penguin, a division of Penguin Books USA Inc.

Nebbe, L.L. 1995. *Nature as a Guide*. 2d ed. Minneapolis, MN: Educational Media Corporation.

Patrias, K. Ed. *Current Bibliographies in Medicine - Human-Pet Relationships*. Bethesda, MD: National Institutes of Health. (US Dept. of Health & Human Services, Public Health Services, National Institutes of Health. National Library of Medicine, Bethesda, MD 20894, (301) 496-6097.)

Dogs

Dunbar, I. Dog behavior booklets and training information. Berkeley, CA: James & Kenneth Publishers. (James & Kenneth Publishers, 2140 Shattuck, Avenue #2406, Berkeley, CA 94704, (415) 658-8588.)

Rutherford, C. and D.H. Neil, M.R.C.V.S. 1981. *How to Raise a Puppy You Can Live With*. Alpine Publications, Inc.

Beck, A.M. and A.H. Katcher. 1984. A New Look at Pet-Facilitated Therapy. In *Journal of the American Medical Association*, 4, 414-421.

Levinson, B.M. 1965. Pet Psychotherapy: Use of Household Pets in the Treatment of Behavior Disorders in Childhood. In *Psychological Reports*, 17, 695-698.

Ryan, T. Booklets: "The Puppy Primer," "The Toolbox: For Remodeling Problem Dogs," "ALPHAbetize Yourself: How to Help Your Dog Regard You as Leader," and "Games People Play...To Train Their Dogs." (Legacy, NW 2025 Friel Street, Pullman, WA 99163, (509) 332-2831.)

1987. *All (160) Breed Dog Grooming*. Neptune City, NJ: T.F. H. Publications, Inc. (Distributed by T.F.H. Publications, Inc., 211 West Sylvania Avenue, Neptune City, NJ 07753.)

1988. *The Doglopaedia - A Complete Guide to Dog Care*. Surrey, England. (Henston, Friary Court, 13-21 High Street, Guilford, Surrey, England.)

Milani, M.M., DVM. 1986. *The Body Language and Emotion of Dogs*. NY: William Morrow and Company, Inc.

Benjamin, C. L. 1988. *Second-Hand Dog - How to Turn Yours into a First-Rate Pet*. NY: Howell Book House.

Diamond Davis, K. *Responsible Dog Ownership.*

Rowan, A.N. Ed. *Anthrozoos*—A Multidisciplinary Journal on the Interactions of People, Animals and Environment. Quarterly. North Grafton, MS: Tufts University. (School of Veterinary Medicine, Tufts University, 200 Westboro Road, North Grafton, MS 01536.) Contact Delta Society office.

Natural PET. Trilby, TL: Pet Publications, Inc. (Pet Publications, Inc., P.O. Box 351, Trilby, TL 33953-0351; Tel/Fax: 904-583-4667. Sample issues available for minimum cost. 6 issues per year.)

Good Dog! Charleston, SC. (Good Dog! P.O. Box 31292, Charleston, SC 29417, Phone (800) 968-1738; bi-monthly.)

Dog Fancy. Irvine, CA: Fancy Publications Inc. (Fancy Publications Inc., 3 Burroughs, Irvine, CA 92718; Subscription service phone number (303) 786-7306; 12 issues per year.)

Off Lead. Rome, NY: American Publications. (American Publications, Inc., 100 Bouck Street, Rome, NY 13440, Sample issue available for minimum cost, Tel: (315) 339-2033; 12 issues per year.)

Pure-Bred Dogs/American Kennel GAZETTE. (Subscriptions (919) 233-9780, 12 issues per year.)

Dogs Today. (Pet Subjects Ltd., 6 Station Parada, Sunningdale, Berks, SL 0EP American contact needed.)

Dog World. Chicago, IL: Maclean Hunter Publishing Corp. (Maclean Hunter Publishing Corp., 29 North Wacker Drive, Chicago, IL, Phone (312) 726-2820. Monthly.)

1990. Canine Source Book. Wilsonville, OR: Doral Publishing. (Doral Publishing, PO Box 596, Wilsonville, OR 97070; Listing and info. on: Specialty & All Breed Dog Clubs, Breed And General Publications and more.)

Rabbits

House Rabbit Society, P.O. Box 3242, Redmond, WA 98073. 1-206-868-4839.

All About House Rabbits (video). Redmond, WA: House Rabbit Society.

House Rabbit Journal. Alameda, CA: House Rabbit Society.

Washington House Rabbit News. Redmond, WA: House Rabbit Society.

Hunter, S. *Hop to it: A Guide to Training Your Pet Rabbit*. Hauppauge, NY: Barron's Educational Series. (Barron's Educational Series, Inc., P.O. Box 8040. 250 Wireless Blvd., Hauppauge, New York 11788. 1-800-645-3476. In NY: 1-800-257-5729.)

Harriman, M. 1985. *The House Rabbit Handbook*. Alameda, CA: Drollery Press.

The House Rabbit Journal. Alameda, CA: House Rabbit Society. (House Rabbit Society, 1615 Encinal Ave., Alameda, CA 94501. $12 donation for 12 issues.)

Percan, S.T. 1984. *The Complete Book on Housetraining Rabbits*. Hermosa Beach, CA: Silver Sea Press.

Lockley, R.M. 1975. *The Private Life of the Rabbit*. NY: Avon Books.

Adams, R. 1972. *Watership Down*. NY: Macmillan.

Cats

Wright, M. and S. Walters, Eds. *The Book of the Cat*. NY: Summit Books.

Caras. R.A. *A Cat is Watching—A Look at the Way Cats See Us and the World Around Them*. NY: Simon & Schuster.

Morris, D. *Catwatching*. NY: Crown Publishers.

Corey, P. 1977. *Do Cats Think?* Henry Regnery Co.

Loeb, P. and J. Banks. *You Can Train Your Cat*. NY: Pocket Books.

Craighead, J. *How to Talk to Your Cat*. NY: George Warner Books. (Publishers Choice, Box 4171, Dept. DN30-PO, Huntington Station, NY 11746.)

Muller, U. *The New Cat Handbook*. Woodbury, NY: Barron's.

Lawson, T. *The Cat Lovers' Cookbook*. Pownal, VT: Storey Communications Inc.

Pirotin, D., D.V.M. and S. Suib Cohen Fawcett. 1985. *No Naughty Cats*. NY: Crest Publishing.

Holland, B. *Secrets of the Cat: Its Lore, Legend and Lives*. NY: Ballantine Books.

Sussman, L. and S. Bordwell. *The Ultimate Cat Catalog*. NY: McGraw-Hill.

Ney, G. with S. Sherman Faden. *Cat Condominiums and Other Feline Furniture*. NY: E.P. Dutton.

Sautter, F.J. and J.A. Glover. 1978. *Behavior, Development and Training of the Cat*. NY: Arco Publishing.

Turner, D.C. and P. Bateson, Eds. 1988. *The Domestic Cat—The Biology of its Behavior*. NY: Cambridge University Press.

Baker, S. *How to Live with a Neurotic Cat*. NY: Warner Books.

Other Animals

Exotic Pets Brochures: "Pet Bird," "Pet Guinea Pig," "Mice," or "Hamsters." Biomedical Communications Unit, 123 Bustad Hall, College of Veterinary Medicine, Washington State University, Pullman, WA 99164-7013. 1-509-335-2624.

Pot-Bellied Pet Pigs. Orange, CA: All Publishing. (All Publishing, 10951 Meads Ave., Box B, Orange, CA 92669.)

Mini-Pig Care and Training. Orange, CA: All Publishing. (All Publishing, 10951 Meads Ave., Box B, Orange, CA 92669.)

Association of Avian Veterinarians, Central Office: Adina Rae Freedman, P.O. Box 299, East Northport, NY 11731. 1-516-757-6320.

The Llama Catalog: A Directory of Llama Products and Services. (International Llama Association, P.O. Box 37505, Denver, Colorado 80237. 1-303-699-9545.)

Brochures by International Llama Association include: "Llama Facts for New Owners," "Llama Housing and Fencing," "Llama Medical Management" and "Feeding Llamas."

Hart, R. 1985. *Living With Llamas*. Ashland, OR: Juniper Ridge Press. (Juniper Ridge Press, Box 338, Ashland, Oregon 97520. They also have video tapes.)

Source to purchase books

Direct Book Service's Annual - Dog and Cat Book Catalog, Your Complete Source for Dog and Cat Books and Videos, Phone number 1-800-776-2665.

Forms

The following pages contain forms that you can use when approaching a facility. You may copy these forms for your own use as a Pet Partner.

1. "Pet Partners Facility Policy Agreement"—helps clarify your responsibilities and the facility's expectations.

2. "Pet Partners"—contains information you can share with facilities that are learning about AAA and AAT. This will come in handy when introducing yourself to someone at a facility.

3. "AAA/AAT Program Report"—will help you document visits.

4. "Animal-Assisted Activities/Therapy Evaluation Sheet"—will help you or the facility evaluate the effectiveness of visits.

5. Pet Partners registration packet.

PET PARTNERS® Facility Policy Agreement

The information on this form will provide the visiting Pet Partners team(s) with important information about your expectations and the team's responsibilities. This information will become the policy guidelines for animal-assisted activity visits to your facility. Please review this information with the team(s) prior to receiving visits. The form must be signed by the contact person and each Pet Partners team.

Staff Involvement

Who will accompany the team on visits?

How frequently?

Who will evaluate and document the visits?

Participation

Who will receive visits?

Who will not?

How will they be identified?

Where will visits be conducted?

Logistics

Where is a safe, outside location for animals to eliminate?

Where is the trash receptacle located to dispose of waste material?

Where are the clean linens kept?

Where is the restroom?

Where is the sign in/sign out register?

Where are the food preparation and sterile supply areas?

Additional Information

Are there any additional requirements the team should be aware of?

Facility Contact

_____   _____
Signature   Date

Pet Partners Team

_____   _____
Handler's Signature   Date

Pet Partners®

A Program of the Delta Society®

Including Pets in Case Management Assists Recovery

Dr. Philip Pizzo, chief of Pediatrics and head of the Infectious Disease section of the National Cancer Institute, believes that children benefit tremendously from contact with animals and that this contact serves as a kind of bridge to their home environment. **"It's a way to comfort children. It simply provides a spiritual fortitude that helps them deal with the difficulties they face. My assessment is that it enhances dignity."**

"These animals are awesome, I would invite skeptics to visit the hospital when the dogs are here. They are so calm. Although the results are hard to quantify scientifically, once physicians see the interactions they will be persuaded to try the program."

-- Dr. Victor Roberts, Medical Director, Brain Injured Rehabilitation Center, Orlando, FL.

"Foothill is a locked psychiatric facility and it is only rarely that our residents are given the opportunity to enjoy the outdoors or friendly animals. [Pet Partners dog] Belle has a calming effect on our patients, who naturally feel anxiety and a lack of freedom. Belle adds unique liveliness and compassion to our treatment facility."

-- Lisa Richardson, Ph.D., Primary Therapist, Foothill Health and Rehabilitation Center, Sylmar, CA

Through Pet Partners, a nationwide registration system for pets and volunteers, compassionate pet owners share the physical and emotional benefits that can result from contact with animals. Pet Partners visit hospitalized children, adults who are ill or lonely, people with disabilities and others. The Pet Partners Program registers companion animals that successfully complete health, skills and aptitude screening, and pet owners who complete volunteer training.

"Registration through Pet Partners gives volunteers credibility with human service professionals," explained Linda Hines, executive director of the Delta Society, the international nonprofit organization which offers the program. "It helps assure these professionals that only well-trained volunteers and animals will be entering their facilities."

The Pet Partners Program includes dogs, cats, birds and other animals. Pet Partners teams visit nursing homes, hospitals, schools, prisons, treatment centers and other facilities to share their animals and their time with people in need. The program is supported by individual donors, foundations and Hill's Pet Nutrition, Inc.

Pet owners of all ages receive training in how to participate in an animal-assisted activities (AAA) or animal-assisted therapy (AAT) program. AAA volunteers visit informally with hospital patients, nursing home residents and people in other facilities. In AAT programs, volunteers and animals work with therapists and become formally involved in patient treatment regimens. Delta Society also trains human service professionals in clinical applications of AAT.

Training is provided by Delta Society certified instructors in many locales in cooperation with humane and veterinary organizations, breed clubs, and health care facilities. In areas where workshops are not available, volunteers can learn at home through the Pet Partners Home Study Course, available from the Delta Society. The course contains articles and a videotape with practical information to prepare volunteers for participation in AAA and AAT programs. Every three years a conference is offered by the International Association of Human-Animal Interaction Organizations (IAHAIO). Seminars and training are offered at Delta Society conferences.

For dog owners, the animal registration process begins with a visit to a Pet Partners Animal Evaluator who gives a skills and aptitude evaluation, a screening procedure written and field-tested by Delta Society's national Activity/Therapy Dog Committee. Then the dog receives a complete health exam and additional tests from a veterinarian. Delta Society also offers seminars on how to train a therapy dog for owners seeking advanced training.

Cats, birds and other animals must pass health, skills and aptitude screening given by a veterinarian and certified Pet Partners Animal Evaluator. Once approved, the animal is given a tag identifying it as a Pet Partner. The owner receives an identification card. After two years the animal and person must re-register.

"They don't witness miracles every day, but Pet Partners volunteers have helped spark remarkable improvements in many individuals' lives," said Hines.

Ann Howie, Delta's first registered Pet Partner volunteer, recently recalled her experience visiting a psychiatric hospital where a young woman was suffering from severe depression. The woman, who had been non-communicative with people, immediately began whispering to Howie's Shetland sheepdog. On a subsequent visit the woman began speaking aloud to the animal.

"In eight weeks time there had been such an improvement in her condition that she was released from the hospital and was able to hold down a job," Howie said.

Delta Society seeks to promote animals helping people to improve their health, healing and independence. For more information about the Pet Partners Program or to subscribe to the Pet Partners Newsletter, full of practical tips on AAA or AAT, contact Delta Society, 289 Perimeter Rd E, Renton, WA 98055-1329; (425) 226-7357.

AAA/AAT Program Report

Date _____

Client/Facility _____

Animal Name and Species _____

Handler Name _____

Approximate Number of Participants _____
  (Include staff, visitors and clients)

Questions

1. How did the clients respond to the visit? (e.g., Were they interested? Interactive? What stands out about this visit?)

2. Were there any negative experiences? (Please explain.)

3. What was the setting like? (e.g., Where did you meet? Were the clients in bed? Were staff present/helpful?)

4. How did the animals react? (e.g., Were they nervous or calm?)

5. What are your suggestions for future visits?

Signed _____

                    Name   Date

Animal-Assisted Activities/Therapy Evaluation Sheet

Date: _____

Legend: ↑ Improvement
         ↓ Deterioration
         O No Change

Client's Name	Socialization	Communication	Anxiety Level	Reality Orientation	Attention	Concentration	Engagement	Affect & Mood

*Adapted from San Francisco General Hospital Psychiatric Unit

Other Comments:

Socialization ---------- Interpersonal relationships; the level and appropriateness of an individual's interrelations within the group.

Communication -------- The client's ability to express him- /herself within the context of the group and the activity.

Anxiety Level ---------- How the individual responds to stimuli and modulates his/her responses.

Reality Orientation ---- The patient's ability to relate appropriately to the context of the group and the surroundings.

Attention Span -------- How long the patient attends to the group and the activity; how long before becoming distracted by other stimuli.

Concentration ---------- How well the patient focuses attention.

Engagement ----------- The relative level of the patient's involvement with the activity; how well s/he becomes an active participant.

Affect and Mood ------ How the patient feels about him- /herself as expressed verbally, by body language, and by facial expressions.

Appendix C

Pet Nutrition*

Your Pet's Health Depends on You

Your Pet Partner animal is especially valued because it provides affection, companionship, assistance and comfort to those who might otherwise not be reached. It is vital to provide your pet, and every other beloved pet as well, with the essentials of good health.

Proper nutrition helps ensure that your pet not only looks healthy, but is healthy. Like regular veterinary care, exercise, and affection, the food your pet eats also directly affects his health and well-being. A healthy, happy pet naturally makes a better Pet Partner.

Eating too much or too little of certain nutrients can make your pet more susceptible to many diseases. Even minor variations in your pet's daily food can influence its wellness, vitality and development. That's why Pet Partners recommends that you feed your pet a nutritionally balanced pet food and look to your veterinarian as your primary source of information on pet health and nutrition.

A pet food that provides the proper balance of nutrients is not only significant to your pet's health, but even more so for animals who will meet the daily challenges of being a Pet Partner.

* This section was written for Pet Partners by nutrition specialists at Hill's® Pet Nutrition, Inc. makers of Science Diet,® Health Blend,® and Prescription Diet.® Delta Society is grateful to Hill's for funding assistance for this *Team Training Course*.

The Challenge for Today's Pets: Nutrient Excesses

Today's veterinarians know that many pets suffer from excesses in the diet, just like humans. Excess salt, fat, protein, calcium, phosphorus, magnesium, and other nutrients and minerals have been linked to serious and debilitating illnesses in pets. Understanding what constitutes a proper diet for your pet is the first, most important step you can take to ensure your pet enjoys a healthy, long life.

Salt and Fat

Much of what has been learned in the field of human nutrition can also be applied to pet nutrition. For example, we know that there are risks of hypertension and coronary disease associated with high sodium and high fat intake. Despite these facts, some pet foods contain too much salt or fat in an effort to improve the taste. Your pet may like the taste, but its long term health may be at risk.

Protein and Phosphorus

Pets need protein to develop body tissue, enzymes and hormones, produce blood, and strengthen their immune defense system. Phosphorus is an essential nutrient for bone development and metabolism. However, excess levels of protein and phosphorus have been linked to kidney disease due to mineral deposits and buildup in the kidneys. Among diseases, kidney disease is the number two killer among dogs today. Since this disease can't be detected in your pet until the advanced stages, proper nutrition is your best preventative measure.

Magnesium

Excess magnesium can predispose a cat to struvite crystal formation in the bladder and an inflamed urinary tract—a condition known as Feline Lower Urinary Tract Disease. This is a painful condition which can be fatal if left untreated.

All Pet Foods Are Not the Same

Federal regulations require that commercial pet foods meet or exceed the minimum amounts of various nutrients recommended by the National Research Council (NRC). The NRC does not suggest maximum levels.

This "over delivery" of certain nutrients often distinguishes lower quality pet foods from those that are healthier for your pet.

Many pet foods available today are developed based on the price and availability of ingredients. These pet foods often have excess nutrients in order to save the costs of nutrient removal. As you've just learned, these excesses can be harmful to your pet over time.

When price and availability of ingredients determine the formulation of a pet food, nutrient balances may be compromised from one package to another. Pet owners may notice extra water or a different consistency in the food and do not realize that this may be attributed to variable formulation. Unfortunately, your pet may not receive proper nutrition on a consistent basis.

Hill's® Pet Nutrition: The Company Inspired by a Guide Dog

"Buddy," one of the first guide dogs for the blind, was the dog that inspired the creation of The Seeing Eye Association. But he's famed for another reason, too. When Buddy became ill in 1948, a veterinarian, Dr. Mark Morris, decided to put Buddy on a special diet. It was one of the first times anyone had tried to treat a dog by changing its food. Because Buddy's kidneys were failing, Dr. Morris carefully reduced the levels of protein and minerals in Buddy's diet.

The improvement was dramatic and the foundation of Hill's foods began. Hill's having pioneered the idea that disease could be treated nutritionally, has proactively developed food that helps maintain good health at every stage of dogs' and cats' lives.

How Much to Feed and How Often

You should feed your pet enough of the proper food to meet its energy needs. Use the feeding guide printed on the package as a starting point only. Thereafter, the amount you feed should be adjusted to maintain ideal body weight. The amount your pet needs will vary depending on its age, size, activity level, temperament, environment, reproductive status, and overall health. Adult pets fed twice per day are usually satisfied.

Switching Pet Foods

Like humans, pets become accustomed to their particular brand and type of food, and may initially resist when offered a new kind of food. It is best to introduce your pet to a new food gradually to allow your pet time to adjust to its taste.

Mix increasing amounts of the new food with decreasing amounts of your pet's current food over several days until you are feeding only the new food.

Complete Pet Care

As a Pet Partners team, you and your pet share your best with people in need. You can give your pet your best care when you make good grooming, exercise, veterinary check-ups, and a nutritionally sound diet regular habits for its health, vitality and well-being.

Appendix

D

Registration Packet

PET PARTNERS® REGISTRATION PROCESS

Materials are subject to change. If your packet is close to a year old, please call Delta Society at (425)226-7357 to receive the current version. To avoid having your packet sent back, be sure to fill out all sections of each form, provide your signature where needed, and include the photo and fee. **Make a copy of your completed registration packet for your records**. If you want a receipt that your materials have been received, please mail it Return Receipt Requested. The turnaround time for processing is 2-3 weeks.

➢ **Step #1: Photo ID Form**

This form contains the information we will use on your identification badge. Be sure to print or type the information to avoid any errors on your ID badge. If you belong to a group and wish to have the name of the group on the badge, please include it. If you do not want your full name and city/state on the badge, please let us know.

➢ **Step #2: Application Form**

Information on this form will be for our records and processing.

➢ **Step #3: Volunteer Policies and Procedures Agreement Form**

Review your Pet Partners team responsibilities as outlined in the *Pet Partners Team* Training Course Manual. Sign and date this form. If you are under 18 a parent or legal guardian must also sign this form.

➢ **Step #4: Volunteer Review**

The questions will review the important material covered in the Pet Partners Team Training Course. Take your time and work at your own pace. Use the review as a way to assure yourself that you are well prepared to visit with your pet.

➢ **Step #5: Handler's Questionnaire**

Complete this form **before** the animal is screened for skills and aptitude. **Make a copy for the Team Evaluator**. This form helps him/her understand your pet's responses. **(Bring this form to the evaluation).**

➢ **Step #6: Animal Health Screening Forms**

You may use your regular veterinarian. It is a good idea to make a copy of the introduction letter and forms and send them to your veterinarian before you schedule the appointment for screening. This will help your veterinarian plan the right amount of time for the procedure. Make sure s/he completes ALL sections of the health screening forms or the entire packet will be returned. NOTE: You may attach a signed health form from your veterinarian which indicates that it meets or exceeds the Pet Partners health requirements.

➢ **Step #7: Volunteer Contact Form**

This form will let us know more about you and your animal teammate.

©Delta Society   August 2002

DELTA SOCIETY®
580 NACHES AVENUE SW • SUITE 101 • RENTON, WA • 98055
PHONE: (425) 226-7357 • FAX: (425) 235-1076
WWW.DELTASOCIETY.ORG

➢ **Step #8: Team Evaluation**

Licensed Team Evaluators will administer the Pet Partners Skills and Aptitude tests. **Licensed Team Evaluators will have the Pet Partners Skills and Aptitude test forms.** Refer to your *Pet Partners Team Training Course Manual* to familiarize yourself with each exercise and the requirements for the evaluation. During the **Skills** and **Aptitude Tests** below, as well as on visits, acceptable accessories for animals in the program are as follows:

- Collar/harness for all animals
- Well-fitted buckle, quick-release connection, or snap closure collars or harnesses made of leather or fabric.
- Martingales (i.e., limited slip) and halters (e.g., Gentle Leader, Promise, Snoot Loop, Halti). Metal buckles, slip rings, and D-rings are acceptable.
- All leather or fabric leashes, no more than 6 feet in length.

Animals such as cats, rabbits, and guinea pigs are encouraged to be carried in a basket and/or on a towel and birds in cages. These animals should be carried such that their urine or droppings will not fall on the floor or on the person being visited. When you are ready to be evaluated, check the course and events schedule on our web site (www.deltasociety.org) or contact Delta Society at (425)226-7357 for a screening near you.

- **Pet Partners Skills Test (PPST)** This role-play test determines whether you and your pet have the basic skills needed when visiting people in different places. **After you have passed the Pet Partners Skills Test, the Team Evaluator will give you a signed and dated copy for you to include in your packet for submission to Delta Society.**

- **Pet Partners Aptitude Test (PPAT)** This role-play test simulates visiting situations to determine you and your pet's ability to work with strangers. **After you have passed the Pet Partners Aptitude Test, the Team Evaluator will give you a signed and dated copy for you to include in your packet for submission to Delta Society.**

©Delta Society   August 2002

DELTA SOCIETY®
580 NACHES AVENUE SW • SUITE 101 • RENTON, WA • 98055
PHONE: (425) 226-7357 • FAX: (425) 235-1076
WWW.DELTASOCIETY.ORG

PET PARTNERS® REGISTRATION OPTIONS

You can register with *no animals, one animal or multiple animals* in any of the following registration categories. Note, there is a $10 registration fee for registering each additional animal or person. Be sure to check the category of your choice on the application form. All fees are for 2 years.

> ## Handler with 1 animal -$45 (Delta Affiliate Group Member*-$40)

For people and their companion animals who are interested in visiting facilities independently or in establishing a people-animal program. Interested people should complete all forms and submit them to Delta Society with a registration fee of $45 for two years. A pet tag and volunteer identification badge will be mailed to the volunteer. A subscription to Delta Society's *Interactions* magazine is included in the registration fee. The registered team can begin visits to local facilities under the Pet Partners name either individually or with other registered teams.

> ## Volunteer without an animal -$30

People who do not have an animal can assist Pet Partners teams by interacting with staff and clients on visits. They organize events, help with workshops and screenings, and provide educational presentations on the benefits of Animal-Assisted Activities and Therapy through the Pet Partners Program. Individuals with no animal must complete the training requirements and pass the volunteer review. They may register at the reduced fee of $30 for two years and will receive an identification badge and a subscription to Delta Society's *Interactions* magazine.

> ## Senior Handler with 1 animal or Handler with a Disability with 1 animal -$30

Senior registration for volunteers 55+ or who have a disability is $30 for two years and includes pet tag and volunteer identification badge. A subscription to Delta Society's Interactions magazine is included in the registration fee. Complete all forms and submit them to Delta Society.

> ## Additional Animal(s)-$10 each

This fee applies when you are registering an additional animal either at the same time or after your initial registration. When registering an additional animal, **complete and** include a photo of each additional animal with handler. NOTE: The Volunteer Review is not required for additional animal applications. Includes pet tag and identification badge for each additional animal registered.

> ## Additional Family Members -$10 each

This fee applies when additional family members are registering with a previously registered animal, either at the same time or after that of the animal's initial registration. If the family member is registering with an additional animal, the total registration fee for that family member and animal would be $20 ($10 for the additional animal and $10 for the additional person within the same family). When registering additional handlers, **complete and submit ALL forms** and include a photo of each additional handler with the animal. NOTE: Each additional family member must complete the Volunteer Review. Includes pet tag and identification badge for each additional family member registered.

*If you do not know whether your group is a Delta Affiliate Group, ask your local group leader or call Delta.

DELTA SOCIETY®
580 NACHES AVENUE SW • SUITE 101 • RENTON, WA • 98055
PHONE: (425) 226-7357 • FAX: (425) 235-1076
WWW.DELTASOCIETY.ORG

STEP #1: PET PARTNERS® PHOTO ID FORM

Information on this form (**except for address**) will appear on your identification badge. Please print or type information to avoid inaccuracies. Attach two color photos of handler and animal, or individual only (if applying for volunteer with no animal): one photo for your ID badge and a candid shot for our files.

Handler's Name: _____   Group Name: _____

Address: _____

City: _____   State: _____   Zip: _____

Work Phone #: _____   Home Phone #: _____

Animal's Name: _____   Species/Breed: _____

Age: _____   ❏ Male ❏ Female   Color: _____

FOR OFFICE USE ONLY	ATTACH PHOTO HERE
ID#: TEAM AREA: EXPIRES: COMMENTS:	Please submit a 3" x 5" color photo for your ID badge (handler and animal or individual if registering without an animal) Please put tape on the back of the photo so as not to distort the picture.

August 2002

DELTA SOCIETY®
580 NACHES AVENUE SW • SUITE 101 • RENTON, WA • 98055
PHONE: (425) 226-7357 • FAX: (425) 235-1076
WWW.DELTASOCIETY.ORG

STEP #2: PET PARTNERS APPLICATION FORM

Information on this form will be entered in our database.
Check version completed: ❐   Home study
                          ❐   Workshop

Handler's Name: _____   Group Name: _____

Address: _____

City: _____   State: _____   Zip: _____

Work Phone #: _____   Home Phone #: _____

E-mail: _____

Animal's Name: _____   Species/Breed: _____

Age: _____   ❐ Male   ❐ Female   Color: _____

Registration Type		Method of Payment (U.S. Funds Only)
❐ Individual	= $45	❐ Check #: _____
❐ Individual w/o animal	= $30	❐ Money Order #: _____
❐ Senior (55+) / Disabled	= $30	❐ Visa ❐ Mastercard
❐ Additional animal	= $10	Card #:_____
❐ Additional person	= $10	Exp. Date:_____
❐ Affiliate Group Member	= $40	Signature:_____
		Total Amount Enclosed: $_____

To avoid having your registration packet returned, please make sure the following forms are included:	FOR OFFICE USE ONLY
1. Photo ID Form	Accepted: ❐ YES ❐ NO
2. Application Form	Reviewed by:_____
3. Volunteer Policies and Procedures Agreement	ID #:_____
4. Volunteer Review	Team Area:_____
5. Handler's Questionnaire	Expires:_____
6. Health Screening Forms	Comments:
7. Volunteer Contact Form	
8. Team Evaluation (Forms from Team Evaluator)	
▪ Skills Evaluation	
▪ Aptitude Evaluation	

©Delta Society   August 2002

DELTA SOCIETY®
580 NACHES AVENUE SW • SUITE 101 • RENTON, WA • 98055
PHONE: (425) 226-7357 • FAX: (425) 235-1076
WWW.DELTASOCIETY.ORG

STEP #3: PET PARTNERS VOLUNTEER POLICIES AND PROCEDURES

I agree to abide by the Policies and Procedures as outlined in the Pet Partners Team Training Course.

I understand that when performing volunteer activities as a DELTA SOCIETY Pet Partner, I am insured by DELTA SOCIETY'S commercial general liability insurance, so long as I am abiding by Delta's policies as referenced above, except in the following circumstances:

1. My pet or I cause a loss to other DELTA SOCIETY volunteers: if that occurs, I will be liable for that loss.

2. My pet or I cause a loss that is in excess of the limits of DELTA SOCIETY'S commercial general liability insurance: if that occurs, I will be liable for losses in excess of those limits.

3. My pet or I intentionally cause a loss or act outside the scope of DELTA SOCIETY volunteer activities: if that occurs, I will be liable for any losses.

Name: _____

Address: _____

City/State/Zip: _____

Signature: _____ **Date:** _____

If under 18, parent or legal guardian must sign below.

Parent or Legal Guardian Signature: _____ **Date:** _____

DELTA SOCIETY®
580 NACHES AVENUE SW • SUITE 101 • RENTON, WA • 98055
PHONE: (425) 226-7357 • FAX: (425) 235-1076
WWW.DELTASOCIETY.ORG

STEP #4: PET PARTNERS® VOLUNTEER REVIEW

You may use the volunteer training manual or the workshop workbook while taking this test. **Circle ALL answers that are correct.** Each question is worth 10 points and you must answer 80 % or more correctly for registration.

1. The purposes of animal evaluations are to:
   1. Show the animal is predictable
   2. Keep certain breeds out of AAA/AAT
   3. Identify where the animal would be most comfortable
   4. Show the animal is under control

2. List the 5 steps in the Pet Partners policy for reporting an injury caused by your animal.

   a.
   b.
   c.
   d.
   e.

3. Identify the characteristics of Animal-Assisted Therapy (AAT) programs.
   a. AAT programs must be documented
   b. AAT programs do not require the supervision of a human service professional
   c. AAT has specific goals
   d. Programs are run by volunteers

4. To prepare your pet for a visit, you should:
   a. Make sure that your pet is clean and well groomed
   b. Check for fleas
   c. Clip and file the nails
   d. Use your mouthwash to freshen your animal's breath

5. You should sign in and sign out when you visit because:
   a. It is required by all state laws
   b. Meets requirements for documentation of therapy
   c. Proves when you were at the facility
   d. Helps the facility record volunteer hours

6. Which are appropriate ways to reduce stress for animals?
   a. Give the animal water
   b. Stop the activity
   c. Provide "time outs"
   d. Give the animal food

©Delta Society   August 2002

DELTA SOCIETY®
580 NACHES AVENUE SW • SUITE 101 • RENTON, WA • 98055
PHONE: (425) 226-7357 • FAX: (425) 235-1076
WWW.DELTASOCIETY.ORG

7.   Your animal should not visit when the following conditions are present:
     a.   The pet has an open wound
     b.   The pet has some dandruff
     c.   The animal refused to eat the night before the visit
     d.   The animal is in heat

8.   When working with children, you should:
     a.   Use active, energetic animals around toddlers and babies
     b.   Help them participate in simple activities with the animal
     c.   Tell them stories about your animal
     d.   Use gentle, quiet animals around toddlers and babies

9.   When talking with a person who uses a wheelchair, you should:
     a.   Lean on the wheelchair
     b.   Ask before touching or moving the wheelchair
     c.   Assume the person needs assistance
     d.   Speak to the person from a sitting or kneeling position

10. Which of the following should you follow as part of infection control procedures?
     a.   Do not visit if you or your pet are sick
     b.   Wash hands after each visit
     c.   Do not visit people who have any kind of infection
     d.   Always wear protective clothing

©Delta Society   August 2002

DELTA SOCIETY®
580 NACHES AVENUE SW • SUITE 101 • RENTON, WA • 98055
PHONE: (425) 226-7357 • FAX: (425) 235-1076
WWW.DELTASOCIETY.ORG

STEP #5: PET PARTNERS® HANDLERS QUESTIONNAIRE

The person who will visit with the animal being tested must complete this form. If you are not the owner, you must provide written proof of permission to handle this animal. Answer all questions as it applies to this animal.

Handler:_____ Owner:_____

Animal's Name:_____ Species/Breed:_____

1. How did you acquire your animal companion?

☐ Breeder ☐ Shelter/Rescue ☐ Pet Store ☐ Friend ☐ Other

2. How long have you had *or* known this animal?_____

3. Have you or your animal trained or practiced at the same location where you are being evaluated?
☐ No ☐ Yes

4. If you are registering with a dog, has the dog ever been encouraged or trained to bite, even as part of a dog sport (e.g., Schutzhund)? ☐ No ☐ Yes

5. List all commands this animal responds to reliably:

6. Is there a specific age group that this animal avoids or seems uncomfortable around?
☐ No ☐ Yes: (*If yes, check all that apply*)

☐ Infants   ☐ Adult Men
☐ Toddlers   ☐ Adult Women
☐ School age   ☐ Seniors
☐ Adolescents   ☐ Other:_____

7. Is there a type of individual that this animal avoids or seems uncomfortable around?
☐ No ☐ Yes: (*If yes, check all that apply*)

☐ People wearing hats   ☐ People using unusual equipment
☐ People with facial hair   ☐ People of a different race
☐ People that move differently ☐ Other:_____

DELTA SOCIETY®
580 NACHES AVENUE SW • SUITE 101 • RENTON, WA • 98055
PHONE: (425) 226-7357 • FAX: (425) 235-1076
WWW.DELTASOCIETY.ORG

8. Has this animal ever acted in a threatening or menacing manner towards an individual or group of individuals? Threatening/menacing includes: overt staring, growling, snapping, snarling, barking at, lunging toward or biting an individual. ☐ No ☐ Yes (*If yes, describe*)

9. What is this animal's favorite game or activity? (*Check all that apply*)

☐ Frisbee/catch   ☐ Pounce games
☐ Chase games   ☐ Find it games
☐ Fetch and return   ☐ Tug of war
☐ Wrestling   ☐ Chew toys
☐ Agility/obstacles   ☐ Other:_____

10. How do you discipline/correct this animal?

11. What does this animal do when it becomes stressed?

12. What do you do when you recognize that your animal is stressed?

13. List any kinds of animals that this animal does not react to well:

©Delta Society   August 2002

DELTA SOCIETY®
580 NACHES AVENUE SW • SUITE 101 • RENTON, WA • 98055
PHONE: (425) 226-7357 • FAX: (425) 235-1076
WWW.DELTASOCIETY.ORG

STEP #6: PET PARTNERS® ANIMAL HEALTH SCREENING FORM

Dear Doctor:

Thank you for performing an examination of this pet for participation in Delta Society's Pet Partners® Program. This is a national visiting animal program in which volunteers and their pets visit people in nursing homes, hospitals, schools, and other institutions.

Delta Society has operated the Pet Partners Program for over a decade. The Program is distinguished by its attention to training the volunteer, evaluating the team every two years, and concern for the health of the animal. By having a systematic process for registering teams, we minimize risk to the patients who are visited by the teams and respect the health and well being of the animals who participate in the Program. The role of the veterinarian is very important in this regard. The animal you are about to examine will be evaluated by a Delta-trained and licensed team evaluator to test the animal's suitability for visiting animal work. The evaluation requires the animal to demonstrate certain basic obedience skills such as, "sit", "stay", and "leave it". The evaluator will note whether the animal accepts being petted, sometimes roughly, and by multiple people simultaneously. Equally important, the evaluator will assess the animal's temperament and aptitude in a simulated healthcare setting. The animal will be observed as it reacts to loud noises, wheelchairs, walkers, and people with stumbling gait and/or speech impediments.

You are being asked to assess the animal's overall health and any notable reactions to the process of physical handling. Please complete the enclosed health screening forms; you may substitute your own forms if you prefer, so long as all issues are addressed. Be sure each section has been filled out. The animal's owner is responsible for mailing the health screening forms to Delta. These forms will be reviewed by Delta staff, along with the results of the evaluation, to determine the team's suitability to do visiting animal work.

As you well know, there is often not a consensus of opinion among those in the veterinarian community about immunizations, and State laws with respect to rabies vaccinations vary. Our Pet Partners are very responsible pet owners and have long-term and trusting relationships with their veterinarians. Rather than attempting to prescribe immunizations schedules for dogs and cats (other than compliance with State laws with respect to rabies vaccination), Delta Society will rely on your medical judgment and knowledge of the animal's health history and status. We want to be assured that the animal's immunity levels are sufficient that participation in Pet Partners will not harm it. Likewise, we need to be sure that Pet Partners' animals will not put seriously ill people at risk. Please also consider that visiting animals may be exposed to zoonotic agents because they visit people in healthcare facilities. As this animal's veterinarian you are the best person to render the overall opinion of the animal's health.

Thank you for your part in making the Pet Partners Program safe and rewarding for thousands of volunteers and hundreds of thousands of people in need. DELTA SOCIETY would be pleased to provide you with information for your office waiting area to encourage more pet owners to become involved in the Pet Partners Program. For information check our web site at www.deltasociety.org or call 425 226-7357.

Sincerely,

Dianne M. Bell ~ Pet Partners® Program Coordinator

©Delta Society   August 2002

DELTA SOCIETY®
580 NACHES AVENUE SW • SUITE 101 • RENTON, WA • 98055
PHONE: (425) 226-7357 • FAX: (425) 235-1076
WWW.DELTASOCIETY.ORG

STEP #6: PET PARTNERS® ANIMAL HEALTH SCREENING FORM

Pet Partner: Complete this section for review by your veterinarian.

Pet Partner's name: _____ Date: _____

Animal's name: _____ ☐ Male ☐ Female

Breed/Species: _____ ☐ Intact   ☐ Altered

Animal's lifestyle: ☐ active   ☐ moderately active   ☐ sedentary

Is animal boarded at kennels?   ☐ No   ☐ Yes If yes, how often? _____

What activities do you do with your animal that would expose it to other animals?

☐ dog/cat shows   ☐ state/county fairs   ☐ other (identify): _____

Does your animal spend time outdoors (other than for routine walks)?   ☐ No ☐ Yes

If yes, please explain: _____

Veterinarian: Please complete the remainder of this form.

Dear Doctor: All sections of this form are to be completed. You may use your own health screening form if it addresses all the categories identified in this form.

How long have you known the handler? _____ the animal? _____

Section 1:   General Health of the Animal

The overall health of this animal is: (select one)

☐ Excellent (No serious chronic diseases or disorders)
☐ Very good (Minor complaints associated with normal aging)
☐ Good (Chronic conditions with occasional flare-ups)
☐ Poor (Serious chronic condition requiring ongoing treatment)

Vital signs:

Pulse:_____ Temperature: _____ Respiration:_____ Weight:_____

Medications: _____

How often do you see this animal?

☐ at least annually
☐ wellness program
☐ only when ill or injured
☐ every _____ months
☐ other (please explain)_____

August 2002

DELTA SOCIETY®
580 NACHES AVENUE SW • SUITE 101 • RENTON, WA • 98055
PHONE: (425) 226-7357 • FAX: (425) 235-1076
WWW.DELTASOCIETY.ORG

Section 2:   General Systems Evaluation

Please check **Normal** for normal findings or **Abnormal** for abnormal. Please list the findings and comment on any abnormal finding, e.g., heart is abnormal—comment, dog has a systolic heart murmur. Note any physical problems that might put the animal at risk, e.g., arthritis, painful ear infection, etc.

System	Normal	Abnormal	Findings/Comments
General appearance	☐	☐	
Skin/coat	☐	☐	
Musculo-Skeletal	☐	☐	
Heart/lungs	☐	☐	
Digestive	☐	☐	
Urogenital	☐	☐	
Eyes/ears	☐	☐	
Nervous	☐	☐	
Lymph nodes	☐	☐	
Mucous membranes	☐	☐	
Teeth/mouth	☐	☐	

©Delta Society   August 2002

DELTA SOCIETY®
580 NACHES AVENUE SW • SUITE 101 • RENTON, WA • 98055
PHONE: (425) 226-7357 • FAX: (425) 235-1076
WWW.DELTASOCIETY.ORG

Delta Society believes that the veterinarian and the pet's owner are in the best position to decide what types of tests and immunizations are appropriate for the animal. **Rabies immunizations, as prescribed by State law, are required for all animals in the Pet Partners Program. Any specifically listed vaccinations and tests are required for that species of animal.** Animals that visit people in hospitals, nursing homes, and other healthcare facilities need to be healthy, clean, and well mannered so that they pose little risk to patients. It is equally important to minimize risk to animals that may be exposed to zoonotic agents that could cause harm to an immune compromised, unhealthy, or highly stressed animal.

Section 3:   Vaccinations and Tests for Dogs and Cats (See following pages for other species.)

Species	Vaccination	Expiration Date	Test	Result
Dogs	Rabies (State law)		Other (list)	
	Other (list)			
Cats	Rabies (State law)		FeLV	
	Other (list)		Other (list)	

Section 4:   Parasite Control for Dogs and Cats

External parasite control will vary depending on your geographic area of the country. For your geographic area please indicate:

Parasite(s) controlled for: _____

Method of control _____

Internal parasite control will have some variation depending on your geographic area of the country. The Pet Partners Program requires annual fecal tests to check for internal parasites such as hook, whip, tape, and roundworms, etc.

DATE OF LAST FECAL EXAM: _____ **Results:** _____

Section 5:   Overall Assessment for Dogs and Cats

In your professional judgment, is this animal a good candidate for the Pet Partners Program?   ☐ Yes ☐ No

Signature of DVM: _____ Date: _____

Address: _____ Phone: _____

©Delta Society   August 2002

DELTA SOCIETY®
580 NACHES AVENUE SW • SUITE 101 • RENTON, WA • 98055
PHONE: (425) 226-7357 • FAX: (425) 235-1076
WWW.DELTASOCIETY.ORG

Section 6:   **Vaccinations and Tests for Other Species**

Species	Vaccination	Expiration Date	Test	Result
Birds			Salmonella	
			Avian TB	
			Chlamydia/Psittacosis	
			Other	
Guinea pigs / rabbits	Rabies		Pasturella (required for rabbits)	
			Coccidiosis	
			Salmonella	
	Other		Other	
Pigs	Rabies		Mites (skin scraping)	
	Erysipelas			
	Pasturella			
	Other		Other	
Horses	Rabies		Other	
	Influenza			
	Tetanus			
	WEE/EEE/VEE			
	Other			
Sheep/Llamas/Goats	Rabies		TB	
	Clostridium		Brucellosis	
	Tetanus		Other	
	Other			

External parasites for llamas and goats: Required screening and control for lice.

Internal parasite control for horses: The Pet Partners Program requires annual fecal tests to check for internal parasites such as hook, whip, tape, and roundworms, etc., however your veterinarian may require more frequent testing and treatment.

DATE OF LAST FECAL EXAM:_____ **Results:** _____

Section 7:   **Overall Assessment for Other Species**

In your professional judgment, is this animal a good candidate for the Pet Partners Program? ☐ Yes ☐ No

Signature of DVM: _____ Date: _____

Address: _____ Phone: _____

_____

DELTA SOCIETY®
580 NACHES AVENUE SW • SUITE 101 • RENTON, WA • 98055
PHONE: (425) 226-7357 • FAX: (425) 235-1076
WWW.DELTASOCIETY.ORG

STEP #7: PET PARTNERS® VOLUNTEER CONTACT FORM

Delta Society receives many requests for information and assistance in developing programs to help animals help people. As a Pet Partner, you have special training in the many ways animals help people.

Handler 's Name:_____ Animal 's Name:_____

Would You Be Interested in Pet Partner Networking?

- ❑ **YES**, PLEASE CONTACT ME, I would like to share my expertise in the areas checked below:
    - ❑ P1 Speak to small groups (15-20) about the Pet Partners Program and my experiences
    - ❑ P2 Accompany a new Pet Partner on initial visit(s)
    - ❑ PT Talk to individuals interested in Pet Partners
    - ❑ P3 Provide information and demonstration of our teamwork to facilities interested in starting a program
    - ❑ P4 Talk to the media about Pet Partners and my experiences
    - ❑ P5 Assist in organizing a Pet Partners Skills and Aptitude Screening
    - ❑ P6 Staff Pet Partners exhibit booth at local fairs and events
    - ❑ P7 Assist in organizing a Pet Partners workshop
    - ❑ CH Help with Delta Society's Annual Conference
    - ❑ P8 Please check here if you want to be listed in the Network. Network lists will be made available to approved facilities seeking quality volunteers or other Pet Partners in your area.
- ❑ **NO**, NOT AT THIS TIME

How did you hear about Pet Partners?
- ❑ Event (Pet or Health Fair/Delta Society Conference)
- ❑ Delta Society Web site
- ❑ Media (Newspaper/radio/television)
- ❑ Friend
- ❑ Other? Explain_____

Additional comments/specifics you would like to share about yourself and your animal teammate:_____

_____

_____

_____

_____

DELTA SOCIETY®
580 NACHES AVENUE SW • SUITE 101 • RENTON, WA • 98055
PHONE: (425) 226-7357 • FAX: (425) 235-1076
WWW.DELTASOCIETY.ORG